Citizenship and Immigration

Citizenship and Immigration

Christian Joppke

polity

Copyright © Christian Joppke 2010

The right of Christian Joppke to be identified as Author of this Work has been asserted in accordance with the UK Copyright, Designs and Patents Act 1988.

First published in 2010 by Polity Press

Polity Press
65 Bridge Street
Cambridge CB2 1UR, UK

Polity Press
350 Main Street
Malden, MA 02148, USA

All rights reserved. Except for the quotation of short passages for the purpose of criticism and review, no part of this publication may be reproduced, stored in a retrieval system, or transmitted, in any form or by any means, electronic, mechanical, photocopying, recording or otherwise, without the prior permission of the publisher.

ISBN-13: 978-0-7456-4234-5
ISBN-13: 978-0-7456-4235-2 (paperback)

A catalogue record for this book is available from the British Library.

Typeset in 11 on 13 pt Sabon
by Servis Filmsetting Ltd, Stockport, Cheshire
Printed and bound by MPG Books Group, UK

The publisher has used its best endeavours to ensure that the URLs for external websites referred to in this book are correct and active at the time of going to press. However, the publisher has no responsibility for the websites and can make no guarantee that a site will remain live or that the content is or will remain appropriate.

Every effort has been made to trace all copyright holders, but if any have been inadvertently overlooked the publisher will be pleased to include any necessary credits in any subsequent reprint or edition.

For further information on Polity, visit our website: www.politybooks.com

Contents

Preface		vi
1	The Concept of Citizenship	1
2	Status	34
3	Rights	73
4	Identity	111
5	Citizenship Light	145
Notes		173
References		186
Index		204

Preface

Citizenship has long been a key entry in the sociological lexicon. In liberal post-World War II sociology, "citizenship" was the answer to the Marxist scenario of polarizing class conflict, which was losing credibility in the context of rising affluence and maturing welfare states. T. H. Marshall ([1950] 1992) canonized the liberal view of citizenship as a device of societal integration, whereby equal civil, political, and social rights become expanded successively to previously excluded groups, especially workers.

Hardly had the ink been dry than Marshall's liberal scenario of internally inclusive citizenship became shattered by the great migrations of the postwar period. Immigration suddenly showed citizenship in a different, less liberal light, as a mechanism of closure and external exclusion that sharply demarcates the world's nation-state societies from one another. Rogers Brubaker, in his now classic comparison of citizenship and nationhood in France and Germany (1992), was the first to articulate crisply modern citizenship's paradoxical duality of being "internally inclusive," providing only one equal membership status for all members of society, and "externally exclusive," blocking interstate mobility and allowing states to exist as relatively closed, self-reproducing units. Brubaker's groundbreaking study created an entirely new field of genuinely cross-disciplinary scholarship on "citizenship and immigration." To review this new academic field is one purpose of this book.

However, more than reviewing a new academic field, the main

Preface

aim of this book is to bring to light some important changes that the institution of citizenship has undergone in the course of the postwar migrations. These occurred in a particular historical context, marked by the rise of universal human rights norms and the outlawing of ethnic and racial discrimination. The combination of both factors – that is, of migrations in a liberal human rights context – had an important impact on citizenship, making the latter more porous and less discriminatory than in the past. It is a truism that in the era of globalization nation-state societies are much less sharply bounded, autarchic units than they used to be, and citizenship has been centrally involved in this transformation, as both dependent and independent variable.

By the same token, changes in the institution of citizenship were much more dramatic in Western Europe than in North America or Australia, simply because European citizenship regimes were much less geared to the reality of mass immigration than their North American or Australian counterparts. Not by accident, the paradigm-setting works on "citizenship and immigration" covered mostly European countries, though they offered sharply divided views on national citizenship as either resilient (Brubaker 1992) or in decline (Soysal 1994; also Jacobson 1996). As opposite as they appear, the "resilience" and "decline" stances jointly failed to see that citizenship, rather than being static or being rendered obsolete, continued to evolve, converging on a liberal model of inclusive citizenship with diminished rights implications and increasingly universalistic identities. This convergence will be demonstrated in this book through a sustained comparison of developments in Western Europe, North America and Australia.

Citizenship is a complex institution with multiple dimensions. In this book, I shall distinguish between the *status*, *rights*, and *identity* dimensions of citizenship. As status, citizenship denotes formal state membership, access to which is regulated by a state's nationality laws. In addition, it denotes certain rights that are typically attached to this status – this is the Marshallian citizenship triptych that has been so influential in liberal postwar sociology. Finally, citizenship denotes certain collective identities on the part of the citizenry, which link the former closely to the semantics of nation and nationalism and the classic question of what integrates society.

Under the ambit of "citizenship studies" separate literatures have evolved about each of these dimensions of citizenship, with very little attention to developments in the other dimensions and an accordingly low degree of attention to cross-dimensional dynamics and impacts. Furthermore, a tendency in much of these literatures is to decouple citizenship from the state, arguing that membership and allegiances are now invested in collectivities and organizational forms smaller than or transversal to the state, such as cities or ethnic groups, or larger than and superordinate to the state, as in the talk of global citizenship. This book offers a counterpoint to exorcizing the state from contemporary citizenship studies. My démarche is to fold citizenship back to what it essentially is: a status denoting membership in a state, and to shed light from there on citizenship's rights and identity dimensions, with particular attention to the changes that all three dimensions have undergone in the context of international migration in the human-rights era.

While its geographic scope is not narrow, this is still a book about the usual suspects, or, as one might say, a view from the comfort zone. No doubt there is dire need to understand better the "upside-down" world of non-Western, developing countries' citizenships, in which "state membership is blurred, the causal relation between status and benefit is sometimes reversed, and people make seamless transitions from illegal immigration to full citizenship status" (Sadiq 2009: 27). Moving the lens from the West to the Rest might not just show a world of difference but also reveal surprising communalities – such as that citizenship "ceases to provide a common national identity" or a lessening "sense of obligation to the state" (ibid.: 197). But this is an inquiry that would require another book and another author too.

Paris, March 2009

1

The Concept of Citizenship

Citizenship is a notoriously polyvalent concept, with many meanings and applications. A recent *Handbook of Citizenship Studies* (Isin and Turner 2002) includes entries on sexual, cultural, and ecological citizenship, to name just a few of the many kinds of citizenship on offer today. However, most definitions of citizenship still conceive of it as "ineradicably political" (Smith 2001: 1857). As Rogers Smith further explicates, citizenship's "oldest, most basic, and most prevalent meaning is a certain sort of membership in a political community" (ibid.). If there is hardly a definition of citizenship that does not conceive of it as pertaining to the political,[1] the question arises: What is "political"?

There are at least two answers: a normative and a factual.[2] The normative answer goes back to the Greek polis, which invented the idea of the "human production of social order" (Popitz 1992: 12). Here the political is about the *Machbarkeit* of order, the possibility to generate order and not just to let it happen. Implicit in this is the notion of something "better," because otherwise there would be no point in change: "To the idea of the political belongs the belief in the possibility to produce a *good* order" (ibid., emphasis added). From here began the search for the best constitution, and the articulation of the principles to evaluate it: justice, rule of law, equality under the law (*isonomia*). This has been the stuff of political thinking from Plato to Montesquieu. However, as the modern experience would show, such normative politics, driven by the search for a better, could eventually not be limited to one sphere. In the age of modern mass democracy, where state and society are not separate but mutually implicated, there is an endemic tendency for normative politics to become ubiquitous, thus dodging our exit proposition of citizenship as "membership in a political community." A normative definition of the political leads to the idea of "citizenships," in the plural, and thus to the hyphenated citizenships of today.

Conversely, only a factual definition of the political allows one to conceive of "citizenship" in the singular, which today means state membership. Key to the non-normative tradition of the political is the idea of order as containment of violence. This tradition's most lucid and penetrating, if controversial, document is Carl Schmitt's *Der Begriff des Politischen*, written on the eve of the twentieth century's darkest moment ([1932] 1963). At the most general level, Schmitt conceives of the political as one of the many spheres of society, much as there are, in addition, religious, cultural, economic, legal, and scientific spheres, to name just a few. Each sphere orders the world from a specific vantage point: "true" versus "false" in science, "good" versus "evil" in religion and morality, "efficient" versus "inefficient" in the economy, etc. The specifically political distinction, this is Schmitt's controversial proposition, is that between "friend" and "enemy." His radical proposal is to separate politics from morality. This has often been misperceived through the lens of Schmitt's dubious sympathy for Hitler and Nazism. However, there is profound insight here into the frail and precarious nature of human existence and sociability, which in modern political thinking had been prominently made by Thomas Hobbes: insight into the physical dangers that human beings represent to one another, and which drives them into the creation of an "artificial body" (Hobbes [1651] 1998), the state, that protects them from the ubiquitous possibility of violence.[3] In this respect, the political is not just one of the many spheres and forms of human association, but the one that is "paramount" because related to the *Ernstfall* of violence and physical annihilation (Schmitt 1963: 39). The political is the terminal human association, the one that cancels out and subsumes all others. In fact, as Heinrich Popitz argues in the Hobbes–Schmittian tradition, the political is tantamount to the "idea of order" itself, which is born out of the "fear of violence" and the "counter-motif of security" (Popitz 1992: 61).

At the same time, more than constituting an own sphere, the political denotes the "degree of intensity" of a human association or disassociation; more precisely, the political is the "most intensive and extreme" (Schmitt 1963: 30) of associations that trumps the others, and which can be "reached from the economy as from any other sphere of society" (ibid.: 72). In this sense, the political is transversal to the other spheres of society, as it can be reached from any point in it. However, short of civil war, in modern society the political becomes identical with the state, as this is the only association that has "power over the physical life of human beings" (ibid.: 48). This involves, internally, what Max Weber called the "monopolization of the legitimate use of violence" (Weber [1919] 1977: 8), whereby domestic society becomes a zone of "peace, security, and order" (which is the definition of *Polizei*, notes Schmitt 1963: 10); and, externally, the *jus belli*, the right of states to declare war. Always the reference of the political is violence and protection from violence. This is no Schmittian prank but the end point of the secular and unsentimental reflection on the political from Machiavelli to Max Weber. As Max Weber summed it up in his *Politics as a Vocation*, "For politics the decisive means is always: violence" (Weber 1977: 58).

If citizenship is "membership in a political community," to reiterate Rogers Smith (2001: 1857), it is membership in that human association that trumps all others through providing elementary security and protection. As in modern society this "paramount" association is the state, citizenship denotes, and should exclusively denote, membership in a state.[4] With Schmittian means one arrives at a parsimonious understanding of citizenship as state membership. Certainly, one may find fault with Schmitt's existentialist, non-normative understanding of the political that is drenched in blood and leaves no space for the routine "politics" in the liberal-democratic state. But one must still acknowledge the fact that state citizenship is the only "citizenship" that is not just rhetorical and metaphorical but formal and institutional, a hard fact in terms of the passport and a state's nationality laws and, by implication, immigration laws from which only citizens are exempt. Furthermore, from a Schmittian angle, one gets a sense of the enormity of the challenge that is posed to citizenship by immigration, because the immigrant is "the other, the stranger," the protection from whom is the whole purpose of the political association (Schmitt 1963: 27). Conversely, one begins to appreciate the enormous civilizing achievement of facilitating, routinizing, and putting on a legal basis this boundary-crossing in today's citizenship and nationality laws.

If reference to (a certain view of) the political allows for a parsimonious understanding of citizenship as state membership, we are still dealing with "citizenship," which is a profoundly liberal institution that centers on the individual, not the group. In Schmitt's well-known scenario, liberalism is the despised "negation of the political," as liberalism celebrates "individualism" (for the various meanings of individualism, see Lukes 1973). By contrast, "political unity" subsumes the individual and asks for his or her "sacrifice of life" (Schmitt 1963: 69f.). As Schmitt rightly sees, liberalism is about "domestic struggle against state power" (ibid.), constraining the latter for the sake of individual freedom and private property. Liberalism thus opens up the black box of domestic politics that was sealed by the sovereign state's internal pacification of society. And here *is* the point of entry for the hyphenated citizenships that had earlier been locked out by tying citizenship exclusively to the political sphere. Schmitt even realized this, in terms of his diagnosis that the classic state, in which the state had overlapped with the political, was giving way to the "blurring of the lines between state and society" in the age of modern mass democracy (ibid.: 25). However, what he misleadingly described as the "total state" that undid the "depoliticizations" of nineteenth-century society was really the arrival of total society, in which the status of political association was leveled to that of any other: economic, religious, or cultural association. In a way, the pluralist state theories of G. D. H. Cole or Harold Laski, which were ridiculed by Schmitt for enmeshing the individual in a plurality of simultaneous groups and associations, of which the political was only one, have come true, thus crossing out the Schmittian "truth" that "there is no political 'society' or 'association', but only a political unity, a political community" (ibid.: 45). In the age of globalization, this fact is registered, if greatly overstated, in terms of the death or demise of the nation-state.

Some three decades before so-called citizenship studies put the hyphenated citizenships of repoliticized society on a pedestal, Ralf Dahrendorf anticipated the latter in terms of "sectoral citizenships," which he profoundly disliked for making modern societies "ungovernable" (1974: 697). Defining citizenship as "the generalized right to participate on equal terms," Dahrendorf argues that there is an inherent tendency of such citizenship to move from its original site, the political sphere of the nation-state, to other sectors of society: "Once the seed of citizenship has been planted in a society, it will grow like ivy, not to say like weeds, until its outgrowth has covered as many members of a community in as large a segment of their social lives as is at all possible" (ibid.: 680). As social structure comes to invade the public sphere, we see the rise of "the economic citizen, the citizen in uniform, the church of citizens" (ibid.: 695), plus – one should add today – the hyphenated citizenships of contemporary identity politics. Citizenship, one could argue, is the medium for the "generalization of suspecting the presence of power" (*Generalisierung des Machtverdachts*) that Heinrich Popitz (1992: 60) found endemic to modern democratic society, in which power is no longer concentrated in the state but has become "societalized" (*vergesellschaftet*).

Of course, these sectoral or hyphenated citizenships cannot be understood in Schmittian terms. They thrive on a normative, infra-national rather than inter-national understanding of politics as resisting coercive power wherever it raises its head, invoking the principles of equality and freedom that are *also* institutionalized in modern citizenship. Citizenship connotes the "rule of law" that is directly opposed to the "political" as the sovereign's non-normative decision about the "exception" (*Ausnahmezustand*).[5] The idea of citizenship is "isonomy" (Hayek 1960: 164), equal laws for all persons, in which the asymmetric power of people over other people is exactly abolished by the symmetric, and thus freedom-enhancing power of the law. While citizenship is notionally tied to the sphere of the political, and at heart is membership in a state as "protection racket,"[6] it also plants the virus of individualism that eventually dissolves this limitation and reduces the import of political association to that of any other association (or, rather, that politicizes the previously non-political spheres of society in a profoundly un-Schmittian sense).

Certainly, what appears here as result of a conceptual analysis is in reality the result of a historical process, the post-World War II transformation of the Western world from a Hobbesian zone of war into a Lockean zone of trade, which makes a Schmittian understanding of politics as group-level "friend–enemy" relationship increasingly implausible.

It is this historical process that forms the backdrop to the story of citizenship and immigration that will be unfolded in this book. At heart, it is a story of the mellowing of citizenship's exclusive edges, which were once marked by nationalism and racism, and of the reverse strengthening of its inclusive thrust, which Linda Bosniak (2006: 2–4) has captured in the oxymoron of "alien citizenship." But, at the onset, one must state the fundamental ambiguity of modern citizenship that is unlikely ever to go away: Rogers Brubaker (1992: ch. 1) characterized it as citizenship's being "externally exclusive" and "internally inclusive." We arrived at this distinction through situating citizenship in the political sphere, as which it is "externally exclusive," but then tracing the reverse dynamics of the individualistic and egalitarian idea of citizenship, as which it is "internally inclusive" and subversive of its exclusive and boundary-setting dimension.

Citizenship in History

To better calibrate the distinct features and dynamics of modern citizenship, it may be helpful to review briefly what citizenship has historically been (a short overview is Gosewinkel 2001). Its birthplace is usually taken to be ancient Athens, in which a citizen was "one who both rules and is ruled," to quote Aristotle's famous definition. Ever since, there has been an intrinsic connection between citizenship and democracy. But, as is well known, classic citizenship was highly exclusive and based on formal inequality, as only the male chiefs of an *oikos* (family household), and thus not women and slaves, could be equal members of the *polis* (city). In the polis, citizens were to abstract themselves from the trivia of economic life and pursue non-instrumental, public goals that lifted human above animal life. Hannah Arendt ([1958] 1981) eulogized this as "acting" and "speaking," pursuing the "good life" that is possible only in collectivity. But in reality, life in the polis was mostly about warfare.[7] What since the eighteenth century has been called society, "this strange intermediate space in which private interests acquire public significance" (ibid.: 36), was locked out of the affairs of Athenian citizenship. The latter was emphatically political, devoted to the affairs of the paramount community, without any interference from the merely private.

However, Athens also invented a more fundamental, lasting aspect of citizenship that is easily forgotten in the focus on the political and democracy: citizens are strangers, rising above the primordial ties of family and tribe. Citizenship is civic. In Ulrich Preuss's (1995: 275) evocative formula, citizenship allows "a kind of community in which aliens can become associates." Or, as J. G. A. Pocock explicated the same condition, a "community of citizens is one in which speech takes the place of blood, and acts of decision take the place of acts of vengeance" (1995: 30). From the start, citizenship is a civilizing instrument that works against the boundaries that are *also* set by it.

If classical Athenian citizenship stressed the importance of political participation and public-oriented virtues, imperial Rome pioneered a more mundane understanding of citizenship as a "legal status, carrying with it rights to certain things" (Pocock 1995: 36). This is much closer to our contemporary, liberal understanding of citizenship (see also Walzer 1970: 205) because of its focus on individuals and their rights, the latter constituting an inner sanctuary, a private sphere into which no one is allowed to intrude. The underlying image of the individual is not one of *zoon politikon*, as group-forming creature, freely and directly associating with other individuals; rather, the image is one of the individual as a "possessor of things" (Pocock 1995: 35) whose relations with other individuals need to be regulated by law, because of the intrinsic competitiveness and zero-sum relationship that property entails. Roman citizenship, in being generously conferred on conquered peoples in return for their expected loyalty, was also the first that foreshadowed a modern understanding of citizenship as legal state membership.

In the medieval age, the classic, polity- or state-centered tradition of citizenship collapsed, as Augustinian Christianity came to relocate the membership that mattered from the corrupted "city of man" to the spiritual "city of God." In the disparaged city of man, feudalism came to constitute a system of particularistic master–servant relationships that is directly opposed to the universalism and equality of citizenship (a concise account is Poggi 1978: ch. 2).

However, close to its etymological roots, citizenship survived as, and now became exclusively equated with, the status of free city-dweller in the Occidental city. As Max Weber famously argued, the Occidental city, with its focus on political autonomy, independent jurisdiction, non-primordial association, and the positive revaluation of economy and trade over the non-productive life of the chevalier and rural nobleman, was a virus that dissolved feudalism and prepared the coming of modern capitalism and state – "city air liberates" (*Stadtluft macht frei*) (Weber [1921] 1976: 742).

Modern citizenship still required an extension of scope from the city-state to the territorial state. A unitary state membership, replacing the multiple and non-territorial master–servant relationships of feudalism, was first established by the absolutist state. Internally, the absolutist state flattened the autonomy and privileges of the old estates and erected a uniform rule of law instead; externally, it created a formal state membership that was based on birth and thus more exacting than mere residency to mitigate the problem of the migrant poor (see Brubaker's discussion of Prussia, 1992: ch. 3). Such unitary state membership became democratically and nationally revalued in the French Revolution, which transformed equal subjectship into equal citizenship, thus producing the modern citizenship that we know today.

Citizenship in Social and Political Theory

Given its rich and variable history, and its centrality for understanding the human infrastructure of the modern state, it is astonishing that citizenship has been touched on only peripherally in classic social theory. Weber was interested mainly in bureaucracy and political leadership in the modern state, glossing over its citizen dimension. Durkheim relegated citizenship to pedagogy and moral education, however important this may be for cohesion in modern society. Only Marx ([1843] 1978) produced a memorable entry on citizenship, if only in terms of a sarcastic denunciation. For him, individuals led a "double existence – celestial and terrestrial" in capitalist democracies, as heavenly "citizen" in the state and as earthly, self-regarding "bourgeois" in civil society. In Marx's view, the formal equality of citizenship served only to mask the substantive inequalities of capitalist class societies. Much against what was ever held possible by Marx, for whom citizenship could never be more than a passive instrument of class rule, his analysis has since become key ammunition for the "complete citizen's" march through the institutions (Dahrendorf 1974), sniffing up coercive power wherever it rears its ugly head, and heralding the many hyphenated citizenships of today.

Social citizenship

The most influential work on citizenship ever written was a direct answer to Marx (without mentioning his name). In T. H. Marshall's *Citizenship and Social Class* ([1950] 1992), originally presented in 1949 as a series of lectures at Cambridge University, citizenship is nothing less than the peace formula that reconciled workers to capitalism. If the social question generated by capitalism was the twentieth century's central fault-line, citizenship was the answer to it. By the same token, if Marshall was the first to make citizenship an entry in the sociological lexicon, it was citizenship in the Roman tradition, as rights and benefits accrued to the individual by the state, and it was citizenship in its "internally inclusive" (Brubaker 1992: ch. 1) dimension only. Migration played no role in it.

In retrospect, one wonders how Marshall's dry and tedious tractate, which includes long digressions on peripheral and by now forgotten pranks of British postwar social policy, could ever have achieved canonical status. The famous triad of successively evolving citizenship rights – eighteenth-century civil rights, nineteenth-century political rights, and twentieth-century social rights – is little more than a sleight of hand, with no presumption of constituting a "theory" that might be valid beyond the provincial English story being told here. Knowing that sociology was "on trial here in my person" (1992: 30) (sociology was still *extra muros* in 1950s Cambridge and Oxford), Marshall reiterated the empiricist and applied diction that had always marked the British social sciences at large. His was a politely conservative (should one say: English?), not a window-smashing, bid for entry.

The overall edifice of a world changed by citizenship is still compelling, precisely because of Marshall's theoretical understatement and empiricist sense for detail. The lodestar of citizenship is equality. In Marshall's definition, citizenship is "basic human equality associated with the concept of full membership of a community" (1992: 6). The politics surrounding such citizenship is profoundly unpolitical in the Schmittian sense, because its thrust is inclusive rather than exclusive, presupposing rather than creating the boundaries that are required for law and rights to be possible. Moreover, the focus is on the individual as unit of the citizenry, not the citizenry as composite. The only vaguely group-level remark is that citizenship "requires . . . a direct sense of community membership based on loyalty to a civilization which is a common possession" (ibid.: 24) and that the evolution of citizenship, in turn, coincides with the rise of "modern national consciousness" (ibid.: 25). But the thrust of this observation is that the ties that bind are not those of "kinship" and "common descent" but those of "free men endowed with rights and protected by a common law" (ibid.: 24). In other words, citizenship is civic, not primordial. If anything, this is a theory of constitutional patriotism, in which the "struggle to win those [citizenship] rights" (ibid.: 25) becomes constitutive of the national narrative itself. No hint is made that a fixed sense of national community might be the presupposition for citizenship rights, which could give ammunition to those who argue today that there is a "progressives' dilemma" between ethnic diversity and welfare – that is, that both together are not possible (Goodhart 2004; see also chapter 2).

Marshall was not worried that citizenship might require something outside of it that it could not itself provide, such as ethnic homogeneity. Instead, he depicts citizenship as a great unifying and homogenizing force in itself, as creating a "unified civilization" (Marshall 1992: 47). If in the nineteenth century the capitalist and working classes faced one another as "two nations" (Disraeli), it was particularly the development of twentieth-century social citizenship rights that forged them into one. The result was not just "equalization . . . between classes as between individuals within a population which is now treated for this purpose as though it were one class" (ibid.: 33).

Marshall's question was what citizenship does to class inequality. His answer to this is differentiated and even partially affirms Marx's rather opposite views on the matter. In the early phase, eighteenth-century England, when the creation of civil rights of free association, contract, and property-holding was key, citizenship did *not* conflict with capitalism. On the contrary, as capitalism is based on contract and property rights, it *presupposes* civil citizenship rights (Marshall 1992: 20). In this respect, Marx is given his due. Marx and Marshall are in agreement that, initially, citizenship and capitalism are interdependent, and that in tandem they mark a fundamental departure from feudalism. In feudalism, individuals were seen as members of groups (or estates) with different rights and privileges – depending on whether you were an aristocrat, a member of the clergy, or a commoner, you lived in a different legal world. Inequality was formally inscribed in the social structure. Since the democratic revolutions of America and France, qua citizenship equality is formally inscribed in the social structure. Inequality becomes informal, and it takes on the shape of class inequality: "Class differences are not established and defined by the laws and customs of the society (in the medieval sense of that phrase), but emerge from the interplay of a variety of factors related to the institutions of property and education and the structure of the national economy" (ibid.: 19). In other words, social class is informal inequality of wealth and education on the floor of the formal equality established by citizenship.

Marshall parts company with Marx only with respect to the further evolution of citizenship, beyond the stage of civil rights. The political rights of citizenship, unlike civil rights, were already "full of potential danger to the capitalist system," entailing "vast changes . . . without a violent and bloody revolution" (Marshall 1992: 25). But a full-scale "war" between citizenship and the capitalist class system emerged only with the rise of twentieth-century social rights. Unfortunately, the "war" metaphor is not explored much beyond the conceptual level: the principle of citizenship is that of a "status," by means of which certain rights and benefits automatically accrue to the person qua citizen, so that social rights especially "imply an absolute right to a certain standard of civilization" (ibid.: 26). This reverses the modern trend from status to contract: "Social rights in their modern form imply an invasion of contract by status" (ibid.: 40). However, Marshall does not empirically trace how social citizenship rights might dissolve existing capitalist class inequalities. Instead, he limits himself to showing that citizenship becomes "an instrument of social stratification" itself, especially with respect to education. This was naively optimistic, foreshadowing later theories of the rise of meritocracy: "[T]he final outcome is a structure of unequal status fairly apportioned to unequal abilities" (ibid.: 38). Marshall thus overlooked the possibility, explored with great acumen in the works of Pierre Bourdieu (especially Bourdieu and Passeron 1970), that existing class inequalities might simply be "reproduced" in the new arena of public education, rather than being replaced in toto by a new form of citizenship stratification. However, the difference may not matter much if judged by the result, which is citizenship's function to put the "stamp of legitimacy" on persisting inequalities

(Marshall 1992: 39). In this respect, citizenship brought peace, not war, to capitalism. Citizenship's march was not, as Marshall falsely believed, "indistinguishable from socialism" (ibid.: 47).

If one rereads Marshall after capitalism's victory over socialism, one notices how much we live in a different world today, beyond the welfare state. The introduction of workfare in the United States and Western Europe, since the mid-1990s, has turned the wheel back "from status to contract" (Handler 2004: 2), and the flip-side to the rights of citizenship – obligations – which Marshall deemed as unlikely as "the Dunkirk spirit [to] be a permanent feature of any civilization" (1992: 46), moved to the fore in a way he completely failed to predict.[8] The discourse of "inclusion," which frames social policy in Europe today, is not about equality as a citizen right, but about reintegration into the paid labor market, with definitional neglect of the increasing inequities of global capitalism (see Levitas 2005). Marshall thought that, more than "class-abatement," the end point of citizenship was "to remodel the whole building" of capitalist class society, from a "skyscraper" of extreme inequality into a "bungalow" with flattened extremes, the only "natural limits" to the chase toward greater equality being the new inequities that resulted from citizenship itself. This was the world of "de-commodification," described by Gøsta Esping-Andersen rather wishfully as one where "citizens can freely, and without potential loss of job, income, or general welfare, opt out of work when they themselves consider it necessary" (1990: 3). It was a world, as Marshall fathomed, with "declining interest in the earning of big money" (Marshall 1992: 48), simply because the "real income" provided by the welfare state would render the "money incomes" provided by the market increasingly paltry and irrelevant, and because there would be a "belief that society should, and will, guarantee all the essentials of a decent and secure life at every level, irrespective of the amount of money earned." While the institutions of the welfare state, and most of its policies, are still with us, the spirit that once fired this enterprise – to make "every man . . . a gentleman" (A. Marshall, quoted ibid.: 5) – is gone. And if it is gone, then also because the very idea of a "unified civilization" (ibid.: 47) was peculiarly provincial, oblivious of the fact that there was a world outside England that stubbornly resisted such compression, and which would soon impose itself, not least, in terms of international migration.

If Marshall's substantive analysis of creeping welfare socialism has proved wrong, his formal understanding of the claims-making nature of citizenship has not.[9] Once the idea of citizenship takes hold, it constitutes "an ideal . . . against which achievement can be measured and towards which aspiration can be directed" (Marshall 1992: 18). This movement can be in two directions, in terms of enlarging the rights attached to citizenship (including, most recently, "multicultural" rights), or in terms of enlarging the categories of persons ("Pandas, Tamils, Women," in Luhmann's [1986] sarcastic diction) to whom these rights apply. "Citizenship" has been the idiom of the twentieth century's great reform movements, from workers to women to racial and ethnic minorities, even for the Eastern European dissident movements (though for the latter the call for the rights of citizenship had, paradoxically, revolutionary implications; see Joppke 1995a: ch. 1).

By the same token, Marshall's concept of citizenship, with its internal focus on rights and inclusion, is an unhelpful point of entry to the topic of this book – immigration and its implications for citizenship – because, from the vantage point of immigration, the world is at first divided into sharply bounded citizenries, each protected on the outside by a state and its intrinsically exclusive immigration and citizenship policies. With respect to immigration, citizenship functions above all as a device of external exclusion, and one that is far more robust and immune to the charge of "discrimination" than the intra-societal exclusions addressed by Marshall and most postwar students of citizenship.

National citizenship

It is the merit of Rogers Brubaker, in his agenda-setting work *Citizenship and Nationhood in France and Germany* (1992), to have broadened the concept of citizenship to make it useful for the study of immigration. He was the first to articulate sharply citizenship's peculiar duality to be "internally inclusive" – that is, to allow for only one formally equal membership status within society – *and* to be "externally exclusive" – that is, categorically to exclude from such equal membership status all foreigners. And he intriguingly suggests that both movements, toward inclusion and exclusion, are intrinsically related. The French Revolution, which invented this dualism, was at the same time democratic and national: "By inventing the national citizen and the legally homogeneous national citizenry, the Revolution simultaneously invented the foreigner" (1992: 46). Of course, this leaves unexplained why the leveling of one boundary, that between master and servant, should lead to the making of another boundary, that between citizen and foreigner. But this question perhaps transcends the boundaries of sociology, as it is ultimately one about the human condition, which is a condition of scarcity and limits *and* the intrinsically unsettling knowledge about it.

While aware of citizenship's duality, Brubaker's innovative contribution is to our understanding of citizenship's externally exclusive dimension. Borrowing Max Weber's concept of social closure, Brubaker conceives of citizenship as an "international filing system, a mechanism for allocating persons to states" (1992: 31). In the context of sociology, this was doubly innovative, as it entailed a new, post-Marshallian vista on citizenship, but also, more generally, a new vista on the state (see Joppke 1995b: 170f.). From Max Weber to Charles Tilly, historical sociology's dominant picture of the modern state had been in terms of a territory-centered rather than a person-centered organization, reflecting the fact that, in the transition from feudalism to the modern state, the basis of political rule shifted from persons to territory, from a polycentric rule of persons over persons that moved with the involved people into a mono-focal, centralized rule over a territory with fixed linear boundaries. This view obscured the fact that the modern state, while being territorial, was at the same time a membership association, and one in which membership was more demanding than mere residence, in being, for most, ascribed at birth.

Closure through citizenship serves both tangible and intangible state interests. With respect to tangible interests, citizenship helps protect "prosperous states from the migrant poor" (Brubaker

1992: x). This is why the pre-national Prussian state had already introduced a formal state membership, and it seems to be of disturbing, if not sharply increased, relevance for the post-national state of our time. In the age of nationalism, closure through citizenship also served the intangible needs of the state qua nation-state, to be "'of' and 'for' a particular, distinctive, bounded nation" (ibid.: 28).

While Brubaker's elaboration of the *why* of closure is unsurprising, his dissection of its *how* is not. He sharply observes that citizenship functions both as "instrument" and as "object" of social closure. As instrument of closure, citizenship allows the state to control access to its territory, because only citizens have a right to enter under international law, and everyone else can be denied entry or be expelled after entry. But citizenship is, in addition, an object of closure, access to which is limited by a state's nationality laws. Such laws provide two ways to accede to citizenship: through ascription at birth for most, and through naturalization for some. The interesting fact is that state membership is usually ascribed at birth. This shows that, contrary to the Enlightenment idea of the modern state as based on a contract, the state is *not* a voluntary association. This makes the state structurally different from, if not "paramount" (Schmitt 1963) to, all other forms of human association. The possibility of naturalization, which is facially a voluntary act, does not change this fundamental fact. Firstly, because naturalization is the exception to the rule of citizenship ascription at birth (all those who naturalize already hold another citizenship by birth). But, secondly, consider the very term "naturalize," whose root word, "nature," denotes the opposite of choice. And, thirdly, a nagging feature of naturalization, even in states such as the US where it is a routine affair with low thresholds, is its discretionary nature. In the end, it is everywhere the state and not the individual who chooses. If, in contemporary political discourse, from Australia to Europe, there is renewed emphasis that citizenship is "a privilege, not a right," this expresses, in positive form, the involuntary essence of state membership.

Taken together, citizenship's instrument- and object-of-closure functions are circular and reinforcing, in that only citizens have unhindered access to the territory, yet only residents (with no such right of access) can ever hope to meet the prerequisites for becoming citizens. "This circularity," Brubaker (1992: 34) concludes, "permits nation-states to remain . . . relatively closed and self-perpetuating communities, reproducing their membership in a largely endogenous fashion, open only at the margins to the exogenous recruitment of new members."

Conceiving of citizenship as a mechanism of social closure is Brubaker's enduring contribution to the theory of citizenship. In a combination of formal-institutional and historical analysis, he shows that citizenship is not ipso facto democratic. In the German language, this formal, unsentimental aspect of citizenship is referred to as *Staatsangehörigkeit*, which is "a legal institution regulating membership in the state, not a set of participatory practices or . . . civic attitudes" (Brubaker 1992: 51). Though nothing new to the lawyer, this is not how sociologists, especially in the wake of T. H. Marshall, had looked at citizenship before.

However, what *Citizenship and Nationhood in France and Germany* is really known for is the much more questionable argument that distinct traditions of nationhood have lastingly locked in states' citizenship laws in either inclusive (France) or exclusive (Germany) directions. At the formal level, this is yet another example of a simple knowledge transfer generating a new insight, this time not from law to sociology but from history to sociology. Historians had long distinguished between the French tradition of "civic" nationhood, in which the state creates the nation in its political image, and the German tradition of "ethnic" nationhood, in which a preexisting nation seeks a state that is expressive of its pre-political (linguistic, ethnic, cultural) features.[10] Giving a new spin to this distinction, Brubaker argues that the emphasis of citizenship laws on either territory or blood in the birth attribution of citizenship is driven by these different understandings of nationhood. Germany's preference for *jus sanguinis*, according to which citizenship is inherited, like blood, from one's parents, is seen as reflective of an ethnic understanding of nationhood. Conversely, France's preference for *jus soli*, according to which citizenship is a function of the political territory into which one is born, is seen as reflective of a civic understanding of nationhood.

The claim that "cultural idioms" of nationhood have shaped French and German citizenship laws is backed by an impressively dense historical analysis of the making and consolidation of these laws in the late nineteenth and late twentieth centuries, respectively. With respect to the French case, an instrumentalist explanation of inclusiveness, which would focus on military and demographic needs in a country notoriously short of people, is skillfully rebutted. And isn't it obvious, already at the conceptual level, that externally exclusive citizenship, which thrives on a boundary, should be subject to a "politics of identity," not just a "politics of interest" (Brubaker 1992: 182)? That boundaries make identities is established wisdom from anthropology (Barth 1969) to social psychology (Tajfel 1970). Why should citizenship be an exception? Empirically, Germany's laggardness in accepting *jus soli*, which relegated even second- and third-generation immigrants to the status of foreigners, and its long-standing preference for co-ethnic immigrants, obviously resonated with an ethnic understanding of the nation, as a "community of descent" (Brubaker 1992: x). Conversely, France's historical inclusiveness toward immigrants, which has been likened to an American-style "melting pot" (Noiriel 1996), and its stubborn refusal to acknowledge ethnic and racial distinctions in public policy up to the present day certainly suggest a civic understanding of the nation, as a "territorial community" (Brubaker 1992: x).

The problem is that, in the reception of this cultural theory of citizenship, much of its conceptual and historical nuance has been lost, and only a stylized and stereotypical contrast of "civic" France and "ethnic" Germany has remained, along with the claim of the iron grip of these nationhood understandings over citizenship laws over the centuries. Patrick Weil (2002: 194) has retorted to this that citizenship laws are, in reality, written by jurists copying or modifying the laws of other countries, thus questioning the entire "politics of identity" frame. Consider that Brubaker's own discussion of the case of Prussia suggests that non-national, non-democratic citizenship – that is, citizenship without identity – is possible (Brubaker 1992: ch. 3). There is no necessity for citizenship to be subject to a "politics of identity," no automatic linkage between nationhood and citizenship, and citizenship's pre-national past suggests the possibility of postnational futures. Secondly, even within the golden era of national citizenship, the tight affiliation of *jus soli* and *jus sanguinis* with civic and ethnic nationhood, respectively, is overdrawn. Brubaker (ibid.: 95) certainly sees, but does not sufficiently highlight, the traditionalism of *jus soli*, which is of feudal origins, and the modernity of *jus sanguinis*, which – as the irony would have it – was invented in the Napoleonic Code civil and became the mainstay of a modern citizenship law throughout nineteenth-century Europe. If anything, *jus sanguinis* empowers the individual, who now transmits nationality like the family name (Weil 2002: 35); there is nothing intrinsically ethnic about it. Finally, the sharp distinction between ethnic and civic nationhood obscures the empirical intermingling of both in the real world. The root word of "nation" is the Latin *nasci* (to be born), which points to descent and intergenerational continuity. In this sense, a nation is ipso facto ethnic. Conversely, in connoting self-rule and internal equality of members, all nations contain a modicum of voluntarism and civicness. Accordingly, Brubaker (1999) later distanced himself from the "Manichean myth" of ethnic versus civic nationhood.[11]

But least plausible of all is the strangely anachronistic picture of self-perpetuating, sharply divergent nation-states, the same that *also* happen to be the engines of European unification – France and Germany. More concretely, Brubaker (1992) attributes an inertia to nationally divergent citizenship laws that does not really exist. When the Gaullist prime minister Jacques Chirac failed, in 1986, to tie *jus soli* citizenship for second-generation immigrants to their expressed *volunté* at majority age, which was a strangely liberal idea imposed on him by Jean-Marie Le Pen's National Front, this was taken as confirmation of an "idiom of nationhood" (ibid.: 162) that stressed the socializing powers of state-level institutions, especially schools. But why then did the same restriction on second-generation *jus soli* succeed the second time around, in 1993?[12] Even more drastic change occurred in Germany, where ethnic immigration has been heavily curtailed since 1992, naturalization rules have been liberalized and – almost unique in Europe – were put on an as-of-right basis in 1993, and, above all, conditional *jus soli* for second-generation immigrants was introduced in a major reform of citizenship law in 1999. The German liberalization of citizenship, which only follows a broader European liberalizing trend, is unintelligible within Brubaker's "cultural idiom" approach to citizenship. Of course, one could argue that, in the meantime, German nationhood has become more liberal and civic to spin forward a more liberal citizenship law. While this is entirely plausible, and probably the case, it is also tautological, because something as intangible as a "culture" can always be found to explain an outcome (which, in turn, is taken to demonstrate the existence of such "culture").

Postnational membership

It is the distinct contribution of Yasemin Soysal's *Limits of Citizenship* (1994) to have pointed to some important "postnational" changes in the institution of citizenship.[13] Hers is, next to that of Brubaker (1992), the second paradigm-setting positioning of citizenship within an immigration context, though with strikingly differing accents and diagnoses. She turns the focus back on Marshallian, internally inclusive citizenship – that is, on citizenship as rights-holding and claims-making. However, contra Marshall, she argues that rights (especially civil and social rights) are no longer invested in national citizenship but rather in universal "personhood," which heralds the coming of a "postnational model of membership" (1994: 3). Her case in point is the postwar European guest workers, lured by bilateral agreements into the booming Northwest European economies between the late 1950s and the early 1970s, who have acquired a safe legal resident status, with civil and social rights that are nearly equal to those of native citizens, without having had to become citizens of their new countries. In her words, "the recent guestworker experience reflects a time when national citizenship is losing ground to a more universal model of membership anchored in deterritorialized notions of persons' rights" (ibid.).

In a "new institutionalism" approach that is strongly influenced by John Meyer's tracing of the workings of world-level cultural "scripts" and institutions (e.g. Meyer et al. 1997), Soysal identifies two "transnational" sources of postnational membership: an increasing density and interdependence of transnational political structures that "constrain the host states from dispensing with their migrant populations at will" (Soysal 1994: 144) and the rise of "universalistic rules and conceptions regarding the rights of the individual" (ibid.: 145) – that is, of a global human rights culture after World War II. Certainly, nation-states are still responsible for "providing and implementing individual rights," but they are mere organizational transmission belts because the "legitimacy for these rights now lies in a transnational order" (ibid.: 143). With respect to citizenship, Soysal (1996) claims that its previous union of "rights" and "identity" has fallen apart, rights becoming institutionalized as human rights at global level, while identities are still particularly bounded, but the national competing with other kinds of identity.

Curiously, Soysal's (1994) claim of postnational convergence, almost like an afterthought, follows upon a differently spirited comparison of national "incorporation regimes" across Europe. The latter shows in the political opportunity structure mold pioneered in recent social movement theory that migrants' participation in host society is conditioned more by host-society structures than by their endogenous cultural features. Accordingly, the claim of convergence toward postnational membership coexists, somewhat uneasily, with the opposite claim of persistent national divergence of immigrant incorporation. While it is not impossible that both trends *may* coexist, simply because they are situated at different levels (organizational versus discursive?), the absence of commentary on their apparent disjunction is strange.

But what *Limits of Citizenship* is known for is not the comparison of nationally divergent incorporation regimes but the claim of convergence toward postnational membership. What Hegel once said about philosophy may explain the success of this strand of her analysis: it is "its time expressed in thought" (*ihre Zeit in Gedanken gefasst*), capturing earlier and better than similar works a postnational moment in the contemporary reflection on state and citizenship. Moreover, because her claim of the postnational transformation of citizenship was so starkly different from Brubaker's opposite claim of the resilience of national citizenship, there was immediately a lively debate on the pros and cons of both sides (Joppke 1998: 7–9, 23–9). This "debate," to the degree that it was one, never quite considered that Brubaker and Soysal dealt with rather different aspects of citizenship – "status" and "rights," respectively – so that both may simply talk past one another.

In retrospect, *Limits of Citizenship* reflects a maximally multicultural mode of European states' approach to immigrant integration, with a low emphasis on citizenship, trust in the universalism of law in work and welfare that made no distinction between citizens and foreigners, and a general distaste for forcing an identity on people. The Berlin Foreigners' Office's free-wheeling motto at the time, *Wir sind Berlin*, is also Soysal's motto, as it "precludes national fixities and allows for shifting categories and fluid confines, and thus can traverse multiple borders" (Soysal 1994: 166). The meaning is not immediately clear. But it hit a nerve.

The irony is that "postnational membership," though articulating the spirit of the nationally uprooted sons and daughters of guest workers, is really the unspoken ideology of their parents, as it spares them the acquisition of a new citizenship without therefore ending up without rights. For second- and third-generation immigrants, postnational membership, if not framed by inclusive citizenship laws, is rather more problematic, as it relegates them to the permanent status of *metics*, second-class members without political rights (which continue to be a citizen privilege). There are intrinsic vulnerabilities to non-citizen status that Soysal glosses over too easily. They first became apparent in the mid-1990s US welfare reforms that excluded legal immigrants from federal welfare benefits (see Martin 2002). And they became even more apparent in the post-2001 era of increased security concerns, with states broadening their powers of expulsion and whittling away the safe residence status of non-citizens (see Cole 2002). Furthermore, just about the time that Soysal (1994) deemed national citizenship on the way out, states rediscovered it as a tool of integration, with distinctly disciplinary and coercive connotations, in a marked departure from the multicultural laissez-faire of the past.

The Concept of Citizenship

Multicultural citizenship

A third agenda-setting work of placing citizenship in an immigration context is Will Kymlicka's *Multicultural Citizenship* (1995). It tackles the question of how to reconcile citizenship with the fact of ethnic diversity, which is partially (but not exclusively) the result of immigration. As it addresses the rights of immigrants, one might think that multicultural citizenship is not so different from "postnational membership" (Soysal 1994). This is not so. Remember that postnational membership is universalistic, in line with the original impulse of the citizenship construct, but driving it beyond parochial national boundaries. By contrast, multicultural citizenship is particularistic, pointing to inherent deficiencies of universalistic citizenship rights for ethnic and national minorities. It addresses instances where the universalism of law, even if extended to non-citizens, is the problem, not the solution. Examples are designated official languages that are not those of long-established national minorities, or public holidays that reflect the religious calendar of the majority group but not that of recent immigrant minorities. For these cases there is a "need to supplement traditional human rights principles with a theory of minority rights" (Kymlicka 1995: 5). The word "supplement" is indicative of the liberal thrust of this theory. This is not a radical or utopian critique of liberalism (as, for instance, Young 1990). Instead, the argument is that liberalism, if it is to remain consistent with its principles of freedom and equality, has to accept minority rights and thus compromise on its axiomatic preference for universalism.

With respect to the first liberal principle, freedom, Kymlicka (1995: ch. 5) argues that free and meaningful choice requires the context of a "societal culture." The latter is defined as "synonymous with 'a nation' or 'a people' – that is, as an intergenerational community, more or less institutionally complete, occupying a given territory or homeland, sharing a distinct language and history" (ibid.: 18). Accordingly, only ethnic and national groups qualify for minority status, not gays, lesbians, or other life-style groups. Against Jeremy Waldron's "cosmopolitan alternative"

(1992), Kymlicka holds that societal culture cannot be a hodge-podge of many cultures or any culture, but has to be "one's own culture" (Kymlicka 1995: 84). This is the culture into which one is usually born, the attachment to it being "based on belonging, not accomplishment" (ibid.: 89). What Kymlicka deems "a fact," grounded in the "human condition" (ibid.: 90), still comes dangerously close to being an apology of nationalism. At least he is toying here with the limits of liberalism. His argument also creates interesting complications for the case of immigrants, who are – realistically – conceived as having "waived" the right to their societal culture through the very fact of having left their homeland (ibid.: 96). However, if "immigrant groups do not [have societal cultures]" (ibid.: 101), how can they be entitled to any minority right? Whatever these complications, the message is clear: if liberal states want to live up to their ideology of freedom, they must secure access for all of their members to "their" societal cultures, majority and minorities alike. And, unlike Charles Taylor's (1992) controversial plea that cultures have an overarching claim for *survivance* that may trump the freedoms of the individual, this is a liberal theory in that the value of culture for the individual, and not of culture for its own sake, is paramount.

But multicultural citizenship is desirable also for advancing a second liberal principle, equality. In a second step, Kymlicka (1995: ch. 6) argues that neutrality or "benign neglect," which is the classic response of the liberal state to religious and cultural difference, is not enough. Even liberal states can never be culturally neutral. In their apparently innocuous decisions about public language(s), holidays, and symbols, states cannot but promote certain cultural identities and thereby disadvantage others. It may have been possible for the liberal state to differentiate itself from religion, which is the model of the "neutrality" response to contemporary cultural difference. But the state cannot equally differentiate itself from ethnicity and nationality: "The state can (and should) replace religious oaths in courts with secular oaths, but it cannot replace the use of English in courts with no language" (ibid.: 111). This critique of neutrality and advocacy for multicultural recognition was invented by radical feminism, which argued that including women on equal terms in work and public life was not enough, because of the inherent male bias built into these institutions (in this spirit, Galeotti 1993). Kymlicka modifies this view in not throwing out state-level particularism, but paying the latter its due respect. He accepts the division of the world into separate states, because one of its functions is "to protect people's cultural membership" (Kymlicka 1995: 125). This provides an "analogy with states" for justifying minority rights, because the same logic that forces one to accept the differentiation of the world into states forces one to accept minority rights within states: "[T]he orthodox liberal view about the right of states to determine who has citizenship rests on the same principles which justify group-differentiated citizenship within states, and . . . accepting the former leads logically to the latter" (ibid.: 124). This ingeniously shifts the burden of proof with respect to minority rights from its proponents to its opponents, simply because citizenship itself "is an inherently group-differentiated notion" (ibid.). The underlying image is that of a pact with the nation-state: its legitimacy is granted, even from a liberal point of view, because it helps secure for the majority the culture that is necessary for their freedom; but, in return, liberal justice commands that minorities are guaranteed access to *their* culture.

Kymlicka's *Multicultural Citizenship* opens a window onto an aspect of contemporary citizenship that is distinct from the questions of access to citizenship and of the extension of citizen rights to non-citizens, which are the focus of Brubaker (1992) and Soysal (1994), respectively. While the work of a political philosopher, and thus primarily normative, it is still of relevance to empirical sociology, for at least two reasons: firstly, because citizenship itself is a normative concept, "an ideal . . . against which achievement can be measured," to reiterate T. H. Marshall (1992: 18); secondly, because Kymlicka can show, with great sense for empirical detail and an honest wrestling with hard cases, that the reality of liberal-democratic states has itself provided the clues for his normative theory.

Of particular importance is Kymlicka's sociological instinct that no single formula can be equally applied to all groups, but that different groups require different rights provisions. The strongest type of minority rights, those of self-government, are reserved to national minorities and indigenous people, who had state borders moving above their heads. But, with an eye on Quebec, Kymlicka concedes that this "most complete case of differentiated citizenship" cannot serve an "integrative function," as there is no "natural stopping point" before full-scale secession (1995: 182). With respect to immigrants, his prescriptions are much more modest. Immigrants are entitled only to "polyethnic rights," such as exemptions from general laws that are at odds with their cultural or religious ways, and they are "usually intended to promote integration into the larger society, not self-government" (ibid.: 31). Again, the status of "right" of these provisions is unclear, because immigrants, unlike national minorities, cannot claim a homeland and "societal culture" that the state must protect. Further, if integration is their purpose, it is not clear why polyethnic rights are, now in line with the self-government rights of national minorities, permanent and not just temporary provisions. This is consistent with these rights' purpose of protecting, rather than eliminating, cultural differences (in contrast to antidiscrimination laws and policies whose thrust is universalistic and whose "taking account of race"[14] is notionally in the interim only, until color-blindness is reached). However, that permanent state-level protection of cultural difference serves the goal of integration is more rhetoric than established truth, and other outcomes than integration are equally possible.[15]

Citizenship in a World of Migration: Status, Rights, Identity

The purpose of this book is to review the evolution of citizenship in the context of international migration after World War II. This caesura is important: it marks the defeat of a regime, Nazi Germany, which sought to remake the world along the principle of race and state-level racism, subduing, if not eliminating, the individual on the way. Conversely, it marks the beginning of the contemporary era of human rights, which establishes the individual and his or her integrity as the benchmark and ulterior constraint of state policy. As a result, citizenship became infused with human rights logic. Racist, sexist or any group-level exclusion became illegitimate. This had enormous consequences once the institution of citizenship encountered the fact of international migration, because the switches for an inclusive approach had been laid.

Of course, the equation of citizenship with human rights is no twentieth-century novelty. Both have a joint ancestry, in the French Declaration of the Rights of Man and Citizen of 1789. What is new, however, is the aggressive pursuit of human rights in both the international and the domestic arena, spurred on by their very annihilation under Nazism. This constrains the sovereignty that states notionally enjoy in matters of citizenship under international law. The paramount expression of this constraint is Article 15.1 of the UN Universal Declaration of Human Rights, which decrees that "Everyone has the right to a nationality." This is a paradoxical "right," because state membership is considered in classic nationality law as a "status" or "condition to which certain rights and duties are connected," so that it cannot itself be a right (A. Makarov, quoted in Joppke 2003: 432). But it correctly shows the intrusion of human rights considerations into a field that previously was at the total discretion of the sovereign state. This would not have been possible without the experience of Nazism, which showed the utter fragility of stateless people, as the German Jews who were targeted for annihilation were first stripped of their nationality. In her somber analysis of totalitarianism, Hannah Arendt ([1951] 1979: 296f.) therefore stipulated the existence of a "right to have rights," that is, "a right to belong to some kind of organized community," which is the spirit that underlies the UN decree of a "right to a nationality."

How has citizenship evolved in the contemporary world of migration? Our theoretical review showed highly disparate and partial answers, and one even wonders how all those discussed could talk about the same thing, "citizenship." T. H. Marshall's "social citizenship," which has set the tone for the entry of citizenship into liberal postwar sociology, depicted the provincial world of a "unified civilization" that was exactly torn asunder by postcolonial immigration. While all the following interventions situated citizenship in a context of immigration, this is about the only thing they have in common. Brubaker's "national citizenship," which turned attention to citizenship's external boundary-setting functions, held that such boundaries lastingly varied according to distinct nationhood traditions, being exclusive and impermeable in "ethnic" Germany and inclusive and permeable in "civic" France. Soysal's "postnational membership" claimed the opposite, that national citizenship was an anachronism, because immigrants now had rights irrespective of their citizenship status. And Kymlicka's "multicultural citizenship" stayed aloof from the question of resilience or decline of citizenship, arguing instead that cultural pluralism required a modification of the rights accrued to citizens (which did not thereby become moot, as claimed by Soysal).

These discrepancies in approach and diagnosis suggest the need to ferret out more clearly which aspects of citizenship are entangled with immigration. Let me distinguish in the following between citizenship as status, rights, and identity.

Status

The most basic aspect of citizenship is that of a status designating formal state membership. This is citizenship as passport-holding. Denoted by the French *nationalité* or the German *Staatsangehörigkeit*, it can go along with an astonishing internal stratification of rights. Most notably, women and racial minorities were once excluded, often far into the second half of the twentieth century, from equal access to the whole panoply of Marshallian rights, especially political rights, even though there never was a question about their formal nationality. Given this internal stratification of rights according to ascriptive group membership, it is no wonder that the same groups faced discrimination in the access to citizenship, in terms of racially exclusive naturalization laws (in place in the US until the early 1950s) or of sexually discriminatory rules of losing or transmitting citizenship (in place in most Western states way into the 1970s).

Rights

A second aspect of citizenship is rights, which has been the classic focus of the political sociology of citizenship since T. H. Marshall. What constitutes a "right" is itself a complex question. Sufficient for us is that, in modern understanding, a "right" is an entitlement that accrues equally to all persons. That is, modern rights are equal rights, in radical departure from a pre-modern understanding of rights as hierarchical and differing from group to group. This raises the question of the relationship between human and citizen rights, because, if confronted with non-citizens, citizens are a privileged "group" no less than the feudal estates of old – as Joseph Carens (1987: 252) put it evocatively, "citizenship in Western liberal democracies is the modern equivalent of feudal privilege." The 1789 Declaration of the Rights of Man and Citizen is mostly about human rights, and an explicit citizen right appears only in Article 6, which is about the constitution of the "general will." Up to the present day, political rights have remained largely citizen rights, whereas – this is the correct observation of Soysal (1994) – most civil and social rights do not show such limitation. However, important civil rights, such as immunity from being randomly "accused, arrested, or imprisoned" (Article 7 of the 1789 Declaration), never had any nationality restriction. This is obscured in Marshall's qualification of civil rights as citizen rights (see the critique by Ferrajoli 1994), and it casts doubt on the novelty of some postnational "personhood" rights. Overall, the calibration of the citizen versus non-citizen line with respect to rights is complicated and variable over time and cross-nationally, not to mention that among non-citizens there is additional variation according to entry, residence, and functional status. To this one must add the final complication that some immigrant rights are not proxies of citizen rights but accrue to immigrants qua ethnic minority, in terms of multicultural and antidiscrimination rights.

Identity

Next to status and rights, a third aspect of citizenship is the shared beliefs or identity that ties the individual to a political community, classically the nation. These beliefs may be of two kinds: the empirical beliefs held by ordinary people, or the normative beliefs that states seek to impute on people. The focus of this book is on state-imputed identities (a rare account of empirical citizenship beliefs is Miller-Idriss 2006, 2009). Since Aristotle, normative citizenship beliefs have been a cornerstone of the republican tradition, which conceives of citizenship as a "virtue" – that is, as ipso facto "good," public-minded citizenship, in which the individual abstracts from his or her merely private interests and inclinations. It thus closely overlaps with political participation and engagement, which – from ancient Greece to present-day representative democracies – is and has remained the classic domain of citizenship. However, from a liberal point of view, virtuous citizenship has always been eyed with suspicion, because of its oppressive, freedom-restricting possibilities – captured in Oscar Wilde's felicitous phrase that "socialism would take too many evenings." The freedom-restricting, public-order producing – in short: integrative – potential of normative citizenship identities has not been lost on states. In fact, their production is the very purpose of nation-building, old and new. This raises the question of what contemporary nation-building, which is specifically geared toward binding immigrants into already nationalized domestic populations, and which is tightly constrained by liberal equality and non-discrimination norms, looks like. Of the works on citizenship and immigration reviewed above, only Brubaker (1992) touches on the identity aspect of citizenship, but in a reductive and static way that by definition forecloses the possibility of change.

Outline

Separate literatures have emerged on each of the three aspects of citizenship, with little mutual awareness and dialogue between them. The fragmentation of contemporary citizenship studies is repeated even when addressing citizenship from the point of view of immigration alone. Interestingly, however, the few attempts at synthesis operate with the same or a similar "status–rights–identity" grid as the one proposed here.[16] The main purpose of the following chapters is to provide a succinct and synthetic picture of citizenship's evolution in each of these three dimensions, and to identify the internal relationships and possible connections between the developments across these dimensions. As obvious as it is, this has rarely been done.

The central claim in this book is that, rather than being reproduced in nationally distinct ways or being set on a global path of decline, citizenship continued to evolve, toward becoming more inclusive and universalistic. In a way, citizenship's internally inclusive core has softened its externally exclusive edges. This is the key development of the past half-century, in Europe and North America alike. However, the liberalizing trend has been especially drastic in Europe, whose citizenship regimes were not originally built for a world of migration, and where the adjustment to the immigration challenge was accordingly of a taller and more difficult order. As a result, not only have intra-European differences melted away, but also the notion that North America differs fundamentally from Europe has to be abandoned. Michael Walzer (1997: 31) once distinguished between the ethnic "nation-states" of Europe, which are "machines for national reproduction," and the "neutral" state of America, which is "committed to none of the groups that make it up." This distinction, if it ever held muster, has become obsolete, as European states are moving into the American direction of inclusive and non-ethnic citizenship (for a similar argument, see Parsons 1971: ch. 6).

The baseline for this development has been a wholesale liberalization of access to the *status* of citizenship, which is the subject of chapter 2. In Europe, ethnically closed citizenship regimes were opened up by the introduction of *jus soli*, an increasing toleration of dual nationality, and a general lowering of naturalization requirements. The underlying imperative is simple: liberal democracy requires the congruence between rulers and ruled, which is violated by the long-term presence of sizeable non-citizen populations, many of them born and raised in the countries of immigration. However, the processes leading to this outcome have been uneven and variegated. Two countertrends will be highlighted. The first is a trend toward new restrictions in naturalization, driven by perceived integration deficits of Muslim immigrants and by security concerns in the wake of Islamic terrorism. The second is a trend toward the "re-ethnicization" of citizenship, by means of which contemporary states seek to retain or strengthen ties with expatriate communities abroad. However, I shall argue that these countertrends are nuances within, not a rollback to, the overall liberalization of the access to citizenship.

Chapter 3 discusses three ways in which immigration has become implicated with the *rights* of citizenship. The first is touched on by the recent debate as to whether ethnic diversity has damaged social rights in the welfare state. While the jury on this is out, it is indisputable that, in the context of immigration, other than social rights have moved to the fore. On the one side, there has been a strengthening of the rights of aliens, which is the bedrock of Soysal's "postnational membership" diagnosis. In approximating aliens to citizens, alien rights indeed render citizenship less important. However, rather than signifying a consolidated new type of membership, alien rights are highly stratified, differing not just across but within countries, according to length of residence, mode of entry, and functional sector. Moreover, there has been a restrictive trend, first in the United States, and later in Europe, which highlighted the essential vulnerability of non-citizens. Thirdly, the fact of immigration has lent new emphasis on minority rights, which accrue to immigrants (but also citizens) qua ethnic minority. These may again be of two kinds, multicultural rights that protect cultural particularity, and antidiscrimination rights that attack discrimination on these grounds. I shall argue that the importance of multicultural rights has been greatly exaggerated, and perhaps there has even been a retreat from them, while antidiscrimination rights are going from strength to strength, lately even in Europe.

Chapter 4 is on the impact of immigration on the *identity* of citizenship. Confronted with increasingly diverse societies, states have recently rediscovered citizenship as a tool of integration, moving away from the multicultural laissez-faire of the recent past. This chapter scrutinizes the citizenship identities that transpire in states' recent integration campaigns toward immigrants and ethnic minorities. I argue that these integration campaigns become caught in a paradox. While the attempt is to bind newcomers into a particular nation-state that is different here from there, all that newcomers can legitimately be expected to adopt and share are the general rules and principles of liberal democracy, which are the same everywhere. Accordingly, a review of state pronouncements of what it means to be "American," "British," or "Dutch" reveals them as at heart identical. In a nutshell, citizenship identities, to the degree that they fall within the ambit of state policy,[17] have become universalistic. However, such identities may still be exclusive, as Muslims in particular currently experience in Europe.

Chapter 5 tackles the question of causality and interconnectedness of the changes of citizenship across its three dimensions, and raises the unavoidable question: What future for citizenship? As citizenship has become more accessible, it inevitably must mean less in terms of rights and identity. A twenty-first-century manifesto of creating a "unified civilization" (Marshall 1992) through citizenship would be anachronistic. European Union citizenship may well herald the future: a "citizenship light" of rights without obligations, in itself socially inconsequential, and devoid of a particular cultural content.

2

Status

For most people in the world, the status of citizenship is never an issue: they are born with it. Birthright is the principal mechanism of attributing citizenship in all of the world's states.[1] At one level, this is due to mere convenience, because birth is the easiest way of allocating people to states. But at a deeper level it reveals a core feature of the state: membership of it tends to be involuntary. This distinguishes the state from most other forms of human association, including the family, which is founded upon a voluntary act – marriage.[2] It also flies in the face of the modern state's own constitutive ideology of contract and consent, articulated in the political philosophy from Hobbes to Rousseau. As Ayelet Shachar (2003: 347) expounds the paradox, "We reject heredity as a determining factor in almost any other admissions criteria (such as those concerning competitive job offers or selective university programs). However, family ties and birthright entitlements still dominate our imagination and our laws when it comes to articulating principles for allotting membership in a state." The distinction between territorial *jus soli* and descent-based *jus sanguinis* citizenship, which tends to be colored today by a preference for the "civic" (because more inclusive) *jus soli* principle, is tangential to the fundamental fact of involuntary state membership – in *both* it is birth, not choice, which makes a citizen.

Access to citizenship becomes an issue only for international migrants, who have left their state of birthright citizenship to enter a state of which they are not citizens. The number of such

Table 2.1 Foreign-born population in selected OECD countries (as a percentage of the total)

	1996	2000	2005
Australia	23.3	23.0	23.8
Austria	–	10.5	13.5
Belgium	9.8	10.3	12.1
Canada	17.4	18.0	19.1
France	–	–	8.1
Germany	11.9	12.5	–
Ireland	6.9	8.7	11.0
Luxembourg	31.5	33.2	33.4
Netherlands	9.2	10.1	10.6
New Zealand	16.2	17.2	19.4
Norway	5.6	6.8	8.2
Sweden	10.7	11.3	12.4
Switzerland	21.3	21.9	23.8
United Kingdom	7.1	7.9	9.7
United States	10.3	11.0	12.9

Source: OECD (2007: 330).

migrants has massively increased over the past few decades, and it shows no signs of abating. Between 1970 and 2005, the number of international migrants has grown from 82 million to 200 million (GCIM 2005: 83). While international migrants still constitute only 3 percent of the world's population, they are overrepresented in the developed world (Europe, North America, and Oceania), into which they are drawn for the obvious reasons – higher wages, security, and the prospect of a better life. Accordingly, between 1980 and 2000 the number of international migrants living in the developed world more than doubled, from 48 million to 110 million; compared to this the parallel increase from 52 to 65 million in the developing world looks paltry (ibid.: 84). In the main immigrant-receiving OECD countries, the foreign-born population share approaches or even exceeds the 10 percent mark (see table 2.1).

Because the category "foreign-born" embraces naturalized citizens, these data are not strictly about "immigrants" (if narrowly defined by non-citizen status); the latter are included in but do not exhaust the "foreign-born." But these data do show the sustained, in most cases even continuously increasing, presence of international migrants throughout the OECD world – even after the 2001 watershed, which has raised new security concerns that might have dampened further intakes. In Northwest European countries, the share of the foreign-born is at about 10 percent of the total population. In Oceania, their share is even around the 20 percent mark, with the United States (12.9 percent in 2005) interestingly being closer to the European than the classic immigrant-country cluster. Luxembourg and Switzerland, with their exorbitantly high foreign-born figures of 33.4 percent and 23.8 percent, respectively, are outliers in Europe (anywhere, for that matter), but many of their "immigrants" are elite functionaries of the international organizations and multinational corporations that are clustering in these small, extremely rich and advanced countries.

If one squares these contemporary immigration figures with the involuntary nature of state membership, one immediately notices that "access to citizenship" is the first and foremost problem generated by the fact of immigration meeting the institution of citizenship. The legitimacy of the modern state hinges on the congruence between the subjects and objects of rule: other than the absolutist state of the past, in which the monarch could say "L'Etat, c'est moi,"[3] this is a state by and for the people (See Dahl 1989: ch. 9). The modern state is a citizen state, with equality as the dominant principle. The presence of permanent second-class members, akin to the *metics* of the Greek polity who were ruled but did not rule (see Walzer 1983: ch. 2), is a thorn in the eye of the equality norm. While it is perfectly legitimate for the liberal-democratic state to ward off first admissions into the territory by means of a restrictive immigration policy, once territorial admission has occurred the second admission into the citizenry is difficult to reject. In a liberal-democratic context, the presence of sizeable, long-settled immigrant populations cannot but exert pressure toward making citizenship more accessible to and inclusive of immigrants, at least where the pertinent citizenship laws do not already show these inclusive features (see Rubio-Marín

2000). This has been, in a nutshell, the experience of the past half-century, especially in Europe.

The classic immigrant countries and Europe were indeed differently prepared to tackle the contemporary immigration challenge. The former possessed historically inclusive citizenship regimes attuned to the fact of immigration, while the latter did not. *Jus soli* birthright citizenship, which has been in place *ab ovo* in all new settler states that owe their origins to British colonialism, dates back to feudalism, where the soil and everything that sprang from it belonged to the lord. This feudal construct was transported by the English settlers into North America and Oceania and retained because it met the integrative needs of a society that had to be made through settlement and recurrent immigration. *Jus soli* citizenship, which automatically turns every newborn into a citizen of the new state, is complemented by historically low thresholds for naturalization. In the United States, basically unchanged for over half a century now, the main conditions for naturalizing are five years of legal residence, the mastery of "ordinary" English, the passing of a civics knowledge test, and "good moral character." Once these conditions are met, there is a legal entitlement on part of the immigrant to be granted American citizenship.

In the age of massive Third-World immigration, which followed upon the liberalization of US immigration law in 1965, there have been surprisingly few changes to the legal contours of American citizenship. In fact, the few momentous changes that did occur over time are entirely unrelated to the new immigration. In 1952, the racial exclusion of Asians from the possibility of naturalizing was terminated,[4] a movement that had started with lifting the ban on China, a wartime ally, a decade earlier. Already in 1922, the Naturalization and Citizenship of Married Women Act (the "Cable Act") had repealed the gender discrimination in US citizenship law that required the nationality of the wife to follow that of the husband (see Sapiro 1984).

Gerald Neuman (1998) thus noted correctly that immigration has had surprisingly "little effect" on US nationality law throughout its history. As is well known, its centerpiece, *jus soli* citizenship, established by the 1868 Fourteenth Amendment to the US Constitution,[5] was meant to enfranchise the descendants of American slaves after the infamous Dred Scott rule of the US Supreme Court.[6] It had nothing to do with including immigrants. The one critical moment in the past few decades was a movement in the mid-1990s Republican-dominated Congress to withhold unconditional *jus soli* citizenship from the children of undocumented immigrants (see Joppke 2000). The intellectual ammunition for this had ironically been delivered by two liberal academics, Peter Schuck and Rogers Smith (1985), who argued controversially that, for the sake of Lockean liberal citizenship, the "jurisdiction requirement" in the citizenship clause of the Fourteenth Amendment had to be understood in a consensual rather than a geographical sense. But this was rebutted by the Department of Justice in hearings of the House Judiciary Committee in 1995, where it was argued that it "would require repudiation of the language of the Constitution itself, the clear statement of the framers' intent, and the universal understanding of 19th and 20th century courts" (quoted in Aleinikoff 2000: 126). In a state created and held together by the Constitution, the very constitutional status of the citizenship clause made it immune to political tinkering.[7] With respect to naturalization, the one notable, though smallish change in the era of post-1965 immigration has been the introduction in 2008 of a redesigned and standardized citizenship test, which was to expunge meaningless memorizing of historical facts and events in favor of "more meaningful, substantive, concept-oriented" elements that should "encourage civic learning, patriotism, and attachment" to the United States.[8] Interestingly, the impetus for this came from Europe, where, in the pursuit of upgrading the role of citizenship in the integration of immigrants, governments such as the British have recently added an American-style citizenship test to their naturalization procedures.

Against the backdrop of institutional continuity and historically inclusive citizenship laws, American scholarship, to the limited degree that it took an interest in citizenship at all, has focused on explaining intra-national variations of citizenship acquisition according to individual and group characteristics. Particular attention has been paid to the fact that Mexicans, for decades America's largest immigrant group, have persistently been the group with the lowest naturalization levels, which has been referred variously to their (anti-Anglo) origin culture, their low socio-economic profile and lack of education, or the geographical proximity of Mexico to the United States.

An interesting, institutional twist to the American "who naturalizes and why" literature has been given by Irene Bloemraad (2002, 2006a, 2006b). In an ingenious comparison of Canada and the United States, she found that around 1950 the propensity of Canadian and American immigrants to naturalize was about even, at the remarkably high level of 80 percent. However, fifty years later only the Canadian naturalization rate remained steadfastly high, at around 75 percent of legal immigrants, while the US naturalization rate had dropped sharply, to under 40 percent.[9] This is particularly puzzling as, in terms of incentives for naturalizing, the benefits of citizenship are rather higher in the US than in Canada, including the possibility of sponsoring a large class of extended family migrants, and considering that, since the mid-1990s, citizenship is required in the US to receive some federal welfare benefits. No group or individual characteristics could explain this "naturalization gap," as it remained constant after controlling for the demographic, socio-economic, and ethnic characteristics of the immigrant populations in both countries. Even the citizenship laws provide no clues for the sharp variation, because the formal thresholds for naturalizing are only slightly lower in Canada.[10]

Instead, Bloemraad finds an explanation in the normative stances taken by both governments toward immigrant integration, the Canadian government proactively furthering the acquisition of citizenship under the umbrella of its official multiculturalism policy. By contrast, the American government, except for a short and gregariously failed interlude under the Clinton administration, has always taken a hands-off and "neutral" stance on naturalization and immigrant integration (see the critique by Murguia and Muñoz 2005). Pampered by a plethora of state-funded campaigns and ethnic organizations, the Canadian immigrants' high propensity for adopting Canadian citizenship is their "way of showing thanks" to Canada's comparatively warmer welcome (Bloemraad

2002: 218). Whereas the American approach furthers at best an instrumental focus on citizenship in terms of "rights and economic opportunities," the Canadian approach furthers a non-instrumental view of citizenship as "obligation to participate and give back" (Bloemraad 2006a: 153). These findings are provocative in two respects. Firstly, they show an astonishing degree of variation between the American and Canadian patterns of naturalization, citizenship, and immigrant integration, which tended to be buried under the "North America" label (or, rather, by a complete ignorance in the United States about Canada). But, secondly, and even more importantly, they show that promoting citizenship and official multiculturalism policies need not be contradictory, as they are in Europe today, but may happily complement one another, if perhaps only in Canada.

The challenge of immigration to citizenship has been of incomparably taller order in Europe than in the classic immigrant nations. This is because, with the exception of France, European citizenship laws had not been crafted with an eye on transforming immigrants into citizens. In the case of Germany, the ethnic tilt of the 1913 *Reichs- und Staatsangehörigkeitsgesetz* (Imperial Citizenship Law), which, however liberalized, is still formally in place today, was even meant to *prevent* undesired Polish immigrants from entering the German citizenry (see Brubaker 1992: ch. 6). The indifference, if not outright hostility, of European citizenship laws to immigration shows in the predominance of *jus sanguinis* as mechanism of birthright attribution, and in a wholly discretionary and erratic naturalization procedure where the post-birth acquisition of citizenship was always the exception. An extreme example of this is Germany, which until the 1999 reform of citizenship law had remained a pure *jus sanguinis* regime, without an inch of *jus soli*, and where until the early 1990s a naturalization could occur only if it was "in the interest of Germany" – furthermore requiring the complete cultural assimilation of the immigrant (see Hailbronner 1989; also Joppke 1999: 200–2).

No wonder that the naturalization rates vary widely between Germany, long one of the most exclusive European citizenship

Status

Table 2.2 Average naturalization rates in select Northwest European states

	1985–90	2000–5
Austria	2.16	4.33
Belgium	2.42	7.28
France	1.22	4.73
Germany	0.36	2.09
Ireland	0.39	1.37
Luxembourg	0.79	0.43
Netherlands	3.52	5.36
Sweden	4.68	7.66
United Kingdom	3.57	4.22

Note: The figures give the percentage of naturalized immigrants of the foreign resident population.

Source: Howard (2009: 217).

regimes, and Canada, the most inclusive New World regime: from 1990 to 2003 (that is, after three successive liberalizations of German citizenship law) there were still only 1,250 naturalizations per 100,000 resident foreigners in Germany, while there were almost ten times as many (11,800) in Canada.[11]

While the greater inclusiveness of North American citizenship regimes is long-standing, the European regimes have undergone an important move in the direction of more inclusiveness in the past few decades (see table 2.2). These data show persistent intra-European variation in naturalization rates, reflecting differently inclusive citizenship laws. But they also show that, with the exception of Luxembourg, the naturalization rates have significantly increased in the past two decades, by a modest 20 percent in Britain (though from a high point of departure) up to a spectacular 600 percent in Germany (admittedly from Europe's lowest floor). Certainly, instead of pointing to a liberalization of naturalization rules, these increasing rates might simply reflect the gradual maturing of the respective immigrant populations, more of them becoming eligible for citizenship with increased residence time.

To assess the influence of institutional change, it is therefore helpful to consult Marc Morjé Howard's "Citizenship Policy

Table 2.3 Changing European citizenship regimes

	1980s	2008
Restrictive:	Germany, Austria, Luxembourg, Italy, Greece, Spain, Denmark	Austria, Denmark, Greece, Spain, Italy
Medium:	Finland, Sweden, Portugal, Netherlands	Luxembourg, Germany
Liberal:	France, Ireland, Belgium, UK	Netherlands, Finland, Portugal, Ireland, France, UK, Sweden Belgium

Source: Howard (2009: ch. 1).

Index" (CPI), which he compiled to assess the direction of citizenship laws in the member states of the European Union over the past quarter-century (Howard 2009: ch. 1). Attributing points (from 2 to 0) to the presence or absence of *jus soli* provisions, the toleration or rejection of dual citizenship, and the relative ease of naturalization, Howard grouped the pre-enlargement states of the EU into three clusters: "liberal" (for the highest scorers, with a total of 4 and above), "medium" (over 1.5 but less than 4), and "restrictive" (scores between 0 and 1.5). Through the lens of Howard's CPI, the European citizenship scene in the 1980s looked like this: most entrants were in the "restrictive" category, with seven states thus classified; four countries were in the "medium," and four in the "liberal" category (see table 2.3).

A quarter-century later, the restrictive category has shrunk from seven to five cases (with Germany and Luxembourg moving up into the "medium" category); the "medium" category is down from four to two cases (with all previous states in this category – Finland, Sweden, Portugal, and the Netherlands – moving up into the "liberal" category); and consequently the number of "liberal" citizenship regimes has doubled, from four to eight, now constituting by far the largest citizenship regime category in pre-enlargement Europe. Most importantly, all six countries that shifted categories between the 1980s and 2008 did so in a liberalizing direction.

Status

This raises two questions. Firstly, what does the obvious liberalization of citizenship consist of? And, secondly, what explains why most European states either liberalized their citizenship laws or retained historically liberal citizenship laws, while a minority did not? After answering both questions in turn, the remainder of the chapter discusses two recent countertrends to liberalization: new restrictions, especially with respect to naturalization, which were introduced after 2001; and a trend toward the "re-ethnicization" of citizenship, which consists of new laws and policies that allow the descendants of emigrants to keep or reacquire the citizenship of their ancestors. I close with the question as to whether these restrictive countertrends outweigh the liberalization of the past two decades.

Liberalization of Citizenship

One must distinguish between two kinds of hurdle to citizenship acquisition that have been successively removed in the past half-century. The most pernicious hurdle to citizenship is group-level discrimination on the basis of race and gender. This has been a shared feature of *all* Western states' citizenship regimes, from Europe to North America and Oceania. Racial discrimination was even more pronounced and explicit in the Anglo-origin settler states than in Europe (with the exception of Nazi Germany). With respect to gender discrimination, in all countries the wife's citizenship used to follow that of the husband, according to the principle of "dependent nationality." Its official purpose was to protect the unity of the family, but in reality it enshrined patriarchy (ILA 2000: 16f.). In addition, a European specificity was unequal descent rules within the predominant *jus sanguinis* citizenship, according to which only men, but not women, could confer their nationality on their children (though similar provisions existed in North America for the – much smaller number of – children born to citizens abroad, in which case citizenship is everywhere accorded *jure sanguinis*). Gender discrimination in Western states' nationality laws had mostly disappeared by the mid-1980s (Vink and de Groot 2008: 9).

Status

The liberalizations to be discussed in the following pages all target restrictions on individuals rather than groups, by means of which immigrants qua immigrants (rather than as members of an ascriptive group) were once kept out of the national citizenry. These are liberalizations that move the European citizenship regimes toward the traditionally more inclusive citizenship regimes of North America and Oceania. The three most important individual-level liberalizations have been, firstly, complementing traditional *jus sanguinis* citizenship with elements of *jus soli* citizenship for the children of immigrants; secondly, curtailing state discretion in naturalization; and, thirdly, tolerating dual citizenship.

Complementing *jus sanguinis* with *jus soli* citizenship

As a state-of-the-art review of citizenship laws across Western states confirms, by the early twenty-first century there had been a "marked movement toward a convergence of citizenship acquisition rules among liberal democracies" (Aleinikoff and Klusmeyer 2002: 7). It no longer makes sense to distinguish neatly between *jus soli* and *jus sanguinis* states because most Western states now combine elements of both. On one hand, many classic *jus soli* states, including Australia and (in Europe) Britain and Portugal, now link the granting of nationality to the newborn children of foreigners to certain legal residence conditions of their parents. Conversely, most classic *jus sanguinis* states of the European continent now grant some kind of automatic birth or post-birth citizenship to the second- or third-generation offspring of immigrants. In particular, most European Union states today grant as-of-right citizenship to second-generation immigrants (see Hansen and Weil 2001).

This is not to say that there is a moral symmetry between both birthright citizenships. Whereas at the dawn of the nineteenth century European nation-state *jus sanguinis* had been the epitome of modernity and progress, at the end of the twentieth century "international law [had] subtly reinforced territorial/civic conceptions of nationality" (Orentlicher 1998: 312).

However, as observed by Aleinikoff and Klusmeyer (2002: 2), the dominant trend is still toward mixed regimes that combine elements of *jus sanguinis* and *jus soli*. The recent European trend toward territorial citizenship, which in 1999 also caught up with the country whose "ethnic" nationhood tradition had made it a most unlikely candidate, Germany does not emulate a pure *jus soli* regime à l'américaine or à la canadiènne. Instead, the territorial attribution of citizenship is linked to a parent's legal residence or his or her place of birth (as in "double *jus soli*," which was pioneered by France in 1889). Or, combining *jus soli* with *jus domicilii*, territorial citizenship is linked to a minimal residence period of citizenship candidates themselves after their birth in the respective state. The preference for a mixed regime reflects the fact that an unconditional *jus soli* system is as much unsuited to a world of massively increased cross-border migration as is a pure *jus sanguinis* regime, the former being as over-inclusive as the latter is under-inclusive. Since the landmark Nottebohm decision of the International Court of Justice in 1955, there is consensus that nationality should reflect a "genuine connection" between an individual and a state.[12] Pure *jus sanguinis* and pure *jus soli* systems equally fall short of that ideal because, next to the random fact of birth, no additional attachment to the state is required in either system. It is therefore no contradiction that pure *jus soli* states, such as Portugal and Britain, added elements of *jus sanguinis* to their citizenship laws in the early 1980s, just when some *jus sanguinis* states, such as Belgium and – a decade later – Germany, moved in the exact opposite direction of incorporating *jus soli* elements. Both movements are part of the same trend toward mixed citizenship regimes that approximate the "genuine connection" requirement in an age of migration.

From discretionary to as-of-right naturalization

In the earliest (and still the best) sociological comparison of access-to-citizenship rules across Western states, Rogers Brubaker (1989b) distinguished between an "as-of-right" approach to naturalization, prevailing in the United States and Canada, and a "discretionary" approach dominant in Europe, especially in Sweden, Germany, Britain, and France.[13] This distinction, while correctly reflecting the routine transition to citizenship in the classic settler states and the exceptional status of naturalization in pre-1990s Europe, no longer holds muster. To a certain degree, it never did, as elastic provisions such as the "good character" clause in the United States had always allowed a modicum of discretion to the state. This discretion reflects elementary state sovereignty, which, according to an international lawyer of her time quoted by Hannah Arendt ([1951] 1979: 278), "is nowhere more absolute than in matters of 'emigration, naturalization, nationality, and expulsion,'" whatever the state or regime in question. Having said this, there has been a steady strengthening of the "as-of-right" component in European states' naturalization rules, curtailing notional state sovereignty in this domain. This change has been especially drastic in Germany, where naturalization had traditionally been an exceptional act of grace by the state, taking into account the "public interest" only, and excluding any consideration of the interest of the citizenship applicant. Since 1993, there has been as-of-right naturalization for long-settled foreigners and their children. In addition, the demanding, individually applied cultural "assimilation" test was replaced by a weaker, generic "integration" requirement. Originally, "integration" was presumed to have happened after a certain residence time and schooling in Germany; but later it was made contingent upon German-language competence, an express commitment to the principles of the constitution, and – after September 2007 – the passing of a civic integration test.

The case of Germany confirms a larger trend toward curtailing state discretion in citizenship acquisition, as well as turning the latter from the jealously guarded exception, in some countries (such as Denmark) even requiring an act of parliament, into an administrative routine. Next to a general lowering of the residence time required for naturalization[14] and a legal standardization of the naturalization procedure, there is a marked tendency toward removing cultural assimilation as a prerequisite for naturalization. Belgium, for instance, first moderated its integration requirement from factual to intentional integration (that is, from *idonéité* to *volonté d'intégration*) in 1985, and later even abandoned any "integration" requirement, deeming the mere fact of continued residence sufficient for the award of citizenship. Only French nationality law still officially asks for the "assimilation" of citizenship applicants. In its case law, however, the Conseil d'Etat, France's highest administrative court, has narrowly interpreted assimilation in terms of "sufficient knowledge" of the French language, further making the determination of "sufficient knowledge" dependent on a person's educational level and social standing. And the Conseil d'Etat, until its spectacular reversal of position in June 2008, repeatedly reined in overbearing magistrates who had refused citizenship requests by Muslim immigrants on the grounds of their wearing a headscarf.[15] In general, abstaining from a cultural assimilation requirement in citizenship acquisition shows an abstention of the contemporary liberal state from aggressive nation-building (as described by Scott 1998 or E. Weber 1977) – that is, the forging of culturally homogeneous citizenries in which individuals are mere replicas of a national standard mold.

Tolerating dual citizenship

The classic immigrant countries have always tolerated dual citizenship, at least with respect to their immigrants (not necessarily their emigrants).[16] The United States, in its oath of allegiance, formally asks its naturalizing immigrants to repudiate their nationality of origin, but it has always closed its eyes to this in practice. In Europe, the attitudes to dual citizenship have been highly uneven, former colonial powers such as Britain and France tolerating it, but the bulk of continental European states having long rejected it. From the late nineteenth century into the 1960s, international opinion and law was sternly pitted against dual nationality. The American statesman George Bancroft famously associated dual citizenship with "bigamy," opining that one might "as soon tolerate a man with two wives as a man with two countries" (quoted in Koslowski 2000: 206). This rejection was legally enshrined in the 1930 Hague Convention, which prescribed that "every person should have a nationality and should have one nationality only." This restrictive line was followed in the Council of Europe's

Convention on the Reduction of Cases of Multiple Nationality of 1963, which outlawed dual nationality among its signature states.

The reason for the rejection of dual citizenship is simple: the latter breaks with the segmentary logic of the classic nation-state, which commands that a person can belong to only one state at a time. This logic was empirically reinforced, in the high age of nationalism, by the fact of warfare being a natural way of interstate relations.

Conversely, the toleration of dual citizenship reflects, in a context of peace in the West after World War II, an invasion of the logic of functional differentiation into the segmentarily differentiated world of nation-states, the functional kind requiring multiple memberships and allegiances.[17] The invasion of functional logic is very visible in the Carnegie Endowment's case for tolerating dual citizenship: "Empirically, modern nations in overwhelming proportions tolerate or encourage a wide range of competing loyalties and affiliations in civil society – to family, business, local community, religious denominations, sports teams, nongovernmental organizations promoting both political and nonpolitical causes – and do not treat such allegiances . . . as bigamous or as incompatible with . . . loyalty to the nation-state" (Aleinikoff and Klusmeyer 2002: 29).

The toleration of dual citizenship is part of the general trend from ethnic toward territorial citizenship, which is driven by states' need to integrate their growing immigrant populations. The linkage between dual-citizenship toleration and immigrant integration is explicit in the Council of Europe's new Nationality Convention of 1997. It justifies the departure from the strict prohibition of dual nationality of its 1963 predecessor in reference to "labour migrations between European States leading to substantial immigrant populations [and] the need for the integration of permanent residents" (Council of Europe 1997: 23).

However, it is not just the strictures of immigrant integration but the demand for equality between the sexes that has driven liberal states in this direction. To the degree that all postwar Western states have abolished patrilinear descent rules in response to feminist concerns, dual citizenship had become a social reality even before this became linked to the immigration problem. There are two reasons why in a world of migration dual citizenship cannot but further increase, whatever stance a state may take on it. The first is the aforementioned sex equality, which has become a feature of all Western states' nationality laws since the 1960s. It inevitably generates dual citizenship in the case of mixed couples, because husband and wife now equally transmit their nationality to their children, *jure sanguinis*. The second reason is the coexistence of primarily *jus soli* or *jus sanguinis* regimes in the world, which is unlikely ever to disappear. It cannot but generate dual nationality, because a child born to foreign parents in a *jus soli* country will obtain the citizenship of that country, *jure soli*, and the citizenship of its parents, *jure sanguinis*. Add to these two reasons the fact of continued immigration, and dual nationality can only keep on growing.

The main possibility for states to restrict dual nationality is through constraints on naturalization: renunciation requirements for immigrants, and automatic loss provisions for emigrants. This leaves states with a small and traditionally recalcitrant subset of the total immigrant population (broadly conceived, including immigrants' children): first-generation immigrants, who are known to avoid naturalizing fast because of a strong return intention, and who are likely to generate dual nationality already through the increasingly territorial birthright citizenships of their newborn children, even in Europe. Conversely, those migrants who are most likely to naturalize fast, and where a renunciation requirement might show teeth – refugees – are allowed under international and national laws to retain their nationality of origin, even in a country such as Germany that is strongly opposed to dual nationality.

As a combined result of equality and human rights considerations, of giving in to the inevitable, and of a growing consensus that the benefits of dual citizenship by far outweigh its costs,[18] toleration of dual nationality is now the dominant trend in Europe (see Howard 2005). While only Sweden endorses dual nationality philosophically (since 2001), most other European states tolerate it for pragmatic reasons. There is, of course, a hard core of pre-enlargement states that firmly reject dual nationality: the two Germanic states, Germany and Austria, and two small states that are in the grip of strong right-wing movements, the Netherlands and Denmark. But this makes only four out of fifteen pre-enlargement states that still reject dual nationality, clearly a minority in pre-enlargement Europe. And even these four nay-sayers are required by Article 16 of the European Nationality Convention to make exceptions where the renunciation of the original citizenship is legally impossible, the conditions for release are unacceptable, or in the case of refugees. Accordingly, around half of the naturalizations in these nay-saying countries entail dual nationality.[19]

Explaining the Liberalization of Citizenship

The very fact of evolving citizenship laws in Europe flies in the face of a "cultural idiom" approach (Brubaker 1992), which conceives of citizenship as locked in by distinct nationhood traditions. Then we would indeed expect stasis and sustained divergence, not change and convergence. However, since the late 1990s, spurred on by the developments discussed above, there has been consensus among scholars on a convergence toward more liberal citizenship laws and policies in Europe.[20] After the German "breakthrough," which as such occurred relatively late, further liberalizing reforms happened in Belgium (2000); in Luxembourg and Sweden (2001); in Finland (2003); and in Portugal (2006). All went into the same direction of strengthening *jus soli*, reducing residence and other requirements for naturalization, and tolerating dual nationality (Bauböck 2006b: 4).

In an impressive comparison of twenty-five countries, Patrick Weil (2001) suggested that three factors, if combined, make for liberalized, non-discriminatory citizenship laws: past and sufficiently consolidated immigration, which creates a high number of permanent non-citizens; entrenched liberal-democratic values, which command a congruence of the subjects and objects of state authority; and, finally, consolidated borders and the absence of unfinished nation-building concerns that might cause a perceived need for national-origin discriminations. This simple scheme has great explanatory power. For example, Germany, which since the late 1950s has had one of the world's largest immigrant intakes and which certainly now must be considered an entrenched liberal democracy, did not overhaul its ethnically closed citizenship regime before the end of the millennium. The simple reason is that the non-congruence between its state and national boundaries stood in the way. Only after German reunification in 1990 was the way free to include its vast immigrant population in the citizenry. Before this turning point, ethnic citizenship was perceived as a bridge to national unification, which was seen as potentially undermined by including too many foreigners with unclear national commitments in the citizenry. Or take Italy, one of the six founding members of the European Community, whose post-1945 credentials as a liberal democracy are likewise beyond doubt, and which – now in contrast to Germany – did not have an unresolved national question. Why did Italy, in 1992, pass a restrictive citizenship law that doubled the residence time required for naturalization (from five to ten years) and that made the road to citizenship significantly more difficult for the children of foreigners born in the country? In terms of Weil's scheme, the inflow of *extracomunitari* (the code word for 'immigrants'), which was unsolicited, massive, and took Italy by surprise in the 1980s, was too recent and too unsettled to be accepted as a long-term fact in the early 1990s (and even today). Finally, Israel, the only stable democracy in the Middle East and a "nation of immigrants" no less than the United States, is unlikely ever to see a liberal citizenship law, because of its structural incongruence of state and national boundaries and the explosive presence of a fast-growing Palestinian minority within its borders and even its citizenry.

Weil's theory correctly identifies the structures that help or block liberalization. But it is silent on the actors that may bring about or prevent change. Its diction is functionalist and teleological – if there is change, then it is because there needs to be change. This overlooks the fact that there is a *politics* of citizenship and with it the possibility of other than liberal outcomes, even if all structural parameters are in place. In Germany, it took a government change in 1998, from one dominated by the conservative CDU to one dominated by the leftist SPD, to pass an immigrant-inclusive citizenship law, the need for which was recognized as early as 1984.[21] In fact, as I pointed out earlier (Joppke 2003), it is mostly governments of the left, perhaps out of a gut internationalism and progressive-mindedness, which have dared to pass immigrant-inclusive citizenship reforms (which tend to be unpopular at the ballot box). Five of the six European liberalizations of citizenship laws between the 1980s and 2008, as observed by Howard (2009: 59), happened under left-of-center or grand coalition governments including the left. Conversely, to the limited degree that it favors more inclusive citizenship laws, the political right tends to privilege the inclusion of emigrants over that of immigrants, in terms of "re-ethnicized" citizenship laws that allow the descendants of emigrants to reacquire the citizenship of their ancestors, often in gross violation of the "genuine connection" norm under international law.

In a compelling comparison of the citizenship laws in the current twenty-seven member states of the European Union, Marc Howard (2009) has further refined and elaborated the "politics matters" argument. In particular, he showed that what matters is not so much the ideological orientation of the government as the existence or absence of a far right party or movement capable of mobilizing an always xenophobic mass public. If faced with a potent far-right challenge, even a left-wing government will cave in and pass a less inclusive citizenship law than it might otherwise have done. A case in point is the long story of Germany's citizenship reform of 1999 (Howard 2009: ch. 6; see also Joppke 2000). It started with an even more daring proposal by the incoming Red–Green coalition government under Chancellor Gerhard Schröder and his Green deputy, Joschka Fischer, to tolerate dual citizenship across the board, for naturalizing immigrants no less than for the children of immigrants who were to become German at birth *jure soli*. This radical proposal to "modernize" German nationality law was derailed by a hugely successful signature-gathering campaign instigated in the state of Hesse by the conservative opposition party, CDU, which even helped bring down the regional SPD government in the *Land* election of 1999. This defeat again changed the majority constellation in the second chamber of parliament, the Bundesrat, so that an agreement of the CDU was required to pass any new citizenship law. The result was a perpetuation of Germany's traditional aversion to dual nationality. With respect to the new *jus soli* provision that was introduced in 1999, the dual-nationality aversion shows in making *jus soli* citizenship temporary at first and requiring that those who want to keep it once they have reached majority age give up their second *jus sanguinis* nationality. If compared with the ethnic citizenship law of the past, this was still "liberalization." But it was one that did not go as far as it might have gone, bearing the restrictive imprint of populist mobilization by the political right. The German and even more restrictive citizenship episodes taking place in the Netherlands, Denmark, or Austria in the 1990s and early 2000s reveal an uncomfortable truth: that democracy is bad for immigrants and for liberal citizenship.

New Restrictions, Post-2001

In the past decade, heightened by religious terrorism post-2001, there has been growing concern about failing immigrant integration in Europe, especially with respect to Muslims. In response, a number of continental European countries, beginning with the Netherlands in the late 1990s, devised "civic integration" courses and tests for newcomers, which over time took on an increasingly obligatory and repressive character, with entry and residence permits being tied to the passing of civic integration requirements (see Joppke 2007a). With the exception of Britain, all countries that have recently included stricter language and integration requirements in their naturalization procedures had first introduced such measures in the context of revamped immigrant integration policies, examples being Austria, Denmark, France, the Netherlands, and Germany. It is obvious that what is expected of immigrants, to speak the language of the receiving country and to have basic knowledge about its history, institutions and everyday life, is asked of citizenship applicants as well.

So there is an internal logic of extending to naturalization the already existing strictures of immigrant integration. But still noteworthy is the changed philosophy underlying tightened naturalization rules. Before the introduction of language and integration requirements, it was presumed, and thus not explicitly tested, that integration would happen in the required legal residence time. There was trust, as it were, that time and informal experience would do what now is expected of an explicit and standardized procedure. Moreover, the previous tenet of naturalization as a tool of integration was replaced by the new tenet of naturalization as the end point of, or reward for, integration – citizenship as "the first prize," as has been the notion in the Netherlands (van Oers, de Hart, and Groenendijk 2006: 403).

Interestingly, a perceived cheapening of citizenship in a previous period of liberalization tends to be the backdrop to the recent tightening of naturalization requirements. It is a check to having made citizenship too readily available in the recent past. The thrust of liberalization was to turn citizenship into a right, which was paradoxical because to have rights cannot itself be a right. The opposite thrust of the new restrictions is to recover citizenship's more fundamental feature of being a privilege, received by the grace of birth, and jealously guarded if granted to people who are not already endowed with it. The new restrictions are a return to the close coupling of citizenship with sovereignty and the self-determination of a political community.

New restrictions as a backlash against citizenship as right are especially visible in the German case. Since a reform in 1993, there has been a right to naturalization in Germany, if certain conditions are fulfilled. This is in contrast to most other countries, where the state can always say "no" to a citizenship applicant, even if all formal requirements have been fulfilled. Next to a language condition, which, curiously, had been removed in 1992 but was reintroduced in 1999, the only integration requirement was a preformulated, written "confession" (*Bekenntnis*) that the applicant shared the liberal-democratic principles of the Basic Law. The tokenist character of this "confession," in the context of weakened state discretion in a rights-centered naturalization procedure, became the pretext of the state government of Baden-Württemberg to issue, in September 2005, inquisitional and discriminatory "interview guidelines" that were to be applied by state officers only to Muslim applicants for citizenship.[22] In scrutinizing the applicant's attitude toward homosexuality, the equality of women, and Islamic terrorism, among other issues, the interview guidelines amount to a morality test that is driven by the strange vision of the liberal state as a state for liberal people only. A nationwide debate about Baden-Württemberg's dubious interview practice led to an agreement among the German *Länder* to introduce the successful passing of a formal civic integration course and test as precondition for naturalization, and thus to apply to the citizenship domain what had already been part of immigrant integration policy.[23]

However, the pacesetter of the new restrictions is not Germany, but the Netherlands, Austria, and Denmark. Consider only the example of the Netherlands.[24] Of all European countries, here the philosophical shift from naturalization as "tool" to "end point" of integration, or from "right" of the immigrant to "privilege" granted by the political community, has been the most extreme. And one can observe the same anti-liberal backlash dynamic as in Germany. Complementing its progressive ethnic minorities' policy, the Dutch Nationality Act of December 1984 had introduced the right for second-generation immigrants to opt for Dutch nationality, while largely decoupling the naturalization procedure for first-generation immigrants from any serious integration requirement apart from a low-key, "reasonable knowledge of Dutch language" condition that hardly anyone failed (van Oers, de Hart, and Groenendijk 2006: 413). However, as the multiculturalism approach to immigrant integration gave way in the late 1990s to a tougher "civic integration" policy, a change that preceded the later populist turmoil in Dutch politics, nationality law could not remain unaffected. The outcome was a new nationality act, which was passed in December 2000 and went into effect in April 2003. While the second-generation right of option remained formally in place, an elastic "threat to public order" proviso made it more akin to ordinary naturalization. Most importantly, the 2000 law adopted the logic of mandatory "civic integration," in terms of a demanding five-hour naturalization exam, which includes four hours of testing the applicant's oral, reading, and writing capacity in the Dutch language, at a level similar to that of the already existing civic integration tests. Crucially, the Dutch government, which since the early twenty-first century has been under the sway of strong right-wing populism, refuses to publish the content of the exam and provides no preparation brochures or materials. As a government official explicated the reason of this refusal, "[o]ne cannot study to be Dutch, one has to feel Dutch" (ibid.: 415). No wonder that the number of applications for naturalization decreased sharply after the new policy went into force, from 37,000 in 2003 to 19,300 in 2004 (ibid.: 419). And of those who nevertheless dared apply in 2003, 50 percent failed the strict naturalization exam (ibid.: 392). Such is the logic of Dutch nationality as "the first prize" (Immigration Minister Verdonk, quoted ibid.: 403): most cannot have it.

Developments in continental Europe must be read as an invasion into the citizenship domain of immigration control concerns, thus fusing two areas that previously had been kept strictly separate. This is demonstrated by the fact that coercive "civic integration" requirements that had first been introduced for new immigrants, and often functioned as a device for fending them off, were simply extended to the acquisition of citizenship.

Britain, which is endowed with a historically liberal citizenship regime that has recently seen a toughening of naturalization requirements, sets an interesting counterpoint to this. Here the sequence has been the reverse: new civic integration measures originated in the citizenship domain itself (well observed by Entzinger 2004: 14–16), and only later did they affect the regulation of permanent legal residence.[25] The Crick Commission (2003), appointed to advise the government on a new naturalization test, expressed the different intention clearly: "[T]he object is not to diminish, and indeed cannot diminish [sic], numbers of people already settled and employed" (2003: 20).

Status

By the same token, the mellower features of British-style civic integration, besides showing the imprint of a Labour government unbothered by a populist fringe party or movement, *also* rest on the fundament of a revamped, Canadian-style immigration policy, which operates on the basis of a points system that selects only the skilled and highly skilled. The government's recent "five year strategy for asylum and immigration" (Home Office 2005a) bluntly states that low-skilled ("Tier 3") immigration "will [be] phase[d] out over time," particularly as ample supply in this category is now available "from the new EU countries"; exceptions to this would be "for fixed periods only" (ibid.: 16). In a nutshell, the low-skilled immigration that may still occur will never be for permanent settlement, and thus it will not come within the ambit of nationality law. In fact, the entire current British integration discourse does not apply to low-skilled immigrants at all (see Ensor and Shah 2005: 10). And with respect to high-skilled immigrants, who have places other than the low skies of Britain to go to, a less control-minded, more "soliciting" logic applies. The more liberal tone in British-style civic integration cannot be decoupled from the exclusive profile of the immigrants to be processed by it.

However, much as in the rest of Europe, the starting point of new thinking on naturalization and citizenship in Britain has been an apparent failure of immigrant integration. This became evident in the 2001 riots in northern England, in which Muslim youths were prominent. The Cantle Commission, set up by the government to investigate the causes of the riots, castigated local-level official multiculturalism policies as part of the problem, recommending a policy that would "reinforce feelings of citizenship and shared elements of nationhood" (quoted in Entzinger 2004: 14). The government heeded the advice, quickly shifting from official multiculturalism to civic integration (Home Office 2002).

Its first expression was more demanding and ceremonial naturalization procedures, as laid out in the Nationality, Immigration and Asylum Act of 2002. Before this law, naturalization hinged on five years of legal residence, "good behavior" (essentially the absence of a serious crime record), and a vague and undefined English-language requirement. A request could always be rejected, as the naturalization process was (and still is) discretionary (though in case of a refusal "reasons" have to be provided). While retaining the residence and behavioral requirements, as well as the discretionary nature of naturalization, the 2002 law introduced formal and standardized naturalization tests to ensure that applicants showed "a sufficient knowledge" of one of the official languages (English, but also Welsh or Scottish Gaelic) and about "life in the United Kingdom." In addition, living up to the words of the then home secretary, David Blunkett, that "[b]ecoming a British citizen is a significant life event" (quoted in Crick Commission 2003: 8), the act introduced a citizenship oath and pledge to be given at American-style, public citizenship ceremonies.

The Crick Commission (2003: 3f.), which prepared the format of the naturalization tests, explicated as rationale of the new approach that "citizenship is more esteemed and valued if it is earned, not given." This notionally resembles the Dutch rhetoric of citizenship as the "first prize." But both approaches are still rather different. Whereas the new philosophy of the Dutch (and of most other continental European states) was that citizenship should be the end point of successful integration, the British philosophy remained faithful to the liberal diction of the past: "[B]ecoming naturalized should not be seen as the end of a process but rather as a good beginning" (ibid.: 14). And whereas the Dutch government espoused the explicitly nationalist diction that one "cannot study to be Dutch," the British government is of the opposite opinion, in offering preparation courses at low cost, along with a brochure, "Life in the United Kingdom," that prepares applicants for the civics part of the naturalization test. Moreover, while Dutch applicants for citizenship can try only three times, there is no such limit for British applicants.

An American observer ridiculed the British civics requirements as being a "set of practical behavior along with correct attitudes toward women and ethnic minorities," comparing it negatively with the "fairly robust" American history and civics requirements.[26] In fact, the stress on "practical knowledge" and distaste for a "memorized history curriculum" (Crick Commission 2003) was deliberate. With respect to the contents of the civics requirement, the Crick Commission established six broad categories in "descending order of difficulty and relevance," with "British national institutions" and "Britain as a multicultural society" being the two most important categories, and "sources of help and information" (such as "use of telephone and help-lines") and "everyday needs" (e.g. "ways of paying bills") being the two least important (ibid.: 14–16).

While in terms of content this is not so different from continental European civic integration, the difference between both approaches is again apparent when considering the more important language part of the naturalization tests. Whereas the continental European approach is to make the language tests ever more demanding and geared toward failing as many applicants as possible, in the British approach "the test is not to be unduly onerous," as a member of the House of Lords put it.[27] Concretely, there is no imposition of one (impossibly high) language standard on all applicants, but a flexible system that respects the individual learning trajectory of each applicant. Accordingly, fulfilling the language requirement for naturalization does not mean reaching an objective minimum standard that is the same for all, but improving one's English skills by one step on an official "English as Second Language" (ESOL) scale after having taken an ESOL course. This takes "future citizens" as "life-long learners," who "will be likely to continue to develop their language skills, and a whole range of other employment, recreational, educational and social skills, long after they have gained citizenship" (Crick Commission 2003: 23). Language competence, in this approach, is not a symbolic marker of "feeling" Dutch or Danish or Austrian, but geared toward maximizing the "economic and social benefit" that Britain expects of its immigrants (see Home Office 2005a: 9).

However, what Britain shares with continental Europe is the new (and old) notion that citizenship is a privilege, not a right, to be "earned, not given," to reiterate the Crick Commission (2003: 3f.), and by now the motto of the new British citizenship policy. Its restrictive possibilities became evident in the new scheme of "probationary citizenship" (Home Office 2008a), which has become a legal reality since the 2009 Borders, Citizenship and Immigration

Act. A clear case of what Margaret Somers called "contractualization of citizenship" (Somers 2009: 2), citizenship is conceived here as a "contract" or "deal," in which "the rights and benefits of citizenship are matched by responsibilities and contributions to Britain" (Home Secretary Jacqui Smith, in Home Office 2008a: 5). Read from the lips of ordinary Britons in a series of "public listening sessions" (ibid.: 14), the concept of probationary citizenship is also, to date, the most drastic invasion of democracy (to choose a friendly term) into the citizenship domain, with questionable implications for immigrants. Probationary citizenship, which is available only for the elite crop of high-skilled migrants, family migrants, and refugees, is a "stepping stone" between temporary residence and either British citizenship or permanent residence. In this period, which for citizenship-bound immigrants is a minimum of one year and for permanent-residence-bound immigrants a minimum of three years, immigrants have to prove that, as a minimum, they are in work and law-abiding. And, commensurate with the idea that citizenship and the rights and benefits attached to it are to be "earned," the minimum period of one year and three years for proceeding from probationary citizenship to citizenship proper or permanent residence, respectively, is possible only if the probationary citizen shows the extra effort of "active citizenship." This consists of "civic activities" through which immigrants "benefit the local community" and demonstrate their "commitment to the UK" (ibid.: 50). While still a voluntary shortcut to citizenship or permanent residence this time around, active citizenship, as part of the probationary citizenship phase, might well become a compulsive "requirement" in the next round.[28] The obvious novelty here, troubling from a liberal point of view, is making virtuous citizenship a condition for legal citizenship.

From Germany to Britain, the examples show that, across Europe, "[v]ague concepts of integration and assimilation . . . have . . . been replaced by standardized language and integration tests" (de Hart and van Oers 2006: 352). To be distinguished from standardized civic integration requirements is a notable tightening of individual behavior and personal integrity requirements for naturalization. Even violations of administrative and foreigner or immigration law can increasingly lead to forfeiture of one's chances for naturalization, not to mention that the threshold of criminal law offences has been lowered dramatically – up to a point that, as in Britain since 2002, even native citizens can be deprived of their citizenship under certain conditions.[29]

There is no doubt that all of these trends bear the mark of post-2001 terrorist fear and a sense that European states have failed to integrate their postwar immigrants into their societies. There is an almost rushed, overcompensating sense that "integration" will not just happen as a result of time and informal socialization, but will have to be furthered, monitored, and – in the case of a negative outcome – sanctioned by explicit state policies, from the point of entry into the territory to that of entry into the citizenry.

However, there is variation in the harshness of the restrictive trend. The European hardliners – the Netherlands, Austria, and Denmark – where an immigration control dynamic and nationalist rhetoric have invaded the citizenship domain, are all cases in which populist right-wing parties have had a direct or indirect hand in shaping legislation. By contrast, the (still) mellower British version originated from a Labour government that was in no way constrained by an extremist right-wing party or kindred discourse. In fact, the new British citizenship regime bears more similarity to the archetype of a liberal, even "multicultural" citizenship regime, that of Canada, than to that of any of the continental European states.[30]

Moreover, there are exceptions to the trend toward more restrictive naturalization rules. The most extreme case is Belgium, which in March 2000 introduced Europe's most liberal nationality regime with the possibility of as-of-right citizenship by mere declaration after seven years of residence. The only further requirement is a hand-written statement to "wish to become a Belgian national and . . . [to] comply with the constitution and the laws of the Belgian people." As a legal critic sarcastically commented, the 2000 law reduced nationality "to a mere confirmation of one's residence" (Foblets and Loones 2006: 91), thus returning to the *jus domicilii* that had been trumped by the introduction of birthright citizenship in early modern Europe.

Status

The increased importance of societal integration conditions for naturalization, which are not new as such, but only in their recently formalized, standardized, and generally more demanding versions, sharpen a paradox that had been inherent in any such condition from the start: to expect more in terms of knowledge, values, and behavioral propriety of newcomers than is or can be expected of native citizens. Citizenship as formal state membership is a "legal-technical connecting concept without a substantive content" (*juristisch-technischer Kopplungsbegriff ohne wesentlichen Grund*) (de Groot 1989: 5). Only communist states went further, tying the mere fact of state membership to certain expectations of virtuous behavior, non-compliance with which could lead to one's deprivation of this status. Liberal states have always abstained from and shunned such practices. But the integrity and civic integration requirements in their nationality laws amount to the imposition of virtuous citizenship, most extreme perhaps in the British proposal of "active citizenship" – the difference, of course, being that it is not native citizens who are affected but only newcomers.

However, one could argue that the new requirements reflect the contractual nature of modern citizenship. Note that the British government has presented its recent invention of "probationary citizenship" as a "deal" (Home Secretary Jacqui Smith, in Home Office 2008a: 5). This is more than the jargon of "market fundamentalism" (Somers 2009: 2). Modern citizenship has always been marked by a tension between an older principle of ascription and a more recent principle of consent (see Schuck and Smith 1985: ch. 1). According to the idea of consent, membership in the political community is contractual and based on a reciprocal *do ut des*. Note how Home Secretary Smith characterized her "deal for citizenship": "This is a country of liberty and tolerance, opportunity and diversity – and these values are reinforced by the expectation that all who live here should learn our language, play by the rules, obey the law and contribute to the community" (Home Office 2008a: 5). According to the logic of contract, in order to reinforce the values and resources that presumably attracted the newcomer in the first place, an already existing community may impose on him or her some conditions for membership. These conditions constitute a state's naturalization rules, old and new. The fact that such conditions are imposed on adults, who in most cases have a citizenship already and are not forced to acquire a new one, minimizes their coercive thrust. So does the fact that the rights of aliens have been greatly strengthened and "constitutionalized" in the past few decades, which has even prompted diagnoses of a "devaluation" of citizenship (the classic statement is Schuck 1989). The irony is still that the liberal, inclusive aspect of citizenship is today invested more in its ascriptive side, in terms of *jus soli* provisions for the children or grandchildren of immigrants, which have largely remained unaffected by the trend toward stricter naturalization rules.

Re-ethnicizing Citizenship

Moments of restricting access to citizenship for immigrants at home are increasingly *also* moments of strengthening the ties of citizenship for expatriate communities abroad. This nexus was first demonstrated for recent nationality law reforms in France, Italy, and Spain (Joppke 2003). But the list can easily be prolonged, including even a classic immigration country such as Australia (see Betts and Birrell 2007). As the re-ethnicizing trend is especially strong in Europe, most of the countries of which are now simultaneously immigrant-receiving and emigrant-sending, it is apposite to concentrate on the old continent further.

The Netherlands, in the same 2003 law that established a demanding language and integration test as a condition for naturalization, also lifted an (admittedly harsh) rule that had prescribed the loss of Dutch nationality after ten years of residence abroad (though only for dual nationals who would not thereby become stateless).[31] As a result, whether intended or not, Dutch emigrants now have the possibility of unlimited nationality transmission abroad, without any generational stopping point. More recently, a planned reduction of exceptions to prohibiting dual nationality for immigrants was explicitly not applied to emigrants

– the argument being that differential treatment of the groups was legitimate because only immigrants, but not emigrants, posed "integration problems" in the Netherlands (de Hart and van Oers 2006: 334). Austria, in a very restriction-minded 2005 reform of citizenship law that extended the "civic integration" requirement from immigration into nationality law, *also* facilitated the retention and reacquisition of Austrian nationality for its expatriate communities abroad. And Finland, while increasing the residence and language hurdles for naturalization in its Nationality Act of 2003, also accepted dual nationality for the first time – but only because of the lobbying by the expatriate Finland Society and the Finnish Expatriate Parliament. As de Hart and van Oers (ibid.: 333) summarized the recent trend, "the position of emigrants appears to have been an important incentive for the Member States (of the pre-enlargement EU) to amend nationality law in recent years."

Because this "re-ethnicization" of citizenship (see Joppke 2003) eases access to citizenship for certain categories of people, it might be seen as a liberalizing rather than a restrictive trend. However, its coincidence with otherwise restrictive nationality law reforms marks it as part of an overarching restrictive trend, in which the ties of territory and socialization are downgraded while the ties of blood and descent are upgraded. In sum, an asymmetric treatment of immigrants and emigrants marks "re-ethnicization" as part of a restrictive trend. A direct measure for this is the toleration of dual nationality for emigrants but not for immigrants. For instance, Spain, in the 2002 nationality law reform passed by the conservative Aznar government, allowed dual nationality for Spanish emigrants seeking naturalization abroad, but notably *not* for immigrants in Spain. A second, even more extreme example is provided by the Netherlands, which shifted from an inclusive policy for immigrants only to one for emigrants only (van Oers, de Hart, and Groenendijk 2006: 404–9; see also Joppke 2008a: 153–5).

Re-ethnicization is not *necessarily* part of a restrictive trend. The trend toward tolerating dual citizenship, which in Europe has been bolstered by the 1997 Nationality Convention of the Council of Europe, mostly entails the symmetric treatment of immigrants and emigrants (Howard 2005). This is because any asymmetric treatment immediately invites charges of "discrimination" against either immigrants or emigrants. A recent example of re-ethnicization that is part of a liberalization of nationality law comes from Portugal. In early 2006, a socialist government, under the banner of fighting "social exclusion," recovered the "very old tradition of *jus soli*" in Portugal (Baganha and Urbano de Sousa 2006: 471), in providing automatic "double *jus soli*" citizenship for third-generation immigrants and conditional *jus soli* citizenship for the second generation. Further, the required residence time for naturalization was reduced from ten to six years (thus abolishing a previous distinction between ordinary immigrants and privileged Lusophone immigrants, who had been allowed to naturalize after six instead of ten years; see Joppke 2005: 135). Simultaneously with these immigrant-friendly, de-ethnicizing changes, the right to Portuguese nationality was extended from the children to the grandchildren of Portuguese emigrants, thus corresponding to a long-standing demand by the sizeable and influential Portuguese expatriate communities. Of course, since the early 1980s Portuguese nationality reforms had been geared toward including emigrants. The novelty was that, notably under a socialist government, immigrants for the first time came to enjoy greater inclusiveness as well. Predictably, this equally de- *and* re-ethnicizing nationality law reform was passed with the great support of the main political parties in parliament, the conservative Social Democratic Party in opposition included.[32]

With respect to granting dual nationality to first-generation emigrants, re-ethnicization is hardly controversial – this is simply part of the secular trend toward tolerating dual nationality. In addition, there is a strong presumption in most states that immigrants and emigrants should be treated equally, particularly if one considers the increasing prevalence of circular migration over the traditional pattern of one-directional emigration or immigration. Re-ethnicization becomes controversial, however, when it involves the grandchildren of former emigrants. Particularly problematic is the absence of any intergenerational stopping point of automatic citizenship transmission *jure sanguinis* or the absence of a residence requirement for the reacquisition of ancestral citizenship. This invalidates the "genuine connection" quality that citizenship should have according to international law, and the corresponding citizenship privileges take on the character of a "right of return."[33] However, developments in this direction have been rare, and they are limited largely to classic emigration countries.

In Europe's quintessential emigration country, Italy, a policy of optional nationality for expatriates abroad or their descendants *without* a prior residence requirement was limited to a short window between 1992 to 1997 (Arena, Nascimbene, and Zincone 2006: 342). Spain, where several reforms of nationality law since the early 1990s have stood under the sign of keeping out the immigrants while allowing emigrants to recover their lost Spanish nationality and pass it on to their descendants, first exempted emigrants from a residence requirement as a condition for recovering lost nationality in 1995, while extending this exemption to their children in 2002 (Rubio-Marin, 2006: 500). These Spanish moves have to be understood in the context of a previously strict rejection of dual nationality, which entailed significant hardship for Spanish emigrants, and a constitution-level mandate not just to "protect" emigrants but to "facilitate their return."[34]

While one should not overstate the degree of re-ethnicization in European states' recent nationality law reforms, their propensity for bashing the immigrant and courting the emigrant is incontrovertible. The courting of the emigrant is even set to increase further, as the political influence of expatriates is growing on account of a trend toward "external voting rights" (introduced, for instance, in Italy as recently as 2001), often (as in the Italian case) within extra-territorial electorate districts for co-nationals abroad (a detailed overview is Bauböck 2007). It is a shortcoming of the emerging literature on "external" or "emigrant citizenship" (see Barry 2006; Fitzgerald 2006, 2008) to focus almost exclusively on the major non-European immigrant-sending countries, such as Mexico, Turkey, or the Dominican Republic, while overlooking the perhaps less visible but equally interesting European instantiations of such citizenship. In Europe, the coincidence of immigration and emigration is increasingly making for contradictory and polyvalent citizenship developments, which sharply polarize the political forces of the left and right.

The contours of emigrant citizenship, which is fed by the "transnationalization" of migration in the era of globalization (see Glick-Schiller 1999), are still largely uncharted, in reality as much as in theory. In an imaginative discussion, David Fitzgerald (2006) embeds emigrant citizenship within the "Roman" tradition of citizenship, which emphasizes passive rights-holding, as against the "Greek" tradition of active participation in the political community. At the same time, the lesser possibilities of the state to mold and monitor its citizens abroad make for a citizenship "à la carte," which is inherently voluntaristic (as one can always avoid it) and necessarily based more on "persuasion" than on "coercion" (Fitzgerald 2008: 174–8). Importantly, the "voluntaristic" quality of emigrant citizenship sets a "structural limit to its endurance over time and generation abroad" (ibid.: 179). De-territorialized emigrant citizenship is thus unlikely to become a long-term competitor to territorial immigrant citizenship.

Liberalization and the New Restrictions

The restrictive trends discussed in the previous two sections are not limited to Europe. Influenced by the European developments, the Australian Citizenship Act of 2007 doubled the required residence time for naturalization from two to four years and introduced a citizenship test stressing English-language competence and "understand[ing] the Australian way of life" (Australian Government 2006). And the Australian extension, in 2002, of tolerating dual citizenship from immigrants to emigrants shows that even a classic immigrant country may be subject to the trend toward re-ethnicization. But few would contest that the Australian citizenship still ranks among the most open and inclusive in the world, in sync with the liberal pattern found in the other classic immigration countries.

To calibrate the restrictive trends in Europe is more complicated, because European citizenship regimes have always varied, some being more liberal, others more restrictive. This variation notwithstanding, the countries that underwent significant changes between the 1980s and today all did so in a liberalizing direction (see Howard 2009). This creates a puzzle: How can there be liberalization and new restrictions at the same time?

The answer is that the restrictive trends occurred within an overall liberal, in some cases even simultaneously liberalizing, framework. The restrictions have mostly remained limited to making naturalization more exacting, and they did not extend to negating dual citizenship or *jus soli*. And even with respect to naturalization, the new civic integration requirements are all individual- rather than group-level requirements; they can in principle be met by all individuals irrespective of ascriptive origin traits.[35] There has been no return to the racist or nationalist group-level exclusions of the past. The new requirements remain within the ambit of liberalism. The only change is *within* liberalism, in that the balance of "rights" and "obligations" in the liberal idea of contract has shifted toward the "obligation" pole (see King 1999: 18).

Even if one takes a less sanguine view of civic integration, a striking feature of many a reformed naturalization procedure is the simultaneous introduction of more restrictive *and* more liberal rules. An interesting example of this is shown by Luxembourg, Europe's smallest state with just 450,000 inhabitants, a staggering 40 percent of whom are foreigners (though some 90 percent of them being from other EU countries). Luxembourg's citizenship law of July 2001 had an overall liberalizing thrust: it reduced the required residence period for naturalization from ten to five years and rendered the latter free of charge, while adopting the liberal mantra that not "assimilation" but only "integration" could be expected of citizenship applicants. However, the same law *also* introduced a rather tight definition of "sufficient integration" required for naturalization: active and passive knowledge of one of the three official languages (French, German, and Luxembourgish) *and* a basic knowledge, supported by a certificate, of the Luxembourgish language. This "nationalist restrictiveness" (Moyse and Brasseur 2006: 380) in an otherwise liberalizing law, which incidentally lifted Luxembourg from the "restrictive" into the "medium" category on Howard's "citizenship policy index," had a predictable origin. It was rammed down the throat of a conservative government under Prime Minister Jean-Claude Juncker (CSV; Christian Conservative Party) by a new populist party (ADR), which had made the defense of the Luxembourgish language its battle cry. Given that Luxembourg's main everyday language is French, and that no government-supported courses on Luxembourgish were immediately available, this constituted a very significant obstacle to citizenship acquisition. The same coexistence of liberal and restrictive features also marks Luxembourg's most recent reform of citizenship law, passed in 2008: while tolerating symmetric dual citizenship, and thus further lifting Luxembourg toward the almost liberal, high end of the "medium" category in Howard's "citizenship policy index," the new law *also* introduced obligatory Luxembourgish language and civics courses, thus fully embracing the pan-European trend toward "civic integration" as a prerequisite of citizenship acquisition.

The list of cases in which restrictive and liberal elements coexist in the same nationality law reform can be extended. Austria, in its overall restrictive nationality law amendment of December 2005, *also* introduced a legal entitlement to naturalization for second-generation immigrants after six years of residence (Çinar and Waldrauch 2006: 53). While this liberal measure is partially neutralized by overall tightened conditions of naturalization, Austria has now joined the majority club of European states that grant the right of citizenship to second-generation immigrants, which has been one of the most significant liberalizing trends in Europe in the past quarter-century. Completing these examples, Finland, whose 2003 Nationality Act for the first time introduced a language requirement, increased legal residence time, and beefed up behavioral and personal integrity requirements (such as the absence of welfare dependency or of a crime record), *also* in the same law accepted symmetric dual nationality (even though, as indicated earlier, the true motivation of this was to please Finnish emigrants) (Fagerlund 2006: 158–69).

The reality of evolving citizenship is complicated, defying any holistic formula. The state-of-the-art review of European nationality laws thus appositely finds that the one discernible trend in the past two decades has been "towards more complex regulation" (Bauböck et al. 2006a: 21).

In an earlier work (Joppke 2003), I suggested that the direction of citizenship reform can be explained in terms of the political ideology of the government in place – leftist governments seeking to include immigrants, rightist governments embracing emigrants. This is a good start for understanding the contemporary politics of citizenship. But it needs to be nuanced.

With respect to the dynamics of "de-" and "re-ethnicization," it has to be emphasized more strongly that, especially in countries with strong emigrant traditions, such as Italy or Portugal, there is a left–right *consensus* on the idea of embracing co-ethnics abroad. The case of Italy is again instructive. After the emigrant-friendly 1992 citizenship law, passed under a center-right government, the left continued supporting even further extensions of co-ethnic preferences in citizenship acquisition. In 2000, a center-left government granted nationality by simple declaration to Italians by origin residing in areas that in the past had belonged to the Austro-Hungarian Empire. In 2006, a center-right government granted nationality by declaration to people of Italian descent in Slovenia and Croatia (Arena, Nascimbene, and Zincone 2006: 347–8). The difference kicks in with respect to immigrants. It was unfailingly leftist parties or governments that defended the cause of facilitating access to citizenship for immigrants, meekly and inconclusively when in opposition in 1992, more proactively (though again without success) in terms of government proposals in 2000 and 2006 to introduce conditional *jus soli* citizenship for second-generation immigrants.[36]

Conversely, the mere existence of a rightist government is insufficient to explain the restrictive trends discussed above. As Howard (2006: 450) correctly pointed out, what matters is whether a rightist government is "*mobilized* on the issue of immigration and citizenship reform." Such mobilization, which in the context of unfailingly immigrant-hostile mass publics is always tilting toward greater restrictiveness, is often the result of the emergence of small far-right parties or movements, which forces the moderate center to cater to the extremists' voters or supporters. Restrictive developments in the Netherlands, Austria, Denmark, and Luxembourg are all explicable in terms of center-right governments acting under the pressure of populist right-wing parties that thrive on anti-immigrant issues.[37]

On the other hand, the case of Britain, where a Labour government unaffected by any noteworthy far-right party or movement introduced civic integration requirements and, step by step, toughened up access to citizenship, suggests that party ideology cum populist mobilization cannot be the entire story behind European states' turn to more restrictive citizenship laws. In addition, there is an emergent consensus that "best practice" in matters of naturalization (and immigrant integration in general) is not just to trust in the informally socializing powers of time and place, as in the past, but to impose formal and standardized language and civics requirements as conditions for the granting of citizenship to adults. In Britain, the introduction of formal integration requirements in naturalization occurred almost Canadian-style – that is, in a mellower and more gentle way than on the European continent, but with no less restrictive effects.[38] However, entirely un-Canadian is a new provision in the 2006 Immigration, Asylum and Nationality Act that empowers the home secretary to deprive a person of their British citizenship if this is "conducive to the public good." This replaces the more rights-respecting condition, which had been introduced in 2002, that such citizenship deprivation had to be in the "vital interest" of the state (see Hampshire 2008a).

The empowerment of the state and converse disempowerment of the citizen is in response to the July 2005 suicide bombings on the London Underground, which were committed by four home-grown British youngsters of Muslim origin. More than the machinations of provincial populists, terror in the name of God has changed the world, leaving its indelible imprints on European citizenship laws.

However, the tightening of access to citizenship also coincides with a further boost toward internationalized economies, which goes under the name of "globalization." As Katharine Betts and

Bob Birrell (2007: 58) characterized the Australian scene under the late conservative Howard government, "We have a Government determined to embrace the global economy yet at the same time turning inwards towards a patriotic stance on citizenship." Even labor, which was long deemed exempt from the logic of global factor mobility, is increasingly sucked into it, as the global "race for talent" (Shachar 2006) testifies. In Europe, the same governments that are outdoing one another in "civic integration" are also reopening their societies, however haltingly, to selective immigration. More than targeting hapless immigrants, the new restrictions may be about adjusting sedentary natives to the inevitable internationalization of the world.

3

Rights

This chapter discusses three ways in which immigration since World War II has become implicated with the rights of citizenship.

Firstly, I review a recent debate among sociologists and political scientists on the impact of ethnic diversity on the social rights of citizenship: Is diversity inimical to social citizenship? While in theory the linkage between ethnic homogeneity and social citizenship is compelling, there is scant empirical evidence that increased diversity is responsible for current welfare-state retrenchments. Still, the overall diminished status of social citizenship is incontrovertible.

Secondly, as captured in the diagnosis of "postnational membership" (Soysal 1994), there has been a strengthening of the rights of aliens in the past half-century, perhaps best expressed in the paradoxical notion of a right to citizenship. However, one must realize that many rights, such as elementary civil rights and certain social rights, have always been separate from formal citizenship status. National citizenship never was the repository of comprehensive rights it is depicted to be in the postnational thesis. More importantly still, it would be wrong to conceive of alien rights as homogeneous proxy to citizen rights. Rather, alien rights are highly stratified, both across states and within states, bearing the indelible mark of the state's immigration powers. And in the age of Islamic terror, security-obsessed states have launched an unprecedented attack on the civil rights of aliens, provoking clashes with law courts that had always accompanied the evolution of alien rights. The post-2001 experience shows the inherent vulnerability of the rights of aliens as compared to the rights of citizens.

Thirdly, postwar immigration has boosted the rise of minority rights, in which immigrants figure not as a legal category externally produced by immigration law but as social groups defined by inherent traits of race, ethnicity, or religion. However, such minority rights are not of one cloth. Instead, their thrust may be either particularistic or universalistic. In the particularistic variant, minority rights are geared towards perpetuating the respective minority trait. This is the gist of multiculturalism policies. In the universalistic variant, minority rights aim to render invisible the minority trait as marker of discrimination. This is the purpose of antidiscrimination policies. I shall argue that the multiculturalism variant is currently in retreat (to the degree that it was ever in place), but that the antidiscrimination variant is going from strength to strength, especially in Europe.

In the following, I address these three aspects of the immigration–citizenship rights nexus in turn.

Diversity and the Demise of Social Citizenship

In a prescient think piece, Gary Freeman argued that welfare states were "closed systems," based on the principle of "mutual aid according to need" (1986: 62). Most importantly, they required for their functioning "some aspect of kinship or fellow feeling" that is undermined by the logic of open economies and free labor mobility. Migration, in particular, could not but be a "disaster" for the developed welfare states of Europe, leading to the "Americanization of European welfare politics," with fractionalized labor movements and greatly diminished social rights and benefits (ibid.: 60–2).

Two more decades had to pass before the debate over the impact of immigration-based diversity on social citizenship started in earnest. In 2004, the British columnist David Goodhart, close to the post-socialist Labour Party of Tony Blair, stated the existence of a "progressive dilemma," in that one had to choose between "solidarity" and "diversity" but that having both together was not possible. This is because welfare solidarity rested on a sense of "prefer[ring] our own kind" and reciprocity that was precisely undermined by immigration-based diversity. And if a public policy choice had to be made, it should be in favor of solidarity, because diversity would happen as a matter of fact.

It is incontrovertible that immigration-based ethnic diversity has detrimental effects on the levels of "trust" between people, which is generally considered a prerequisite for accepting the redistribution mustered by the welfare state. One study of "generalized social trust"[1] in sixty countries found that "high trust" countries were precisely characterized by ethnic homogeneity, among other features (Delhey and Newton 2005).[2] Before Robert Putnam's (2007) landmark study on diversity and trust in the United States, the dominant wisdom was that, because of competition for scarce resources, diversity fostered in-group solidarity but out-group distrust (referred to by Putnam as "conflict theory"). Conversely, the earlier "contact hypothesis," stating that diversity had the opposite effect of weakening ethnocentric attitudes and fostering out-group trust and solidarity, was largely discounted. Putnam's representative survey of the United States confirmed the negative impact of diversity on out-group solidarity, but added the important nuance that "diversity might actually reduce *both* in-group *and* out-group solidarity" (2007: 144). Rather than triggering in-group/out-group divisions, as conflict theory had assumed, according to Putnam's "constrict theory," diversity breeds "anomie" and "social isolation." As Putnam put it, "people living in ethnically diverse settings appear to 'hunker down' – that is, pull in like a turtle" (ibid.: 149), distrusting their fellow ethnics as much as they distrust the members of other ethnic groups.

While Putnam's findings are controversial, instantly employing a cottage industry of refutations and amendments, most scholars agree that "ethnic diversity appears to have a negative effect on generalized trust" (Miller 2003: 27).[3] The question is whether the negative relationship between diversity and trust must translate into lack of support for the welfare state. An even greater leap is from increased diversity to actual reductions in social spending.

However compelling both inferences may be in theory,[4] there is little evidence for them in reality. With respect to attitudinal support for the welfare state, a review of public opinion surveys across a large number of states found that there was "no systematic negative association between multiculturalism policies and redistributive attitudes" (Crepaz 2006: 108).[5] With respect to welfare-state expenditures, a study of the impact of immigration on changes in social spending across OECD countries from 1970 to 1998 found that there was no relationship between them: "There was simply no evidence that countries with large foreign-born populations had more trouble sustaining and developing their social programs over these three decades than countries with small immigrant communities" (Kymlicka and Banting 2006: 291). Growing out of the same research program, a study of twenty-one OECD countries found that there was likewise "no consistent relationship between the adoption of multiculturalism policies and the erosion of the welfare state" (Banting et al. 2006: 65). On the contrary, the countries with the strongest multiculturalism policies (Australia and Canada) saw the largest rise in social spending as part of GDP and showed the greatest strengthening of redistributive effort in terms of taxes and transfers.

In fact, most of the literature that connects diversity with welfare-state minimalism has drawn its evidence from the United States, where the levels of social spending across states and cities are indeed negatively correlated with the presence of racial or ethnic minorities (especially blacks and Hispanics) (see the brief overview in Hero and Preuhs 2006: 121–6). An important recent work in this genre compared the US and Europe with respect to "fighting poverty," seeking to explain why there has been significantly less redistribution from the rich to the poor in the United States than in Europe (in the US, government spending constitutes only 30 percent of GDP, while in Europe it is around 45 percent – almost two-thirds of this difference arising from spending on welfare) (Alesina and Glaeser 2004: 2). Notably, the two economists discount economic explanations, and instead hold political institutions and race jointly responsible for America's lesser welfare largesse. In a statistical analysis, they find that 50 percent of the US–European difference in welfare spending is a result of different political structures, most notably the absence in the United States of proportional representation (which in Europe favors the growth of welfare-friendly, leftist parties). The other half of the difference is explained by the higher "racial and ethnic fractionalization" in the United States, the argument being that "individuals are more generous towards members of their own racial or ethnic group" (ibid.: 10).[6] A third factor that *might* explain the US–European difference is referred to as "culture and attitudes," in that there is a propensity in the US to stigmatize the poor as "lazy," whereas Europeans are more inclined to exculpate the latter as merely "unfortunate."[7] However, Alesina and Glaeser argue that such views are not freestanding but are themselves conditioned, on the one hand, by institutions that favor the political right in the US and the left in Europe, and, on the other hand, by the racial heterogeneity in the US that allows politicians to underscore the moral failings of the (racially concentrated) poor. Accordingly, the authors reaffirm "institutions and race" as the two primary factors driving the US–European difference in welfare spending (ibid.: 12).

However, Alesina and Glaeser's (2004: 218) grinding quest for "first causes" eventually dethrones even institutions, because the latter are "themselves the result of the profoundly different geographies and ethnicities of America and Europe." Lesser geographic distance and ethno-racial difference have favored stronger labor movements in Europe that, in turn, have helped create the "institutions that support the European welfare state" (ibid.: 129). Geography and race are thus, in the end, key to explaining the strength of social citizenship in Europe and its weakness in the United States.

Projecting the American experience onto Europe, Alesina and Glaeser predict the demise of social citizenship in Europe to the degree that the latter grows more ethnically diverse: "[If] Europe becomes more heterogeneous due to immigration, ethnic divisions will be used to challenge the generous welfare state" (2004: 11), especially on the part of a strengthened New Right. However, this projection is questionable. Against a facile application of America as "model for Europe," Banting and Kymlicka have argued that context and timing matter: "Where minorities are newcomers rather than historically enslaved groups, and where state institutions are strong rather than weak, the impact of increasing heterogeneity may be quite different" (2006: 28). Note that even in the United States the stigmatizing "lazy" is attributed only to the descendants of African slaves, and not to voluntary immigrant groups (see Gilens 1999). With respect to timing, the European immigration challenge meets mature and entrenched welfare states, whereas in the United States the fact of race has hampered welfare-state development from the start. This is a decisive difference. Consider that while the New Right may be anti-immigrant, it certainly is not anti-welfare (at least in its more recent incarnation), favoring strong states as a shelter from globalization. Moreover, as Peter Taylor-Gooby (2005: 671) pointed out in a statistical re-examination of the data used by Alesina and Glaeser (2004), once the strength of the political left is factored into the analysis (rather than seen as a mere reflection of the level of racial diversity), the effect of diversity on social spending almost disappears: "In effect, the presence of the left appears able to insulate welfare systems against the impact of greater diversity among citizens."

Thus the expectation of an Americanization of the European welfare state on account of immigration appears misguided. As John Myles and Sébastien St-Arnaud emphasized, the key question is whether increased diversity generates "new ethno-racial political cleavages powerful enough to erode social solidarity" (2006: 341). And the emergence of such cleavages is not simply a function of the presence of immigrants or of multiculturalism policies on their behalf. Rather, it hinges on immigrants' "level of . . . economic and political incorporation," which, in turn, is multiplex, depending on their selection, on whether multiculturalism policies are perceived as "fair," and on the electoral strength of minorities (ibid.: 353). In short, the linkage between ethnic diversity and welfare-state development is not direct but mediated by many other factors, which work out differently here from there.

This is not to deny the current reality of welfare-state restructuring and retrenchment – only that immigration is at best peripherally involved in it. A key development in this respect has been a transformation of social citizenship from "status" into "contract" (Handler 2004), thus exactly reversing social citizenship's earlier triumph over market inequalities. In social citizenship as status, social benefits were rights attached to the status of citizenship, the logic being one of "decommodification" (Esping-Anderson 1990: 3). In social citizenship as contract, of which contemporary "workfare" programs are a prime example, social benefits are in return for obligatory reintegration into the labor market. They thus follow an opposite logic of commodification. In OECD Europe, the backdrop to this change has been permanent high unemployment, which shot up from only 3 percent on average in the 1970s to over 9 percent in the 1990s (Handler 2004: 99). Now the focus of social policy became the problem of "exclusion" of certain social categories from work and society – single parents (the root cause of child poverty), youth, and immigrants and ethnic minorities. If the focus of social policy becomes the inclusion of the excluded, and thus straddling the boundary that separates the included from the excluded, it is necessarily blind on what goes on in the included sector, such as persistent or even widening inequalities *there*. A further feature of inclusion is that individuals meet it as an obligation, and as something for which they themselves are deemed responsible. "Inclusion" is thus the exact opposite of classic social citizenship: an obligation, not a right; an effort of the individual, not of society.

In an interesting discussion of the Dutch case, Han Entzinger (2006a) showed that there is a striking coincidence between welfare-state restructuring along such lines and the decline of multiculturalism policies – only that there is no causal connection between the two. First, Entzinger provides disconcerting evidence of the typically European overrepresentation of immigrant minorities in the welfare system. In the early twenty-first century, the relative claim on disability allowances among migrants of non-Western origin was 24 percent higher than among the Dutch; their relative claim on unemployment benefits, rent subsidies, and public assistance was higher still, at 57 percent, 184 percent, and 337 percent, respectively (2006a: 191). And 40 percent of those entitled to public assistance ("welfare" proper) are of non-Western origin, while the latter constitute only 10 percent of the Dutch population (ibid.: 193). One can further observe that, between 1983 and 2003, public spending on schemes with high minority participation (especially unemployment benefits and public assistance) was reduced more than spending on other programs. But this was less the result of a substantial reduction in benefits than of successfully redirecting people from welfare to work, which became the focus of Dutch social policy in the 1990s. As a result of the successful welfare-to-workfare transition in the Netherlands, only people "at a great distance from the labour market" are still entitled to social benefits – and these tend disproportionately to be immigrants, most of whom are low-skilled or otherwise impaired when competing in the labor market. "So we find ourselves in the paradoxical situation," Entzinger (2006a: 195) concludes, "that the immigrant share in some of the most prominent parts of the social security system has increased as a result of the successful reform of that system." Whatever the paradoxical outcome of welfare reform may be, Entzinger's important message is that immigration has not been a consideration in this reform. Instead, the impetus has been the globalization-related concern of making the Dutch workforce more efficient and competitive.

While until now there has been little evidence that diversity, either as fact or as policy-guiding norm, has damaged the welfare state, it is not ruled out that diversity could not have such effect in the future. As Philippe van Parijs (2003: 382) surmises, perhaps more time is required for the underlying "sociological processes to work themselves out." In considering why diversity could damage social citizenship in the long run one must direct one's attention back to the principal tension between the two. The tension between diversity and welfare has been well formulated by the French historian Pierre Rosanvallon (2000). He argued that the classic welfare state was based on the idea of an "insurance society": risks were shared, and a "veil of ignorance" obscured who would eventually take advantage of social benefits. Because risks (of unemployment, disability, disease, etc.) were equally distributed and predictable, everyone was willing to pay for their accommodation. In essence, self-interest in a context of *shared risks* and *opacity* produced the solidarity that sustained the welfare state. The problem today is that both conditions no longer exist. Firstly, risks are not shared but stratified: exclusion concerns specific groups (including immigrants and ethnic minorities). Secondly, the "veil of ignorance" has been lifted and opacity no longer applies: knowledge personalizes risk and makes it predictable (we *know* that smoking causes cancer; we *know* that certain genes cause disease; etc.). Why then should someone who, through behavior or luck, is outside the risk zone pay for those who are inside?

This new constellation has two consequences: the target of social policy is not entire populations but individuals or specific groups; and to the degree that, with the retreat of opacity, self-interest dissipates, there is an extra need for solidarity to make people support an increasingly redistributive, tax- (rather than insurance-)based welfare state. According to Rosanvallon, there are two ways to respond to this situation. The first is "victimization" (2000: 35–7). This is the politics of multiculturalism, in which compensation steps in for insurance, and in which a culprit substitutes for bad luck. The second solution, advocated by Rosanvallon, is welfare in return for obligatory reintegration into the workforce, and thus a variant of social citizenship as contract, as discussed above.

Rosanvallon (2000: 19–21) rightly identified the source of social citizenship's current difficulties as "the curse of knowledge of the differences among men," which can only be fuelled further by immigration-based diversity. And he rightly reminds us that social citizenship historically evolved in "leaps and bounds," especially in the aftermath of wars that boosted the requisite solidarities (ibid.: 28). Citizenship rights, in general, are concession or reward for having suffered for the collectivity: "[W]ork, war, and reproduction have been the primary avenues for the construction of citizenship, its bounds and rights" (Abraham 2002: 7).

In a multicultural society, the sense of collectivity required for social citizenship to prosper inevitably weakens. In particular, the focus shifts from redistributive social rights to procedural civil rights. Rosanvallon (2000: 36) eloquently describes the changing ethos of this society: "The central social values are tolerance rather than solidarity, and impartiality rather than equality. The 'good society' is the society that allows the peaceful coexistence of differences, not the society that guarantees inclusion. The principle of citizenship no longer implies a demand for redistribution . . . but is reduced to common trust in autonomy."

The Rights of Aliens: Stratified and Reversible

In her gloomy tractate on the lot of stateless people and of national minorities in early twentieth-century Europe, Hannah Arendt argued that the "rights of man" were nil if not encoded as citizen rights by nation-states. Those deprived of their state were "rightless, the scum of the earth" (Arendt [1951] 1979: 267). In turn, as the experience of the newly founded state of Israel demonstrated, the "restoration of human rights" could happen only by means of the "restoration . . . of national rights" (ibid.: 299). As Arendt bitterly concedes, Edmund Burke, veteran critic of the French Revolution and its high-minded Declaration of the Rights of Man and Citizen, was correct that the "rights of an Englishman" counted infinitely more than the "abstraction" of human rights (ibid.). However, if membership in a nation-state is the source of rights, how can there be a "right to have rights" (ibid.: 296), "a right to belong to some kind of organized community" (ibid.) – that is, a right to citizenship? As Hohfeld (1919) pointed out in his acidic analytic of rights, a "right" presupposes a "duty" on others, the enforcement of which requires a state that is exactly found wanting in Arendt's scenario. The "right to have rights" is vitiated by circularity. Yet what other conclusion to draw from Europe's dark century?

One has to keep in mind the Arendtian equation of human rights with citizen rights to realize the enormous provocation that is inherent in the contemporary claim that "postnational membership" (Soysal 1994) has come to trump national citizenship, and that states matter less in view of an international human rights regime. There is certainly a slice of truth in this. This slice of truth

Rights

is revealed when scrutinizing the rights component of citizen rights. Consider Cass Sunstein's definition of rights, which is as good as any. He defines rights pragmatically as "legally enforceable instruments for the protection of their claimants" (Sunstein 1995: 739). When probing deeper into the content of this protection, Sunstein finds that rights pertain to "important human interests" (ibid.: 736). If this is the case, citizen rights notionally blend with human rights. Qua reference to "important human interests," citizenship as rights is inflicted with the virus of universalism that eventually bursts the shell of nationality and asks for the equal consideration of all human beings. The universalistic core of citizenship inevitably pushes toward something akin to "postnational membership" (Soysal 1994) or, even more provocatively, "alien citizenship" (Bosniak 2006).

Historically, the trigger for unleashing this dynamic was the mid-twentieth century's delegitimization of race as marker of social differentiation, which had meant the exact denial of shared humanity. While the distinction between citizens and aliens remains valid under international and domestic law, the threshold for attributing lesser rights to aliens, at least outside the narrow nexus of immigration law, has massively increased because it is now tainted by the smell of racial discrimination. In the famous 1971 decision *Graham v. Richardson*, which restored state-level welfare rights for legal immigrants, the US Supreme Court likened immigrants to a "discrete and insular" minority, discrimination against which on the basis of "alienage" was "inherently suspect," much "like those based on nationality or race."[8] Precisely because political rights continued to be the privilege of citizens, which subjected aliens to the whims of xenophobic citizens in the political arena, there was a heightened need for their protection in the legal arena. Supreme Court Justice Blackmun articulated this spirit in a post-Graham decision:

> The very powerlessness of a discrete minority, then, is itself the factor that overcomes the usual presumption that even improvident decisions affecting minorities will eventually be rectified by the democratic process. If anything, the fact that aliens constitutionally may be – and

83

generally are – formally and completely barred from participating in the process of self-government makes particularly profound the need for searching judicial review of classifications grounded in alienage. (Quoted in Katyal 2007: 1373)

This is the inherently legal versus political dynamic that has marked the evolution of alien rights in America and Europe since World War II (see Joppke 2001b).

However, what the diagnosis of postnational membership leaves out is the role, if not the revenge, of the state. As Randall Hansen put it sarcastically, postnationalists have reduced the function of states to that of "policy waiters following the orders of universal persons" (Hansen 2009: 4). But these universal persons are still "aliens" on the state's radar. Ultimately subject to the state's immigration powers, aliens never quite reach the position of comfort allotted to them by postnationalists. Certain rights are always precluded, most notably political rights, absolute protection from expulsion, and rights of diplomatic protection. This last may never be relevant to most people, but when needed – say, in the "human rights horror that is Guantánamo Bay" (ibid.) – postnational membership is not enough to escape death or unjust punishment, because only formal citizenship status entitles one to diplomatic protection.

But even the rights that indisputably belong to postnational members, especially civil and social rights, are in reality stratified rights that bear the heavy mark of the state's immigration powers; and, through being concessions by the state, they are always reversible. In the following, I will discuss both limitations of alien rights in turn.

Stratified rights

In a dry but compelling comparison of migrant rights in Germany, Britain, and Italy, Lydia Morris argued that "the rights and protections afforded by the state to different 'entry' categories constitute a system of stratified rights closely associated with monitoring and control" (2002: 19). Her important insight is that migrant rights are stratified rights that are inherently fused with the state's control and surveillance interests. These rights vary cross-nationally and, within the state, according to entry category and functional sector. For instance, most Western states have recently passed laws to attract high-skilled immigrants, who are given certain residence, family unification, and other (often even tax) privileges that are denied to less desired, low-skilled, not to mention illegal, immigrants (Shachar 2006). In addition to stratification by entry category, migrant rights are stratified by functional sector, as different conditions apply to the access to residence, work, or welfare. If the "granting and withholding of rights" is indeed "a possible basis for the management of migration" (Morris 2002: 19), one even wonders whether there are any "rights" of migrants at all, and whether one should not better conceive of migrant rights as a whole as contingent "concessions" by the state. This goes too far. The floor of rights not to be undercut by the state is set by the intervention of law courts, which have mobilized constitutional and international convention clauses against states' restrictionist intentions. There *is* a nucleus of alien *rights*, properly understood as "trumps" (Dworkin 1984), that the individual may hold *against* the state and the democratic majority that the state stands for. But this nucleus is much smaller and more brittle than thought by postnationalists.

To give a flavor of the complexity and fluctuating nature of alien rights, let us review their stratification only by functional sector.[9] The two sectors where alien rights are most precarious are residence and access to the labor market. There is a sharp division in this respect between the classic immigration states, which hand out legal permanent immigrant status plus full and equal access to the labor market *from the start*, and European states, where residence status and labor market access are at first limited and grow only over time. Of course, in no state is there a right to first entry and residence; instead, everywhere the issuance of the necessary permit is fully discretionary. Only gradually did European states create a status akin to permanent legal residence in the US, and the transition periods to acquire the most favored status initially differed widely (three years in France, four years in Britain, eight years in

Germany, ten years in Switzerland).[10] In some countries, such as Belgium, Germany, the Netherlands, and Austria, long-term residence status has been made available as of right; in others, such as Switzerland and Britain, it remains fully discretionary. France, while fast in handing out the possibility of most-favored residence after three years of stay, grants a legal entitlement to the latter after only ten years. In most European countries, including Germany, France, the Netherlands, Austria, and Britain, acquiring long-term residence status is contingent on not being welfare-dependent; Germany further asks for sixty months of pension payments, an unlimited work permit (*Arbeitsberechtigung*),[11] and, even preceding the recent civic turn, German-language competence.

There has been a move over the past three decades toward narrowing the initially huge gap in Europe between at first rightless foreigners and citizens in the domain of residence. Even France, Europe's major immigrant-receiving country since the nineteenth century, did not have a permanent residence permit until 1981 (when the famous *carte de dix ans* was introduced under President Mitterrand). In Germany, only the Aliens Act 1990 introduced an individual right to permanent residence, while casting into law the court-engineered notion of status improvement over time. In its new Immigration Act of 2004, Germany even became the only European country to issue permanent residence permits at entry (if only for a very small number of high-skilled immigrants), thus reversing the European logic of gradual status consolidation. These positive developments with respect to residence rights point to a kernel of truth in the postnational thesis. However, as Ulrike Davy (2005: 133) points out, "even the best status available to non-nationals is still different from the status of nationals." Most notably, not even permanent residents are ever quite safe from the most drastic of the state's immigration powers: deportation. Certainly, weighty reasons have to be mustered, in terms of severe violations of public security and order, to deport best-status immigrants. But Germany in particular has shown few qualms over exercising this possibility, even with respect to second-generation immigrants born in Germany who had never seen the "country of origin" to which they were deported (ibid.: 139, n. 95).

Similar strictures apply to immigrants' access to the labor market. Since the official stop of guest worker recruitment in 1973, in all European states the employment of immigrants is generally prohibited unless expressly allowed and a so-called *Inländerprimat*,[12] which requires a prior search for a domestic worker before a foreigner can be employed, is in place. Even Germany's new Immigration Law of 2004, which otherwise eschews the old notion that Germany is "not a country of immigration," has not formally lifted the three-decade-old recruitment stop. When a work permit is issued to a foreigner, it is always at first precarious and limited in time and tied to a specific employer, type of work, or economic sector. As with respect to residence, entitlements grow over time. Generally, with achieving the most-favored residence status either the need for a work permit lapses or such a permit has to be granted as of right and without any limitations. An interesting exception to this is provided by Austria, whose most-favored employment permit for foreigners, the so-called *Befreiungsschein*, while issued relatively easily, is always only temporary and thus revocable. Particularly sensitive and highly varied across states is labor market access for family migrants, who in some countries are at first excluded from the right to work (as in Austria or Germany), while in others are immediately allowed to work (as in Belgium, Britain, France, or the Netherlands). But perhaps the most drastic variation is with respect to public sector employment. In Britain or the Netherlands, such employment is or has been made accessible to non-citizens without much ado. By contrast, in France and Germany, despite pressure for opening it up, such employment tends to be reserved for citizens (and, to avoid a violation of EU law, other member state citizens).

In the United States also, the question of access to public sector jobs for legal immigrants has been restrictively answered, thus constituting an exception to the general lifting of state-level discrimination after the Supreme Court's momentous 1971 *Graham v. Richardson* decision. Shortly after this ruling, the Supreme Court issued the so-called political function exception, according to which state-level jobs that touched on "basic governmental processes" (quoted in Bosniak 2006: 61) could be reserved to citizens. This exception has subsequently been interpreted expansively to include state troopers, school teachers, and deputy probation officers, thus "swallow[ing] up the entire proposition [set by *Graham*] that alienage classifications are suspect" (G. Rosberg, quoted ibid.: 63).

The political function exception raises the larger question, which has perennially followed the evolution of alien rights in the United States and elsewhere, of how far the border should reach in vitiating the status of aliens compared to that of citizens. As elaborated by Linda Bosniak, this question may be answered either in terms of a clear "separation" of immigration from other social spheres, for which above all *Graham* stands, or in terms of a "convergence" of immigration with all social spheres, which is exemplified by the political function exception. However one answers the border question, alienage is ineradicably a "hybrid legal status" that is a creature equally of the "world of borders" and of the "world of social relationships" (Bosniak 2006: 38f.). To eradicate the border from the concept of alien is the major shortcoming of the postnational thesis.

But the crown of postnational membership is generally taken to be social rights. Soysal (1994: 127) even argues that their bestowal on immigrants reverses the Marshallian citizenship logic, because for immigrants in Europe social rights arrived earlier and perhaps more completely than civil or political rights. In the United States, the decisive moment was, again, the Supreme Court's 1971 *Graham v. Richardson* decision, which invoked the Fourteenth Amendment's equal protection clause to strike down state statutes that withheld welfare benefits from resident aliens. However, the ensuing welfare inclusion was valid only at state level and perhaps not even primarily because immigrants were "persons" protected by the Constitution, but because otherwise the state would arrogate to itself immigration powers that are the privilege of the federal government.[13] Promptly the same Supreme Court that had negated state-level discrimination permitted it at the federal level, in its *Mathews v. Diaz* (1976) decision that, by virtue of its "plenary power" over immigration, the federal government was free to exclude resident aliens from Medicare benefits if it so wished. This suggests yet another axis of stratification with respect to alien rights, though one specific to American federalism – namely that these rights may be of varying strength at different (state versus federal) government levels.

However, with respect to the stratification of the social rights of aliens, perhaps even more important is an internal distinction between contributory and non-contributory benefits. Health care, unemployment compensation, and pensions are in most countries insurance-based, the triggering factors being labor market participation and territoriality, not nationality. Such contributory social benefits never had any nationality restriction. Accordingly, this is the one domain where aliens fare no worse than citizens, simply because nationality is not and never has been a relevant consideration. Peter Baldwin (1997: 109) even argues that contribution-based benefits, which are tied to formal employment and whose amount grows with working years and wage, should be excluded from the ambit of "social citizenship," reserving the latter to non-contributory benefits, which are "distributed regardless of any effort made in return" (ibid.).

Indeed, aliens fare notably worse with respect to non-contributory and thus genuinely redistributive welfare benefits, as their granting is often made contingent on citizenship status. This has been the site of extended and often fiercely contested jurisdiction by the European Court of Justice,[14] which has greatly restricted European states' powers to treat their own citizens better than other member state citizens, even in critical nation-building domains such as education and family planning. With respect to non-contributory social benefits, Ulrike Davy finds that "almost all legal orders [in Europe] contain discriminatory rules and mostly openly discriminatory rules at that" (2001: 947), though there are, again, variations. In some countries, such as the Netherlands and Britain, there were initially no restrictions for such welfare benefits for temporary or even illegal migrants – not out of largesse but out of sheer non-consideration of atypical claimants. Until the late 1990s, the Dutch social security system did not include many rules or conditions specifically related to aliens, so that even illegal immigrants had full and equal access. This changed with the so-called Linking Act (*Koppelingswet*) of 1998, which made the entitlement or access of aliens to non-primary education, housing, rent subsidy, health care, and national assistance dependent on their legal status. The target of this measure was illegal immigrants, so that temporary migrants continued to be covered (Groenendijk and Minderhoud 2001: 540f.; see also Engbersen 2003). Britain, initially allowing a similarly inclusive access to social security, went even further in excluding, with the Immigration and Asylum Act 1999, temporary migrants from access to all non-contributory benefits. Technically speaking, all persons "subject to immigration control" (that is, all immigrants not entitled to an "indefinite leave to remain") are no longer entitled to non-contributory benefits, known as "public funds," which include child benefit, council tax benefit, disability living allowance, housing benefit, income-based job-seeker's allowance, and income support (Goldsmith 2008: 57). This made Britain by far the most restrictive country in Europe with respect to immigrants' access to welfare.

As limiting welfare benefits to citizens may appear blatantly discriminatory, there is a marked tendency to make the "immigration authority" the "watchdog of the welfare state" (Baldwin 1997: 111) or to build a "wall around the welfare state" (Engbersen 2003). An interesting case is Germany, where the entire welfare function (contributory *and* non-contributory) had never hinged on nationality. Even illegal immigrants continue, in principle, to have access to non-contributory social aid (*Sozialhilfe*). However, this universalism is neutralized by restrictive immigration laws that prescribe termination of residence for non-citizens who make use of such benefits. More precisely, temporary immigrants may ask for social aid, but at the risk of losing their residence permit and being deported. Social rights are thus indirectly restricted through immigration law, which precisely in this respect has become more restrictive in recent years (see Davy 2005: 137f.).

In sum, the "social rights" granted to immigrants look rather different from the social rights that have crowned the civilization-making citizenship evolution according to T. H. Marshall. As Ulrike Davy (2005: 137) showed in the German case, social rights for immigrants are at best "contingent upon economic value,"

Rights

because immigrants have to prove "time and again," from the point of entry to the prolongation of at first temporary residence to the eventual granting of a permanent residence permit, that they will "not burden public funds." The same logic applies to most other European states, not to mention the United States, which pioneered the wholesale exclusion of immigrants from federal welfare benefits in 1996.

Reversible rights

If alien rights are to an important (though never absolute) degree concessions by the state, they are in principle reversible. The notion that alien rights are reversible is inherent in the notion that they are stratified. To date the most dramatic expression of the wide possibility of states to reverse alien rights is the recommendation of the Goldsmith Commission (Goldsmith 2008), called by the British government to advise on citizenship policy, to abolish the very category of legal permanent resident. As the commission's report bluntly states: "Permanent residency blurs the distinction between citizens and non-citizens. We should expect people who are settled in the UK for the long-term to become citizens." Only those who cannot acquire British citizenship because their first country of citizenship does not allow dual nationality should be allowed to live on as "associate citizens." Should such proposal become law, it would signal the end of postnational membership. More than any other Western state, Britain is growing impatient about the luxury of welcoming people who may enjoy most of the rights that citizens hold, but who lastingly refuse to commit themselves to their new country by becoming its citizens. Most annoyingly, postnational membership "blurs" the meaning of citizenship, as a bold line may divide the rights of citizens and those of temporary migrants, but not the rights of citizens and those of permanent residents (Goldsmith 2008: 11). This is "a muddle that probably exists for honourable reasons," submits Lord Goldsmith (ibid.: 77). But, considering that the "blurring" of citizenship had already been extended to the realm of "protection and loyalty,"[15] it was time to draw the line where it should be drawn: between citizens and non-citizens. This would mean confronting immigrants with the choice either to stay on temporarily or to opt for citizenship. However, if immigrants choose the first option, "they will not obtain the broader access to entitlements that currently comes with permanent residence" (ibid.: 78).

The radical dethroning of postnational membership through throwing out the status of legal permanent residence has not yet happened anywhere, and probably it never will. However, a distinct mark of the post-2001 period and the US-led "War on Terror" is a "growing vulnerability of noncitizens" (Goldstone 2006). The United States responded to the unprecedented attack by nineteen Arab non-citizens on 11 September 2001 by resuscitating the Schmittian notion that the citizen bind is the quintessential political bind, in which "friends" are sharply distinguished from "enemies." Aliens now were potential enemies, as in the gruesome notion of "unlawful enemy combatants,"[16] beyond the pale of the rule of law, and subject to blanket registration, heightened surveillance, indefinite detention, or summary deportation. The "law for enemies" dispensed on aliens differs from ordinary criminal law in not intending to rehabilitate, to reform, or even to punish; instead, its purpose is to "banish" danger (Eckert 2008: 20).[17]

If the post-2001 obsession with security is often considered as sacrificing liberty for security, this is at best a half-truth. Because, as David Cole (2002: 955) described the US response, "in practice we have selectively sacrificed non-citizens' liberties while retaining basic protections for citizens." The opening shot was President Bush's Military Order of 13 November 2001, which established military commissions to try suspected international terrorists, and in which the military acts as prosecutor, judge, jury, and executioner in one, without appeal to a civilian court. Crucially, only aliens, not citizens, were subjected to this regime. This was not because of legal constraints but political expediency, or, if you like, plain nationalism. Nationalistic, at least, was Vice President Dick Cheney's defense of singling out aliens: "Somebody who comes into the United States of America illegally, who conducts a terrorist operation killing thousands of innocent Americans – men, women, and children – is not a lawful combatant . . . They don't deserve the same guarantees and safeguards that would be used for an American citizen" (quoted ibid.: 959f.).

Upon President Bush's Military Order[18] followed the US Patriot Act, which renders non-citizens deportable merely for associational activity, excludable for pure speech, and detainable on the Attorney General's say-so that they are suspected of having engaged in "terrorist activity," without a hearing and without a finding that they pose a danger or a risk of absconding. Association with an organization designated as terrorist was so widely conceived that "an alien who sent a toy train set to a day-care center run by a designated organization would be deportable as a terrorist, even if she could show that the train set was used only by three-year-olds" (Cole 2002: 967). And "terrorist activity" was so laxly defined that "a permanent resident alien who brandished a kitchen knife in a domestic dispute with her abusive husband" would qualify (ibid.: 971).

The dubious novelty in the American response to terror is the denial of elementary civil rights to aliens, showing no mercy even to their previously most protected subset, legal permanent residents. David Cole made an important distinction in this respect between rights that stem from a contract, and which are better conceived of as privileges, and rights proper, which inhere in an inviolable integrity of the person. Political freedom, due process, and equal protection under the law, which are undercut by the American revival of its late eighteenth-century concept of enemy alien, are "best understood not as special privileges stemming from a specific social contract, but from what it means to be a person with free and equal dignity"; they are "human rights, not privileges of citizenship" (Cole 2002: 957). Accordingly, the denial of "equal justice under law" to enemy aliens is of a different order from no longer "handing out a 'goody'" (Katyal 2007: 1375), which is the gist of excluding immigrants from welfare benefits. By the same token, the enormity of this move consists in undercutting the generality of the law, which had hitherto been a staple of the rule of law as such, and surely is no innovation of the postnational age. Supreme Court Justice Jackson had stated some sixty years ago that laws of general applicability were the best protection against tyranny: "[T]here is no more effective practical guarantee against arbitrary and unreasonable government than to require that the principles of law which officials would impose upon a minority must be imposed generally" (quoted ibid.: 1370). The dethroning of postnational members (worse, the deprivation of all aliens' elementary civic rights) thus bears risks for the citizenry at large.

These risks became evident in Britain, where an indictment of similarly selective anti-terrorism laws by the country's highest court was responded to by the government not by lifting the incriminated emergency provisions but, on the contrary, by extending them from aliens to citizens.[19] Section 23 of Britain's 2001 Anti-terrorism, Crime and Security Act, hastily passed a few months after the terrorist attacks on the United States, allowed indefinite detention, without an indictment, of suspected international terrorists who cannot be deported. All that was required was that the home secretary "reasonably believes" (without grounding in objective fact) that a person is a terrorist who poses a risk to national security. As in the US anti-terror laws, this heavy-handed measure first applied only to non-citizens, in this case using the less protective framework of immigration law. A government report defended this limitation with respect to "the damage" that the extension to citizens of such "draconian powers" could inflict on "community cohesion" (Home Office 2004: 9). In less circumscribed words, aliens were victimized on the altar of domestic Muslim appeasement. To achieve this, the government had to derogate from Article 5 of the European Convention for the Protection of Human Rights (ECPHR), which protects the "right to liberty and security" (and prohibits indefinite detention), and it had to invoke article 15 of ECPHR, which allows derogation for the sake of a "public emergency threatening the life of the nation." But, more than repudiating an unloved European convention import, the power to detain people indefinitely without charge or trial, which was stipulated by Section 23 of the anti-terrorism act, called into question "the very existence of an ancient liberty of which this country has until now been proud: freedom from arbitrary arrest and detention."[20] In fact, much as the US government had done in its War on Terror, its British deputy sheriff lifted ancient habeas corpus rights, and this – also as in the United States – selectively for aliens.

Concretely, the operation of Section 23 of the 2001 anti-terrorism act meant that by late 2004, when the House of Lords condemned the measure, twelve detainees had been held for three years under prison-like conditions as suspected terrorists, without any criminal charge having been brought against them. This situation could possibly have continued indefinitely, because the non-refoulement norm of international refugee law prevented their deportation. In a widely noted decision of 16 December 2004, the House of Lords declared Section 23 of the 2001 Anti-terrorism, Crime and Security Act in violation of Articles 5 and 14 of the European Convention for the Protection of Human Rights, which prohibit compromising the right to liberty and discrimination on the grounds of national origins, respectively. Importantly, the Law Lords bemoaned that Section 23 selectively targeted aliens, while leaving outside its ambit suspected terrorists who are citizens and who might pose an equal security threat. This was not deemed "proportionate" to the intended purpose of providing domestic protection from the terrorist threat, as about half of all terrorism suspects at that time were believed to be British nationals.[21] And, in exempting suspected citizen terrorists from its reach, Section 23 unduly discriminated against suspected non-citizen terrorists for no other reason than their nationality. Citing US Supreme Court Justice Jackson's famous plea that the law should be "equal in operation," Lord Bingham affirmed that the habeas corpus protection that in Section 23 was selectively lifted for non-citizens did not allow such rationing: "Every person within the jurisdiction enjoys the equal protection of our laws. There is no distinction between British nationals and others. He who is subject to English law is entitled to its protection."[22]

However, even after the incorporation into domestic law of the European Convention for the Protection of Human Rights, British courts still do not have the powers to strike down an act of parliament. So the House of Lords' condemnation of the British government's singling out of aliens in its anti-terrorism measures was merely an opinion, without direct effect. Home Secretary

Charles Clarke promptly refused to bow to the Law Lords' judgment, vowing that the detainees who had taken the government to court would remain in prison.[23] In fact, the government responded to the discrimination charge simply by extending the emergency provisions of the anti-terrorism laws from aliens to citizens, in terms of the Prevention of Terrorism Act of 11 March 2005. As one observer sarcastically characterized this outcome, "it puts an end to a double judicial system: rule of law for citizens and pure violence for foreigners. The suppression of habeas corpus is extended to the whole population" (Paye 2005: 4).[24]

Even if counteracted by vigilant courts, as in different measures it was in the United States and Britain alike, the attack on the civil liberty rights of aliens after 2001 still proves their inherent vulnerability. Almost thirty years ago, long before postnational membership was on the map, the legal scholar John Hart Ely identified the root cause of aliens' vulnerability in their exclusion from the political process, so that their representation was at best "virtual" or entrusted to independent judiciaries (quoted in Cole 2002: 981, n. 114). This analysis remains as true as ever, especially as international terror has moved the world a step back to the situation described by Hannah Arendt more than half a century ago, when aliens indeed were "rightless, the scum of the earth" ([1951] 1979: 267).

Minority Rights: Multiculturalism versus Antidiscrimination

Through bearing or adhering to a distinct ethnicity, race, or religion, immigrants often constitute a minority group in the society into which they move. A classic text defined a minority group as "a group of people who, because of their physical or cultural characteristics, are singled out from the others in the society in which they live for different and unequal treatment, and who therefore regard themselves as objects of collective discrimination" (Wirth 1945: 347). Louis Wirth's definition aptly captures the role of discrimination and inequality in the making of a minority. In this view, a minority only arises out of the discriminations inflicted on it by the majority. One may then conceive of minority rights as protections from race- or culture-focused discrimination.

By the same token, Wirth (1945) may overstate the other-defined, discriminatory origins of minority groups. For instance, Mary Waters found that the ethnic identifications of today's European-origin Americans are entirely self-made and optional, and she distinguishes their "symbolic ethnicity" sharply from the "real and often hurtful" consequences of "being Asian or Hispanic or black" (Waters 1990: 156). Of course, one may well refrain from calling self-defined Italian- or Polish-Americans a "minority group" at all.[25] But it would be unhelpful to make the modicum of self-definition that is required for being a minority even in Wirth's (1945: 347) account solely a function of external discrimination. Witness the recent relabeling of American blacks as "African-Americans," which shows the need for positive self-definition even among a group that would not exist except for the gross discrimination that is slavery. There is likely to be a continuum between positive self- and negative other-definition in the making of any minority, and it is implausible to eradicate from it a positive sense of self that is not reducible to discrimination but that articulates a shared ethnicity, language, religion, or history.

The distinction between positive self- and negative other-definition in the making of a minority is not just academic. It points to the fundamental ambiguity of how the state should respond or relate to a minority: should it be protected or should it be abolished in the name of equality? The first response may be called "multiculturalism," the second response "antidiscrimination." Let me comment on each in turn, with special attention to the indirect ways in which even notionally group-destroying antidiscrimination cannot but be factually group-making.

Multiculturalism

In the post-World War II era, Western states abstained from forcing immigrants to abandon their culture of origin as a price of entry. The mantra was "integration" not "assimilation," which left the cultural integrity of immigrants intact. The question was only whether such integration could be achieved within the established rules of private and public, according to which immigrants were free to follow their cultural demons in private, on their own effort, while the state stayed neutral on such matters; or whether a further, proactive stance on part of the state was required, which would reshuffle the existing private–public distinction. "Multiculturalism" proper is the second response, according to which the state should not stay aloof but publicly "recognize" the minority group. To a certain degree, even international law moved in this direction. One of the first codifications of minority rights, the 1966 International Covenant on Civil and Political Rights, only asked states *not* to do certain things, namely that minorities "shall not be denied the right" to their culture, religion, or language.[26] The 1992 Declaration on the Rights of Persons Belonging to National or Ethnic, Religious and Linguistic Minorities contains the stronger and more proactive language that states shall "protect" and "promote" these minorities.[27] This may come down to little change in reality (see the critique by Kymlicka 2007), but the distinctly more multicultural diction in 1992 is unmistakable.

What marks multiculturalism as a political stance has been influentially formulated by Charles Taylor (1992). Multiculturalism is depicted as an expression of the "modern preoccupation with identity and recognition," which derives from modernity's collapse of social hierarchies and a new ideal of authenticity (1992: 26f.). The novelty is not the *quest* for identity and recognition, which is grounded in the "dialogical" nature of human life, but that it can *fail*, because identity is no longer immutably fixed by one's social position (ibid.: 35). Under modern conditions, recognition engenders two different kinds of politics, a "politics of universalism" that strives for the equal dignity of *all* individuals, and a "politics of difference," which asks that the unique identity of *this* individual or group be recognized. Both politics are internally connected, as "the universal demand powers an acknowledgment of specificity" (ibid.: 39). However, and this is the rub, the politics of difference operates in terms of a polemic against the politics of universalism, which is accused of being a "particularism masquerading as the universal" and of "imposing a false homogeneity" (ibid.: 44). While such a stance can equally be found in radical feminism, Taylor traces it to Frantz Fanon's indigenous critique of colonialism. Much like Fanon's *The Wretched of the Earth*, multiculturalism attacks "the imposition of some cultures on others, and . . . the assumed superiority that powers this imposition" (ibid.: 63). Positively phrased, multiculturalism, at least in the Taylorian variant, asks for the "presumption" of "equal worth" of the cultures denigrated by the West (ibid.: 68).

Of course, this is only a variant of multiculturalism, and one in which the latter is a radical alternative to and critique of liberalism.[28] In addition, there is a liberal variant, in which multicultural minority rights complement rather than substitute liberal rights and citizenship (Kymlicka 1995; see my discussion of both in Joppke 2001a). But constitutive of all variants is that minority identities have to be publicly recognized in a kind of special deal apart from the general rule of law, which does not know group distinctions. Even in Kymlicka's liberal variant, "benign neglect," the classical liberal state stance on religion, does not work with respect to culture. Try as it might, the liberal state can never be neutral in the choice of its public language, holidays, and symbols, which inevitably privileges the majority group. If equal justice is to prevail, the culture of minority groups needs special protection by the state.

To have one's identity recognized by the state has always been an implausible stance, not only with respect to immigrants. As Chandran Kukathas (2003) retorted to Taylor and Kymlicka alike, "recognition" is not something the liberal state can deliver:

> The liberal state . . . should take no interest in the character or identity of individuals; nor should it be concerned directly to promote human flourishing: it should have no collective projects; it should express no group preferences; and it should promote no particular individuals or individual interests. Its only concern ought to be with upholding the framework of law within which individuals and groups can function peacefully. (Kukathas 2003: 249)

Liberalism, Kukathas sums up, is at heart a "politics of indifference" (ibid.: 250).

What Kukathas formulated as an "ought-to" captures well the factual uneasiness that has always surrounded liberal state responses to multicultural claims. By definition an asymmetrical stance, recognition, in singling out one group, must whet the appetite of other putative groups to be recognized too. Recognition thus not only vitiates the symmetry of the rule of law but is "almost always dangerous" in the real world, as Kukathas (2003: 251) argues with a particular eye on the rougher quarters of Southeast Asia. In fact, groups are often called into existence only by the recognition game itself. And this is a game that helps transform mundane interests, which are open to compromise, into ethereal identities, which are not.

While an unlikely stance to take in the liberal state at large, recognition becomes especially implausible if applied to immigrants. Kymlicka (1995) actually admits this in his pragmatic concession that immigrants, in voluntarily leaving their homeland, have "waived" the right to have their culture and identity resurrected abroad. The "polyethnic" rights that are granted to immigrants, such as exemptions from general laws that unduly restrict their cultural or religious ways or public funding for their cultural practices, are intended to promote "integration into the larger society, not self-government" (Kymlicka 1995: 31). However, in this healthily minimalist account it is not clear why such measures are couched in the language of rights; perhaps they are better conceived of as pragmatic concessions by means of which states seek to further the integration of immigrants.

The "rights" worth the name with respect to accommodating immigrants as cultural minorities are not special "polyethnic" rights, granted only to them and not to others. Instead, the most effective protections are the general rights of free expression and association, of privacy and family life, and of religious belief and practice that the liberal state grants to all individuals, be they immigrants or natives, residents or citizens.[29] Much of the accommodation of Muslims in liberal societies has proceeded along this individual rights track. This has regularly brought courts, as the

Rights

defenders of individual rights, into conflict with rights-constricting public authorities, with the courts and their minority clients getting the upper hand most of the time. Especially in continental Europe, with entrenched systems of judicial review and written constitutions, courts have routinely given in to Muslim parents' wishes to exempt their daughters from parts of the school curriculum that are considered in violation of their religious beliefs; allowed exemptions from animal protection laws that stand in the way of a religious diet; or forced public and private employers to accommodate the ritual needs of their Muslim employees (see Joppke 2009b: 120–5).

A particular case in point is the accommodation of the Muslim veil. If it is allowed, even on the part of state agents who are expected to be neutral in their appearance, then it is because the right of free religious expression is deemed superior to the rights of other involved parties or public order concerns. By the same token, if the veil is prohibited, as it has been for public school students in the French anti-veiling law of 2004 and for public school teachers in several regional anti-veiling laws in Germany in 2004 and 2005, this is because third-party rights or public order considerations have won the upper hand (see Joppke 2009a). Overall, the highly publicized headscarf restrictions, all passed in the turmoil after 2001 and the global proliferation of Islamic terror, obscure the silent accommodation of most Muslim claims (including the claim to wear the veil) through the legal systems of Western states. The individual rights provisions of the liberal state have done much of the work claimed by the multiculturalists, only more quietly and effectively.

Antidiscrimination

Whereas the thrust of multiculturalism is particularistic, seeking to perpetuate minority groups, the opposite thrust of antidiscrimination is universalistic, seeking to render minority groups invisible and in this sense to destroy them. The great ancestor of all contemporary antidiscrimination policies is the American civil rights laws, passed in the early to mid-1960s to end the racial segregation of American blacks. Their target is not so much "expressive" racism, such as defamation or assault, as "access" racism,[30] which denies to minorities equal participation in key societal sectors like employment, education, and housing. If multiculturalism is situated in the lofty realm of culture and identity, antidiscrimination moves us into the mundane world of interest conflict over scarce resources.

It is safe to say that, in the wake of post-World War II immigration, antidiscrimination laws and policies have massively increased throughout the Western world. Of particular significance is the development in the United States, where a policy that had originally been conceived as a color-blind measure to combat discrimination against "any individual," on the basis of his or her "race, color, religion, sex, or national origin,"[31] quickly turned into color-conscious "affirmative action," in which specific, historically disadvantaged groups are selected for preferential access to important societal resources, most notably employment, business contracts, and higher education. US antidiscrimination policy was thus transformed from a notionally group-destroying measure into one that was factually group-making, no longer content with securing "equal opportunity" but providing "equal results" by means of quota and strict time-tables.[32]

While this transformation went along with an obvious change of philosophy, it was still more the product of accident than of design. As the historian Hugh Davis Graham (1990) showed, the change from color-blindness to color-consciousness stemmed from the difficulties that federal agencies faced in effectively implementing the civil rights laws: "The problems and politics of implementation produced a shift of administrative and judicial enforcement from a goal of equal treatment to one of equal results" (1990: 456).[33] It was much easier to identify discrimination by its (presumed) result than by its motivation. The watershed in this shift was the Supreme Court ruling *Griggs v. Duke Power Company* in 1971, which invalidated hiring practices and intra-company promotion schemes that were "fair in form, but discriminatory in operation."[34] Thus the notion of indirect discrimination was born. It did not require the identification of a discriminatory intention on the part of the employer; instead the statistical underrepresentation of the discriminated group in the workforce was sufficient. Of course, such statistical discrimination, which happens whenever there is a "disproportionate" negative impact of a facially neutral measure on a minority group, is still attributed to originally overt discrimination. As the Supreme Court drew the linkage in *Griggs*, employment practices with such an impact "operate to 'freeze' the status quo of prior discriminatory employment practices."[35] This is a rather daring leap of faith because eyes are closed to numerous other factors that might cause the statistical underrepresentation of a minority group.

But the crucial matter in *Griggs*'s invention, not of the name but of the concept of indirect discrimination,[36] is "abolishing the analytical distinction between antidiscrimination and affirmative action" (Sabbagh 2007: 123). Remember that antidiscrimination, in being color-blind, cuts both ways, prohibiting discrimination against whites *also*. By contrast, affirmative action necessarily discriminates against whites – so-called reverse discrimination. Prohibiting indirect discrimination erases the distinction between antidiscrimination and affirmative action, in that antidiscrimination now "requires *selection* of a limited number of reference groups within which all individuals will enjoy a specific kind of protection not available to members of other conceivable groups" (ibid.). There can be no statistical underrepresentation without a preformed sense of the "groups" that are subject to this. And these groups are precisely those that once were targeted for overt, intentional discrimination. In a nutshell, there cannot be a fight against indirect discrimination that is not group-making or at least group-reinforcing.

The impetus of the transformation from antidiscrimination into affirmative action, much as of the original civil rights laws, was to help out the original victims and, even today, most disadvantaged members of American society, the descendants of African-American slaves. However, affirmative action was immediately extended to other historically disadvantaged groups – American Indians, Hispanics, and Asians. The logic of this extension has never quite been revealed. In John Skrentny's (2002) stellar account of the American "minority rights revolution," it is not the pressure of social movements but the "anticipatory politics" by enlightened state administrators that is responsible for this extension. They included groups "analogous to blacks," following a mostly implicit "logic of appropriateness" not unlike that of "bugs are not food" (2002: 9–12). All non-black groups "were basically free rides, requiring virtually no lobbying or protest at all" (ibid.: 141). And if white ethnics, such as the working-class descendants of Polish or Italian immigrants who had heavily lobbied for inclusion in affirmative action between 1965 and 1975, were shown the door, then it was because "they simply had not suffered enough" (ibid.: 264).

Whatever the logic of carving out, and delimiting, the American affirmative action universe, immigrants were in it from the start (see Graham 2002). This is because constitutional and statutory rights protections, including those provided by the 1964 Civil Rights Act and its creative reinterpretation by the civil rights bureaucracy, had always targeted "persons," not just "citizens." This meant that 70 percent of the 20 million immigrants entering America between 1965 and 1995 immediately profited from affirmative action (Sabbagh 2007: 39). This is because, after the de-racialization of US immigration law in 1965, most newcomers came from Latin America and Asia, filling the "Hispanic" and "Asian" racial categories that are entitled to affirmative action – even though the individuals occupying these categories could not look back to a history of injustice at the hands of white America, which long was the main rationale of affirmative action.

However, the justification of affirmative action underwent a momentous shift in the *Bakke* decision of the US Supreme Court in 1978.[37] The famous swing opinion by Justice Powell, which tilted an evenly divided Supreme Court to support a qualified version of affirmative action, radically departed from the previous paradigm of corrective justice for minorities. As Powell pointed out, the "white 'majority' itself is composed of various minority groups, most of which can lay claim to a history of prior discrimination."[38] If anything, the United States was a "Nation of minorities," each having had "to struggle – and to some extent [struggling] still – to overcome the prejudices not of a monolithic majority, but of a 'majority' composed of various minority groups."[39] If everyone was a member of a minority, they could not all receive preferential treatment. The only way in which "race" could be salvaged as a positive factor in college admissions was as a "plus" that helped the university to build a "diverse student body" conducive to its educational mission of fostering a "robust exchange of ideas."[40] Thus was born the notion of diversity, which has since become the main justification of affirmative action.

The new diversity paradigm had several advantages. As Justice Powell outlined in *Bakke*, it dispensed with "the kind of variable sociological and political analysis" that was required for determining who was "minority" or "majority" at any point in time, and which was beyond the scope of "judicial competence" and better accomplished by Congress.[41] Diversity was, as Daniel Sabbagh (2007: 38) sharply observed, a device for keeping race and antidiscrimination in the legal as opposed to the political arena. But in addition to this strategic advantage there were other, more substantive advantages. Most importantly, only within the diversity paradigm did the inclusion of immigrants in affirmative action constitute no anomaly, which it had to be under the old corrective justice paradigm (ibid.: 43). And diversity legitimized the inherent tendency of affirmative action, fed by the apparatus engendered by it, to be in it for the long haul, as now there was no need to identify the (necessary if impossible) moment when the last trace of past injustice had been eradicated.

Finally, diversity provided the "missing link" between antidiscrimination and multiculturalism (Sabbagh 2007: 163). It had always been more than a coincidence that affirmative action had evolved side by side with multiculturalism, which in the United States is institutionalized above all in "minoritized" public school and college curricula and in a plethora of women's and ethnic studies programs at the country's universities, especially the very best. Through Sabbagh's rather dark lens, American multiculturalism, with its penchant for fostering "self-esteem" through ethno-racial perspectivism, is "rationalization of the failure" that many an affirmative action kid experienced at the elite university into which they came to be admitted (ibid.: 156). This is most certainly exaggerated.[42] However, diversity's foot in both camps is evident in Justice Powell's strange inference from race to a viewpoint, and the ensuing equation of race with culture, which is a staple of multicultural discourse. To the degree that *Bakke* helped boost the multicultural notion of viewpoint diversity, American multiculturalism is indeed "partly a side effect of the juridicialization of political conflicts over the reduction of race-based inequality" (ibid.: 162).

Turning to Europe, antidiscrimination has never had similarly strong grounding in a domestic race problem. There is nothing akin to American apartheid, which might have whipped European states onto the road of result-oriented racial equality. In fact, the command never to morph into affirmative action has from the start accompanied the first European antidiscrimination policy, which is that of Britain (see Teles 1998). While European antidiscrimination policies mostly target immigrants and their offspring, it is still noteworthy that their earliest incarnations all occurred in countries where immigrants, through colonial linkages, either arrived as citizens or could acquire citizenship easily. Only if there is a sense that racial discrimination is located within the "political community", which is conditional on "open" citizenship laws (Gehring 2009: 103), is there a likely push toward antidiscrimination. Accordingly, in Germany, until recently a country with closed citizenship laws that kept immigrants and their offspring out of the political community, a rather belated move toward antidiscrimination, which was due only to external pressure by European Union law, was heavily contested and denounced by an otherwise moderate mind as "legal vandalism" (Ladeur 2002: 1).

While, in European states with a colonial legacy and with historically open citizenship laws, antidiscrimination has domestic roots, antidiscrimination became a European-wide trend only with the EU Race Directive passed in 2000. It imposes the Anglo-Saxon type of civil-law-based fight against "access racism" also on countries that had previously proceeded differently,[43] if at all. The EU Race Directive requires member states to pass legislation that outlaws "direct or indirect discrimination based on racial or ethnic origin" within a narrow time frame.[44] Its scope is sweeping, including employment, education, social protection, health care, and access to vital private goods and services such as housing and insurance. As in the British antidiscrimination law on which the European law is modeled, the burden of proof is on the accused party, which has to rebut "presumed" discrimination, and member states are obliged to create "a body or bodies for the promotion of equal treatment."[45]

The most important feature of the EU-led fight against discrimination is its inclusion of indirect discrimination.[46] This raises the question of whether Europe is now destined to go down the American road of latently group-making antidiscrimination policies. Interestingly, the EU Race Directive is at best permissive about the next logical step in tackling indirect discrimination, dubbed "positive action," which member states are "not prevent[ed]" from but also not mandated to engage in.[47] France, with its long-standing republican aversion to recognize groups that stand in between the citizen and the state, deems itself immune to the virus of group recognition in the principle of indirect discrimination. This is because of a clause inserted at its behest in the Race Directive, which leaves "[t]he appreciation of the facts" about direct or indirect discrimination "a matter for national judicial or other competent bodies, in accordance with rules of national law or practice."[48] In a word, France does acknowledge the existence of indirect discrimination but is not forced to collect the requisite statistical evidence to corroborate this fact (see Joppke 2007b: 262). But if one considers the EU campaign to "promote diversity" (European Commission 2002), which has accompanied the European foray into antidiscrimination, there is no doubt that eventually it cannot but be group-recognizing – this is simply inherent in the notion of diversity that has apparently branched out from North America to Europe.

The so-called Veil Committee (chaired by *femme d'Etat* Simone Veil), charged with advising the current French president, Nicolas Sarkozy, on the wisdom of inserting a "diversity" clause into the French constitution that would allow him to venture "positive discrimination," recently rejected both resoundingly. The committee argued that the official recognition of race and ethnicity was a vestige of countries that had once practiced legal racial segregation. In France, by contrast, it threatened to "weaken national unity" (*affaiblissement du vivre-ensemble*) and to foster group conflict (Veil 2008: 70). However, this defensive stance faces the triple pressure from ethno-racial organizations such as the *Conseil représentative des associations noires* (CRAN), statisticians and demographers who ask for ethnicity- and race-sensitive measurements, and corporations that push for "ethnic marketing" strategies and diversity as a tool to enhance their competitiveness.[49] Above all, the French president himself has vowed to continue with his project of injecting more "diversity" into the government and top-level public functions: "I am not in favor of quotas, which make no sense. But one can also not pretend that [a better representation of minorities in the French elites] will happen by itself, it will not happen by itself."[50] Interestingly, as the United States is increasingly questioning the wisdom of race-focused affirmative action, France, which had long prided itself on avoiding the Anglo-Saxon ways, is now cautiously but steadily moving in this direction.

Decline of multiculturalism and the rise and rise of antidiscrimination

So we are left with the startling fact that multiculturalism is in retreat, while antidiscrimination is on the rise and rise. This discrepancy is especially marked in Europe, where the few countries that had pursued official multiculturalism policies in the past have recently shifted to civic integration policies, but where European Union law in conjunction with domestic pressures have boosted antidiscrimination to an unprecedented degree.[51] The root of the cooling down on multiculturalism is that liberal states are intrinsically geared "to treat people as individuals rather than as members of a class" (Starr 1992: 156), leaving the constitution of social groups to the individuals themselves. This is the gist of universalistic citizenship that had once replaced the particularism of groups under feudalism. At the same time, driven by their commitment to equality, liberal states seek to rectify inequalities and injustice. This makes them favor antidiscrimination. However, the distinction between multiculturalism and antidiscrimination is not as neat as it appears. This is because antidiscrimination tilts liberal states in the direction of group recognition, which philosophically they abhor, forcing them to accept an unavoidable de facto multiculturalism.

Let us explore this paradox further. The fact that discrimination and inequality often "follow cultural boundaries" makes liberal states captive to a "dilemma of recognition" (de Zwart 2005: 142, 137). If they embark on "targeted redistribution policies," examples of which are affirmative action in the US or the positive discrimination that even France is poised to take now, states cannot but engage in "definition, recognition, and even mobilization of the groups concerned," which often accentuates the ethnic or racial distinctions that the policies seek to attenuate or even eradicate (ibid.). As de Zwart argues, states have three possibilities of coping with the dilemma of recognition: they can "accommodate," which is multiculturalism; they can "deny," which is liberal color-blindness; or they can "replace" ethno-racial group distinctions with artificial categories that avoid the freezing of ethno-racial distinctions, which seems to be the drawback of accommodation. As both multicultural accommodation and liberal denial apparently proved inadequate to redress discrimination and inequality, states are increasingly pushed toward replacement strategies. Examples of this are the refocusing of affirmative action from race to class, which is gaining ground in the US, and the use of geographic and socio-economic proxies to which France has long resorted in her aversion to ethnicity and race (and that it now finds wanting), and which the Netherlands recently adopted in lieu of its old ethnic minorities' policy.

However, de Zwart's (2005) global review of replacement strategies finds them incapable of resolving the dilemma of recognition. In the Netherlands, for instance, the "general policy" that replaced the group-focused "categorical policy" in the 1990s foundered on the rock of having to identify target populations for effective policy intervention. As the mayor of Amsterdam explained why subsidies for ethnic and sub-ethnic "self-organizations" persisted despite the nominal turn away from them: "we needed to contact society and in the turn we as government . . . created the self-organizations ourselves, as it were" – and the groups that emerged were exactly those that stood to be replaced (quoted ibid.: 155).

By the same token, the modicum of group recognition that persists in antidiscrimination is pragmatic, not philosophical; it is by-default recognition in the pursuit of effective remedies to discrimination. Such pragmatic recognition is a far cry from the principled "politics of recognition" decreed by Charles Taylor. Recognition proper does have its field of application, but it is much more narrowly drawn than propagated by the multiculturalists. In fact, it closely overlaps with the politics of reparations, by means of which states have redressed historical injustice to particular groups (Torpey 2005). The mistake was to extend this paradigm to immigrants. The fact of mobility has shown immigrants to be actors, not victims. And, as we saw, they are actors with rights, which obliterate the program of multiculturalism.

4

Identity[1]

The liberalization of access to citizenship and the strengthening of the rights of immigrants and ethnic minorities, however qualified and punctured by new restrictions both may be, feed the picture of unbounded, centrifugal societies in which everyone and everything flees the center. Hence the question: Does the center hold or, even more fundamentally, What is the center? This leads us into the third and final dimension of citizenship to be investigated in this book: citizenship as identity.

Classically, the unity and integration of modern societies was provided by loading citizenship with the semantics of nation and nationalism. Citizenship in this respect was not just state membership but "nation membership," in which "[t]he political community should be simultaneously a cultural community, a community of language, mores, or belief" (Brubaker 1989a: 4). However, the increasing universalism of citizenship, which we could observe on its status and rights dimensions, cannot but affect the identity of citizenship, diluting its national distinctness. As we shall see in the following, states have responded to the centrifugal tendencies of immigrant societies with attempts to upgrade the meaning of citizenship through ceremonies and tightened civics and language requirements. Yet in doing so states had to learn that they could not but provide universalistic (and thus paradoxical) answers to the question of identity.

The reason for this is simple: liberal states ought to be (and increasingly are) neutral with respect to what lives their citizens should live. Before immigrant diversity would dramatize this fact at the exterior boundaries of the citizenry, it was at first experienced in the interior sphere of private morality. Take the case of 1950s Britain, where the 1957 Wolfenden Committee Report famously suggested abolishing the crime of homosexuality (which had been on the books since 1885, and one of whose illustrious victims had been Oscar Wilde): "It is not, in our view, the function of the law to intervene in the private lives of citizens" (quoted in Sacks 2007: 38f.). This provoked a passionate debate about what kind of society Britain was or, rather, was to become. Defending what Britain was at the time, Lord Devlin objected to decriminalizing homosexuality, because Britain was not just a sack of individuals but a society: "Society means a community of ideas; without shared ideas on politics, morals, and ethics no society can exist." And, anticipating what Britain was to become, the legal scholar H. L. A. Hart defended the Wolfenden Committee, appositely by restating J. S. Mill's harm principle: "[T]he only purpose for which power can be rightfully exercised over any member of a civilized community against his will, is to prevent harm to others. *His own good, either physical or moral, is not a sufficient warrant*" (Mill quoted ibid.: 39; emphasis added). The very meaning of liberty is that the individual, and not the state, decides about his or her "physical or moral good." While Mill's advice remained unheeded in Victorian England, his 1960s successors prevailed. In 1961, suicide was legalized; in 1967, homosexuality became legal, as did abortion. This was the "end of England as a Christian country" (ibid.: 40). More than that, it was the end of a society kept together by "shared ideas on politics, morals, and ethics," to reiterate Lord Devlin. And it was the beginning of the "procedural state," marked by "principled neutrality on matters of identity and morality" (ibid.: 19).

It is important to see that this development occurred at first apart from immigration, even though immigration would, of course, mightily reinforce it. In fact, the procedural state that is reluctant to force a culture and an identity on people, and which prefers integration over assimilation, has been the backdrop to the hands-off, de facto multiculturalism that has framed the reception

Identity

of immigrants in Western societies since the 1960s (see Joppke 1999: part II). Only most recently, when especially in Europe the failure to integrate the second and third immigrant generations became obvious, was this approach (more often not approach, but absence of a coherent policy) found wanting. This was the moment of the citizenship and integration campaigns to be examined in this chapter.

In the first part, I address what kind of unity and integration, if any, a liberal society can have. In the second and main part, I scrutinize the citizenship and integration campaigns conducted by various Western states today, with a focus on their propensity to become caught in the paradox of universalism. In the third part, I argue that liberalism, which is the content of the citizenship identities promoted by most Western states today, may still be exclusive, like every identity – as Muslims in Europe can attest to. I close by hinting at the implications of this analysis for nationhood and citizenship.

Unity in the Liberal State

Perhaps we should drop the vocabulary of unity and integration. Certainly, the notion of integration figures centrally in the annals of academic sociology, especially the line of Emile Durkheim. Even long before this, Thomas Hobbes had started modern political philosophy by asking why there is order and not chaos. But to the degree that there *is* integration, it is safe to say that no one knows why, and there is no agreement on any one answer. The grand sociology of Talcott Parsons, who had argued, much influenced by Durkheim, that integration occurs through shared cultural values, is discredited. Michael Mann (1970) pointed out that values such as "equality" and "achievement" are too general to legitimate any concrete social structure; that in embodying absolute standards they bear no compromise and thus are likely to breed conflict rather than cohesion ("equality" clashing with "achievement," etc.); and that, if there is cohesion, it is perhaps more because of insulation from than commitment to core values. The working class in particular displays, at best, "pragmatic acceptance" of core values, on account of the lack of a "realistic alternative," which is a far cry from their "normative acceptance," as decreed by Parsons (Mann 1970: 425).

It is useful to reiterate these sociological trivia at a time when "integration" has become the unquestioned mantra toward immigrants. From a liberal perspective, integration talk is suspicious because it rests on the premise of unity that cannot but exclude. As Chandran Kukathas (2003: 21) observed, a notion such as "body politic," since Hobbes a common metaphor for unity, overlooks the fact that "bodies are not generic but sexed." This leaves only two options for women: de-feminizing incorporation or exclusion. Obviously, "it is not a metaphor which can accommodate deviance, or diversity, or difference – for it cannot accommodate the most evident form that difference takes: sex" (ibid.).

But what alternative do we have? Kukathas (2003) opts for a view of political society as an "archipelago" of independent but mutually tolerant jurisdictions, not unlike states that coexist in international society. This is a model of domestic as international society, or rather one that does not acknowledge the distinction between the two. This does take seriously that liberalism is at heart "an internationalist creed" for an "open society" that bears no boundaries and caging of people (2003: 39). But it conflicts too radically with the way the world is politically organized, as a world of sovereign nation-states, to be a realistic alternative. Because states cannot be wished away, we have to buy into state elites' unity and integration talk.

At a theoretical level, the problem of unity and integration in a liberal society is crisply captured in John Rawls's idea of political liberalism. If one stipulates that in a liberal society individuals are free to choose the ends of their actions, the state has to remain neutral about competing conceptions of the good life ("comprehensive doctrines," in Rawls's terminology) that inform such choices. Social unity, then, cannot derive from a consensus on some conception of the good; in any society there will be a multiplicity of conflicting and incommensurable conceptions of the good. Instead, social unity and stability can derive only from an "overlapping consensus" on principles of justice, the first and foremost of which is that "each person has an equal right to a fully adequate scheme of equal basic rights and liberties" (Rawls 1985: 227). Such an "overlapping consensus," Rawls claims, can in turn be derived from the substantive moral or religious doctrines to which people may adhere, as long as these doctrines (or the people that hold them)[2] are "reasonable."

There is an evolution in Rawls's thinking about the nature of liberalism that undergirds this theory, ethical and grounded in a metaphysical conception of the person (as "autonomous" or "individualistic") (Rawls 1971), or political and independent of any such conception of the person (Rawls 1993). And communitarian critics have pointed to the difficulties of the political version of liberalism, which forces individuals to abstract from their moral and religious views for the purposes of public life, in which they are supposed to embrace the ethereal "ideal of public reason" (see Sandel 1994). But one may respond to this that some form of "public reason" or "transcendence" (Schnapper 2006) is precisely the abstraction upon which modern citizenship, as the space where "aliens can become associates" (Preuss 1995: 275), is based – political as against ethical liberalism may further accentuate but does not create this abstraction.

Most importantly, the neutrality mandate of the state applies to both versions of liberalism, ethical and political. Rawls's enduring suggestion is that nation and nationalism cannot integrate a liberal society: "[T]he hope of political community must indeed be abandoned, if by such a community we mean a political society united in affirming a general and comprehensive doctrine. This possibility is excluded by the fact of pluralism together with the rejection of the oppressive use of state power to overcome it" (Rawls 1987: 10). This is another way of saying that social unity in a liberal society cannot derive from the "good" of nation and nationalism, but only from a consensus on the "rights" that accrue to each individual. This is a vision of the world in which morality trumps politics, but – *pace* Kukathas – it may be what liberalism boils down to if transported into the world of politics.

Jürgen Habermas (1987) has formulated the same idea in terms of "constitutional patriotism."[3] It shares the Rawlsian divorce between culture and politics, arguing that the social bond in a liberal-democratic state should be "juridicial, moral and political, rather than cultural, geographical and historical" (quoted in Laborde 2002: 593). "Constitutional patriotism" holds that the ultimate motives for attachment to a political community are universalistic and not particularistic: in the last instance, one sticks to it because its values, goals, and outlook are rationally justifiable, not because they are contingently what they are. By the same token, perhaps taking more of a republican than a strictly liberal stance (so argues Kopper 2008: 106–16), Habermas is more optimistic than Rawls that this universalism can effortlessly blend with other, more particularistic motivations, and he is less exacting than Rawls in shutting the latter out of the realm of "public reason." In fact, "constitutional patriotism" was first offered, not for everyone, but for Germans after the Holocaust. The usual riposte against "abstract" and "bloodless" constitutional patriotism forgets that it was born in a specific historical context, the German Historians' Struggle of the 1980s, in which Habermas defended the historical singularity of the Holocaust as the revolving axis of German postwar identity. In this particular, the German context, any other stance, in which commitment to the here and now trumps the strictures of reasoning, would exculpate the loyalty to the racist *Volksgemeinschaft*. Habermas thus could claim that "constitutional patriotism [must be] situated in the historical context of a nation of citizens in a way that [it] link[s] up with those citizens' motives and attitudes" (quoted in Lacroix 2002: 949f.). One could formulate it as a paradox: the German particularism is to be condemned to universalism because of the latter's (or, rather, the Jewish people's) brutal annihilation by the Nazi regime.

Whatever you call it, "overlapping consensus in a political conception of justice" (Rawls 1987: 9) or "constitutional patriotism" (Habermas), the idea is that, in a liberal society, the ties that bind can only be thin and procedural, not thick and substantive. Otherwise individuals could not be free. A communitarian critic of the "unencumbered self" stipulated by the procedural liberalism of Rawls clearly articulated the necessary link between state neutrality and individual freedom: "It is precisely because we are free and independent selves, capable of choosing our own ends, that we need a framework of rights that is neutral among ends" (Sandel 1994: 1769).

However, this is frustrating advice for contemporary states attempting to foster integration and unity in diverse societies. The shortcoming of procedural liberalism has been neatly identified by a variety of "civic nationalists," who point to its incapacity to motivate a preference for "this" over "that" collectivity.[4] For instance, Will Kymlicka, advocate of the most concise and influential theory of minority rights, admits that "social unity" in a multi-ethnic state is a "valid concern" (1995: 173). But, to achieve it, "shared political values" à la Rawls or Habermas are not enough. Following Wayne Norman's (1995) devastating critique of the Canadian "ideology of shared values," Kymlicka points to the arresting example of Quebec. In the very moment that political values of the liberal-democratic kind have converged across Canada, the province of Quebec, self-defined by the "French Fact," came to insist ever more stridently on its independence, close to the point of seceding from Anglophone Canada. Kymlicka thus concludes that social unity must consist of more than "shared political values"; it requires a "shared identity," a "communality of history, language, and maybe religion" – that is, "the things exactly not shared in a multination state" (1995: 188f.).

Identity, one could say, is what does not happen twice in the world. S. N. Eisenstadt and Bernhard Giesen (1995: 75) depicted it as "the center, the present, the subject," which form the excluded third in the dichotomies of "left and right," "past and present," "God and the world," by means of which human beings structure their worlds. From this point of view, the notion of collective identity has to be categorically distinguished from that of rule of law (and one must beware of fusing both, as do "political liberalism" or "constitutional patriotism"), identity setting the boundary within which the law can be effective.[5]

States, like persons, are locked into singularity because they do not happen twice in the world.[6] The question is how far "identity" hinges on singularity. An extreme case for equating identity with singularity has been made by Alasdair MacIntyre (1995). He defined "patriotism" (the function of identity in which states are most interested) as "a kind of loyalty to a particular nation which only those possessing that particular nationality can exhibit" (1995: 210). Such patriotism is not virtue but vice from the point of view of (liberal) morality that requires impersonality. Even a Germany that calls for allegiance to its *Kultur* or a France that prides itself on its *civilisation* is not engaging in (or seeking to instill) "patriotism," because an "ideal and not the nation" is the primary object of allegiance, and because anyone subscribing to these ideals can be enlisted in the respective cause. For MacIntyre there is a contradiction in terms between the "morality of liberal impersonality" and the "morality of patriotism," and as a result liberal democracies require "systematic incoherence in the form of public allegiance to mutually inconsistent sets of principles" (ibid.: 228). Whatever the "conceptual confusion" in the foundation of the liberal democratic polity, liberal morality will always tend toward "the dissolution of social bonds," while patriotism is required for the polity "to continue functioning effectively" (ibid.). As MacIntyre put it darkly, "the political survival of any polity in which liberal morality had secured large-scale allegiance would depend upon there still being enough young men and women who rejected that liberal morality" (ibid.: 226). One sees the enormous provocation inherent in the concept of "constitutional patriotism," which tries to overcome the contradiction between patriotism and morality.

However, MacIntyre (1995) perhaps unduly particularizes the identity of a patriotic citizenry. At least, patriotism devoid of any "tension between the transcendental and mundane orders" cannot be found in any of the "axial" world civilizations, Jewish–Christian, Hindu, Buddhist, or Islamic (Eisenstadt 1999: 3). All modern nationalisms involve a secularized element of axial-age universalism, in which an abstract ideal is held against a deficient reality along with the mandate to rework reality in light of the ideal: "[P]atriotic themes were promulgated in universalistic terms and the respective nations presented as bearers of universalistic values" (ibid.: 43). In this respect there is a direct continuity between religious axial-age transcendentalism, its secularization in modern nationalism, and – one should add – the contemporary possibility of integrating immigrants in a postnational society.[7]

Georg Simmel's ([1908] 1971) classic discussion of identity makes a similar point: identity always combines difference *and* sameness. Simmel locates identity first at the individual level, in terms of an "individuality" that results from social differentiation.[8] As people become more specialized, they come to differentiate themselves from one another. At the same time, they are charged with multiple roles and affiliations, the "sensation of a personal ego" (1971: 290) being a sense of sameness underneath these multiple involvements. In sum, difference and sameness make identity, but only in the context of the "large circles" of a complex society (without which the individual would remain an appendix of social structure). Identity thus is a modern phenomenon, comprising an element of "difference" (celebrated by nineteenth-century romanticism and nationalism) *and* of "autonomy" (the subject of eighteenth-century Enlightenment universalism) (ibid.: 271f.). Simmel's message is that to deprive identity of its universalistic element (autonomy and sameness) distorts its modern meaning.[9]

But what about group-level identity? In a next step, Simmel argues that "individuality" (now obviously reduced to a romantic sense of difference) may be situated at the level of either the person or the group – but apparently not at both at the same time. At one extreme, highly distinct groups tend to go along with undifferentiated, serial individuals. Take the example of Quakers, where individuality is invested at the level of the group, not the individual. As individuals, Quakers are subordinate to the group, and they are indistinguishable from one another with respect to education, marriage choices, or occupation. As group members, however, Quakers are easily distinguishable from non-group members, and in this sense they carry the individuality of the group. In the large circles of modern society it is the other way around: highly individuated individuals leave no space for individuated groups. Simmel articulates the zero-sum relationship between individual and group identity in terms of a "phenomenological formula":

"[T]he elements of a distinctive circle are undifferentiated, and the elements of a circle that is not distinctive are differentiated" (Simmel 1971: 257). This obviously glosses over the intricate ways in which the making of individual and group identities is interdependent rather than zero-sum.[10] But the plausibility of his scheme is difficult to refute: a complex society where a high degree of difference is invested at the level of individuals and subgroups will have difficulty in sporting a distinct sense of collective self, simply because a common denominator cannot be found. Or, if one can be found, it is bound to be so abstract as to be indistinguishable from that of any other society.

Will Kymlicka's (1995: 188f.) argument that social unity requires not just political values but identity obviously reduces identity to pure particularism, not unlike MacIntyre's extreme account of patriotism. This creates instructive problems. Consider Jonathan Sacks, who argues much like Kymlicka: "[T]he trouble with values as a source of identity is that they are not the source of an identity. Values are universal; identities are particular. They are about this place, this land, this language, this landscape, this history" (Sacks 2007: 95). And, beyond Kymlicka, Sacks provides a compelling reason why identity is particular: identities are narrative; they are the story by means of which individuals and groups retroactively make sense of themselves (on the importance of narrative in the making of collective identity, see also Smith 2003). It is the narrative structure of identities that locks them into particularism, because a narrative cannot but be a particular narrative. However, having plausibly cleared the path "from values to stories," Sacks's fictitious narrative of a robust but inclusive British identity in an age of migration lapses into inconsistency: "What stayed the same, though, were the *values*: the freedom, the independence, the tolerance, the respect for difference. Those . . . were non-negotiable. They were what gave the place its core *identity* and without them the project wouldn't work, wouldn't even be worth doing" (Sacks 2007: 170; emphasis added). Indeed, not any narrative would do for Britain (as presumably for any Western state), but only one whose lodestar is universalism, in terms of the securing of liberal democracy against its many challenges and challengers.

Identity

In offering a "religious defense of liberal democracy," Jonathan Sacks (2007: ch. 19) at the same time displays a sane sense of the limits of state intervention on the treacherous ground of identity. Unlike the Greek polis, which conceived of itself as the embodiment of virtue and the good life, the liberal-democratic state is marked by "modesty": "It is a system in which politics makes no claim to embody the true, the beautiful and the good. Political involvement promises neither salvation nor redemption. It claims merely to keep the peace between contending parties" (ibid.: 221). In a nutshell, identity cannot be legislated.[11] All that the liberal state can produce with its own means is the procedural "hotel" that Sacks (like many a liberal nationalist) finds wanting; it cannot build the "home" that makes people feel more than transient. Sacks's "covenantal" remaking of Britain, though bearing some formal resemblance to the current Labour government's attempts to strengthen British citizenship, is a religious project whose site is "civil society," not the state. In this sense, if the envisaged "integration without assimilation" requires a "strong sense of national identity" (ibid.: 234), it is not something that the state can provide. The state campaigns for unity and integration, in Britain and elsewhere, which I shall discuss in the following, have yet to grasp this insight.

At the same time, much as it cannot force an identity on people, the state still "cannot avoid coercing citizens into preserving a national culture of some kind" (Scheffler 2007: 111). Even in Rawls's account there is always a "public political culture" that the state cannot but support.[12] And the content of that culture must be particular because "[a] country is a contingent historical formation" (ibid.: 113).

This invites a reflection on what, if anything, distinguishes identity from culture. Robert Bellah (1998) asked whether there is a "common American culture." His answer is "yes," simply because of the power of institutions – education, state, media, markets – to be "purveyors of common culture" (1998: 615). But that does not mean that "we are all the same" (ibid.: 620). On the contrary, he identifies as one of the core features of common American culture the "absolute centrality of religious freedom" (ibid.: 617).

Religious freedom has since been extended to all kinds of secular "freedom of conscience" issues that drive the contemporary "identity politics" of multiculturalism, such as the right of abortion, gay marriage, etc. Bellah thus suggests that a culture is not an identity, because a culture may comprise many an identity. Samuel Scheffler argues similarly that "'culture' is a descriptive, ethnographic category, not a normative one" (2007: 120). Cultures are conventions. This distinguishes them from "justificatory structures," such as religion, that provide "guidance about how to live" (ibid.: 119). Accordingly, and echoing Bellah, Scheffler finds that cultures don't have a "uniform normative outlook" but contain much "moral, religious, and philosophical diversity" (ibid.: 120). While he does not spell out the implications of this view of culture for the meaning of identity, one could extrapolate that an identity is a "justificatory structure" that, by being grounded in ethical conscience, is not something which the liberal state can force upon people.

If an identity is a "justificatory structure" (Scheffler), the notion of "national identity" becomes awkward, at least to the degree that it falls under the ambit of state policy. This is because such an identity, which cannot but be grounded in individuals' innermost sphere, their conscience, is more than a cultural convention that immigrants may be legitimately expected to respect. In an intriguing account of what binds societies together, Rogers Smith (2003) pointed to the importance of "ethically constitutive stories" of peoplehood. They differ from merely "economic" or "political power" stories of people-making in pertaining to an identity, not just an interest. The basis of ethically constitutive stories is particularistic, unchosen features, which are seen as "intrinsic to who a person is" (2003: 98), and which are loaded with the meaning of "intrinsic propriety and goodness" (ibid.: 102). In this sense, an identity is an ascribed particular that is endowed with ethical significance. Quite similarly, Anthony Appiah (2005: 14) argues: "Identities make ethical claims because . . . we make our lives *as* men and *as* women, *as* gay and *as* straight people, *as* Ghanaians and *as* Americans, *as* blacks and *as* whites." The one oddity in this list is "Ghanaians" and "Americans." It is one thing if identities pertain to groups, of which individuals may or may not consider themselves to be a part – this is what we usually refer to as "identity groups" (Gutmann 2003); it is quite another thing if identities are institutionalized at the level of the state, which has the power to force them on people. This would precisely violate the ethical core of identities, because the dictate of the state replaces the dictate of conscience. The spectacle of groups struggling over institutionalizing "ethically constitutive stories" of peoplehood may be as old as human history (see Smith 2003). But it is precisely the ethical nature of identities that sets limits to their imposition in the liberal state.

Upgrading Citizenship and the Paradox of Universalism

If, indeed, a distinction can be drawn between culture and identity, this has surprising implications for the citizenship tests that are currently mushrooming from Europe to Australia: to ask citizenship applicants to familiarize themselves with the basic facts of the national culture of the citizenship-granting state is unobjectionable from a liberal point of view; what is pernicious is to require – and verify by means of an inquisitive procedure – a certain identity on part of the citizenship applicant, even if – as we shall see – "liberalism" tends to be the content of that identity in many Western countries today.

But before addressing the pitfalls of liberal citizenship identities, let us first review contemporary state campaigns to upgrade citizenship as part of the process of immigrant integration. Of particular interest to us is their difficulty in finding other than universalistic answers to what it is that immigrants are to be integrated into. This faithfully reflects the ethical neutrality of the liberal state. But it is mostly experienced as a deficiency and an incapacity adequately to name the center that is to keep a centrifugal society in check. Overall, the same forces that have brought about a sense that the center does not hold restrict the possibilities to beef it up: public neutrality, non-discrimination, and positively valued diversity.

Identity

Citizenship tests fare centrally in these campaigns. As already touched on in chapter 1, from Europe to Australia there has been a rush to introduce formal citizenship tests as part of the naturalization procedure. Only in the United States and Canada have such tests been on the books for long. With respect to the United States, one must first note the irony that the "covenantal" nation par excellence, celebrated by Sacks (2007) as a model for Britain, has always followed a most perfunctory line on citizenship. Perhaps just because there is so much trust in the assimilatory powers of American society, there is no need to invest too much attention on the formal process of citizenship acquisition. Certainly, "good moral character," "attachment to the principles of the Constitution," the ability to "read, write, and speak . . . in the English language," and "knowledge and understanding of the fundamentals" of US history and government have always been required components of the naturalization exam. But, compared to the more exacting standards now deployed in Europe, the cognitive and loyalty requirements are low indeed. The Oath of Allegiance, in which the naturalizing citizen, rather antiquely, "renounce[s] and abjure[s] all allegiance and fidelity to any foreign prince, potentate, state, or sovereignty," is merely ritual, and dual citizenship is routinely tolerated. The language requirement, in which citizenship applicants are given three chances to read and write a sentence correctly in English, is as low as it could be, and routine exemptions are made for illiterate or elderly people. In the (oral) civics exam, six of ten questions have to be answered correctly, out of a master list of 100 questions that are publicly distributed, along with the correct answers.

A recent reform of the US citizenship test, put in place in October 2008, deliberately abstains from making the test more difficult. In the post-2001 climate, such moderation is astonishing. The main motivation was to move from "rote memorization" of facts to a "focus on concepts, such as the rights and responsibilities of citizenship."[13] In the words of Emilio Gonzales, director of the Citizenship and Immigration Services unit in the Department of Homeland Security: "Our goal is to inspire immigrants to learn about the civic values of this nation so that after they take the oath

Identity

of citizenship they will participate fully in our great democracy."[14] But there is an important substantive change in the meaning of citizenship underlying the new test design, from "power-" to "principle-centered" citizenship (Wonjung Park 2008). In the old citizenship test, which dates back to 1986, citizenship meant "allegiance to a strong federal government headed by a powerful executive in a post-war community" (ibid.: 1003). Its thrust was particularistic: the first seven questions in the old master catalogue infamously were about "our flag," how many stars and stripes were on it, and in what colors.[15] Twenty-six questions focused on the executive branch of the federal government, twenty-two of them on the US presidency alone. There was no reference whatever to local or state government, not to mention "checks and balances" or division of powers. The image of citizenship conveyed in the old citizenship test was, indeed, one of "nationalistic" and "patriotic citizenship" (ibid.: 1010).

By contrast, the new US citizenship test betrays an "effort to define citizenship in terms of neutral, abstract principles" (Wonjung Park 2008: 1014). The very first question in the new master list is about the constitution, not the flag, and great emphasis is placed on individual rights, the rule of law, and divided powers. Only eight questions are about the presidency. As in the old test, there are sections on geography, history, and symbols. And there are questions about the original victims of American society, African-Americans and American Indians. There is no reference at all to immigrants, European no less than non-European. This proves to Wonjung Park (ibid.: 1014f.) that "the effort to define citizenship in terms of neutral, abstract principles . . . is premised on the exclusion of certain historically disfavored groups from the citizenship community." In sum, the truth of universal citizenship is "white citizenship" (ibid.: 1031). However, as black and native Americans are included, this cannot be true. And the knee-jerk racism charge glosses over the *really* astonishing fact that, in one of America's most nationalist moments, and under a president who has done much to fan the flames, a citizenship test was introduced that breathes "universalistic ideology" (ibid.: 1030).

Identity

Much the same could be said about Australia. Promoted by a center-right government, under Prime Minister John Howard, that has moved from multiculturalism to nationalism, the new Australian citizenship test, which came into force in October 2007, shows a typical incapacity to define distinctly "Australian values." In contrast to the United States, there had previously been no formal citizenship test, and Australia acquired one only by "aping British and Dutch models."[16] Indeed, the Australian road to the citizenship test resembles closely the standard European road: a fatigue with multiculturalism, concern about home-grown Islamic terrorism, and the need to reconcile unconvinced natives with a simultaneous opening for new legal immigration. Strikingly, a key event in Australia also was the bombing of the London Underground in July 2005, which triggered a move toward restricting access to Australian citizenship (Cheng 2009).[17] The language of upgraded citizenship is indistinguishable from the European. In his introduction to the government paper that launched the move toward the citizenship test, the immigration minister, Andrew Robb, stressed that "Australian citizenship is a privilege not a right," and that the acquisition of "English skills" and "understand[ing] the Australian way of life and our shared values" were indispensable on the part of immigrants (Australian Government 2006: 5).

Katharine Betts and Bob Birrell (2007) see the Australian government moving from "proceduralism" to "patriotism" on citizenship. Previously, a Labor prime minister, Bob Hawke, had defined an Australian as "someone who chooses to live here, obeys the law and pays taxes" (2007: 47). The new line, under the conservative Liberal Party prime minister John Howard, was that Australians were "a union of people who have something of a family feeling for each other" (ibid.). Symbolizing this shift, in January 2007 Howard renamed the Department of Immigration and Multicultural Affairs as the Department of Immigration and Citizenship.

However, the "Aussie" test was quickly ridiculed for its incapacity to provide any but universalistic answers to the "Australian values" that immigrants were to adopt. A leader of the Sikh

Identity

community declared that he had no problem with universal values, "but when you say Australian values, no one knows what those values are."[18] In fact, the government brochure "Becoming an Australian Citizen," which helps applicants prepare for the citizenship test, has little on offer beyond the universalistic standard brew. While becoming Australian is presented as "joining a distinct national community" (Australian Government 2007: 1), here are the "Australian values" to be adopted: "respect for the equal worth, dignity and freedom of the individual," "freedom of speech," "freedom of religion and secular government," and eight more values of the same kind. For those who had not noticed, this list of values "should not be seen as a quest for conformity or a common set of beliefs" (ibid.: 5). And, when elaborating on each of these values in turn, only the last one, "tolerance, mutual respect and compassion for those in need," is given a slightly Australian edge, in terms of the "egalitarian ethos" of "mateship" that stems from the convict and working-class background of Australia's first European inhabitants (ibid.: 7). With respect to the concession that these values are "shared to some extent by all liberal democracies" (ibid.: 5), one wonders: why only "to some extent"?

In fact, a comparison of Australia's new citizenship test with that of Germany finds its young Australian author baffled that "the tests are similar in content," and that "In both Australia and Germany what are considered to be the most important 'national' values are the liberal values of democracy, freedom of religion, freedom of speech, and the equality of men and women" (Cheng 2009: 62). The road to Germany's citizenship test, which was put in place in September 2008, has still been rocky, and it included digressions into moral inquisition and cultural nationalism that stood to be corrected. The opening shot was Baden-Württemberg's introduction, in September 2005, of a morally inquisitive citizenship test that targeted only Muslim applicants (to be discussed further below).[19] The *Land* government of Hesse followed, in March 2006, with a proposal for a general citizenship test (*Einbürgerungstest*) to be applied to all applicants. Though it scaled back the element of moral inquisition,[20] the Hesse proposal stirred up controversy in requiring a cognitively demanding immersion into the German *Kulturnation* (cultural nation). Among the open-ended questions were to name works by Goethe and Schiller and to identify the "central motif" in a painting by Caspar David Friedrich that shows a landscape on the Baltic island of Rügen.

However, a federally standardized German citizenship test, on which the interior ministers of the *Länder* quickly agreed in May 2006, deliberately abstains from the dual pitfalls of moral inquisition and cultural nationalism.[21] With regard to the rejection of cultural nationalism, the Framework Curriculum for the Citizenship Test (2008)[22] explicitly states that the questions under the rubric "Individual and Society" (*Mensch und Gesellschaft*) should rest on a concept of "culture" that "includes [only] areas that centrally shape the life of participants."[23] In other words, this "culture" was to be understood in an anthropological sense as everyday experience. Though still allowing for questions of the type "What do Germans do at Easter?," such culture contains a reference to "differences and communalities in the context of migration processes."[24] And there are rather trivial questions on how to respond to a wrong tax assessment, what is "not" included in the fringe costs of a rented apartment, and where to register your dog.

Most importantly, the German citizenship test deliberately abstains from addressing "matters of conscience."[25] The section on "History and Responsibility" even comes close to the "national constitutionalism" that the Israeli jurist Liav Orgad, in a sensitive and instructive discussion of Europe's new citizenship tests, considers apposite in the liberal state: "Every state has a constitutional uniqueness reflecting its history, development, traditions and contextual background" (Orgad 2010: 19). Asking the citizenship applicant for knowledge about its particular road to democracy realizes the fact that they seek entry not in *any* but in *this* political community. National constitutionalism is, according to Orgad, next to language, the one particularism that the liberal state may legitimately impose on citizenship applicants. In this sense, asking for the meaning of the photograph showing Chancellor Willy Brandt's famous *Kniefall* (kneeling) at the

Identity

monument commemorating the victims of the Warsaw Ghetto, which is one of the 300 possible federal citizenship test questions, is not like asking what Germans do at Christmas or Easter. Instead, knowledge of this event refers to Germany's unique story of becoming a liberal democracy. In its intrinsic linkage to universalistic liberal-democratic values, this type of question differs from asking for knowledge about German composers, car-makers, or painters – all entries of the heavily criticized and never practiced Hesse proposal, which had endorsed a cultural particularism that is unrelated to the precepts of liberal democracy.

Britain's citizenship test, in place since 2005, goes even further in avoiding history and "national identity." This is both surprising and unsurprising. It is unsurprising because of the historically weak sense and late institutionalization of British citizenship. However, it *does* surprise if one considers that, of all European countries, in none has there been a similarly strong attempt to promote national citizenship as an antidote to immigrant diversity. As Sir Bernard Crick, who chaired the commission that recommended the new citizenship test, describes the diction: "We didn't deal with national identity and that was quite deliberate. I said we're not dealing with nationality, we're dealing with a skill, a knowledge, an attitude for citizenship" (quoted in Kiwan 2008: 62). So, next to emphasizing liberal-democratic values and procedures (which are the same in Britain as they are, say, in Sweden), there is a focus on practical knowledge to master everyday life. For example, one might have to answer the following question: "What do you do if you spill someone's pint in the pub? A. You offer the person another beer. B. You offer to dry his wet shirt with your own. C. You prepare for a fight in the car park" (the correct answer is A).[26]

What is interestingly left out in Britain's dual focus on abstract principles and everyday practice is any reference to the distinctly British road to democracy, or what Orgad (2010) called "national constitutionalism." This is all the more astonishing as the "need for a national story of identity" has been widely recognized (Straw 2007). Jack Straw's "story of British freedom" would go like this: "That means freedom through the narrative of the Magna Carta,

Identity

the civil war, the Bill of Rights, through Adam Smith and the Scottish enlightenment, the fight for votes, for the emancipation of Catholics and non-conformists, of women and of the black community, the Second World War, the fight after that for rights of minority groups, the fight now against unbridled terror" (ibid.: 16). Of this story there is rather little in the British citizenship test.[27]

The case of Britain – of course, a proverbially liberal state – is instructive for the difficulties of liberal states adequately to name the center and instill a sense of it on newcomers. The Crick Commission defined "British" as having "respect [for] the laws, the elected parliamentary and democratic political structures, traditional values of mutual tolerance, respect for equal rights and mutual concern; and that we give our allegiance to the state (as commonly symbolized in the Crown) in return for its protection" (Crick Commission 2003: 11). This way of being British contains only one particularism: "the Crown," which appositely appears only in parenthesis, subsumed under an anonymous, exchangeable "state."

The British state, like all Western states trying to upgrade citizenship for the purpose of more successful immigrant integration, is caught in the paradox of universalism: it perceives the need to make immigrants and ethnic minorities parts of *this* and not of *any* society, but it cannot name and enforce any particulars that distinguish the "here" from "there." This paradox is visible in most of the government pronunciations of what it takes to be British, of which there have been many in the past few years. Take, for instance, the Home Office's recent *Strategy to Increase Race Equality and Community Cohesion* (Home Office 2005b). It stresses, again, that a "greater sense of inclusive British citizenship" does not imply "assimilation of cultural difference" (ibid.: 21). In fact, "no one set of cultural values," including that of the majority, is to be "privileged more than another" (ibid.: 42). And the "essential values of Britishness" not up for negotiation are nationally anonymous. In fact, they are applied political liberalism: "[the] values of respect for others and the rule of law, including tolerance and mutual obligation between citizens" (ibid.). Surely, this goes along with stepped-up efforts to strengthen the ceremonial aspects of citizenship, introducing (in October 2005) a Citizenship Day, in addition to public citizenship ceremonies (which have existed since February 2004). But, as if to apologize for the pomp, it is held to be government's "first priority" to "keep people safe," by means of a more rigorous persecution of racially motivated offenses (ibid.: 49).

The paradox of universalism also permeates the legacy statement on race relations of the departing prime minister Tony Blair, which is appositely a reflection on the meaning of integration, particularly with respect to Muslims (Blair 2006). In a reiteration of political liberalism, it renounces the idea that to be British is a matter of "culture or lifestyle." In fact, the very notion of identity is reserved to the level of the group – "Christians, Jews, Muslims, Hindus, Sikhs" are said to have a "perfect right" to it. Conversely, to be British is presented not as a matter of identity but of "essential values," which – again – are mostly universalistic: "belief in democracy, the rule of law, tolerance, equal treatment for all, respect for this country and its shared heritage." Of course, smuggled into this invitation to "continue celebrating" multicultural Britain, which was not by accident delivered at one of British multiculturalism's intellectual bastions, the Runnymede Trust, were themes less germane to the etiquette of multiculturalism – that there is a "duty" to integrate, that "forced marriage" was no good thing, that "religious law" had no place in the UK, that "unacceptable actions" would lead to expulsion, that a language test would henceforth be a requirement for permanent residency (and not only for naturalization), and that the burka was a barrier to "communicat[ing] directly with people." However, these qualifications to the "right to be different" were in the name not of a British particularism but of the universalism of liberal democracy.

If, as Blair (2006) concluded, "being British" is a combination of "the right to be different" and "the duty to integrate," this also suggests that the integrationist component in this is experienced more as a constraint and a duty than as affective loyalty and an identity. Instead, one's identity continues to rest on one's membership in one of the religious or ethnic groups as the conglomerate of which "Britain" is conceived.

While meant to be a qualification of multiculturalism, Blair's legacy statement really demonstrates the unfettered reign of unreconstructed multiculturalism in Britain. This is visible in the final report of the Commission on Integration and Cohesion (CIC 2007), which was set up by the British government in 2006, one year after the bombings on the London Underground, to find remedies to the domestic sources of Islamic terrorism. "Groups" are presented here, in classic multicultural fashion, as the building blocks of society, with "cohesion" as the envisioned state where "different groups . . . get on well together" (ibid.: 38).

However, there is a noteworthy new source for "cohesion" and "integration" identified by the Commission on Integration and Cohesion: the future. Indeed, if the past, in nationalist as much as in multicultural diction, is what makes people different, and if the present is by definition paltry (otherwise no need for a policy), the only temporal source of unity left is the future. Accordingly, the report, programmatically entitled *Our Shared Future*, stipulates: "the concept of a shared future will be what binds local communities together whatever their histories" (CIC 2007: 45). While the idea is compelling, one is astounded to learn what this "shared future" might consist of. Candidates for "a chance to deepen a sense of our shared futures" (appositely in the plural) are the European Year of Intercultural Dialogue (in 2008) and the Olympic Games in London (2012). These are not just rather thin and spotty "futures," they are also devoid of a genuinely national dimension. In fact, these motley "shared futures" suggest that the future, if anything, is likely to hold more national unbounding in stock.

A more serious vision to forge unity by means of the future is Jonathan Sacks's idea of re-creating society through a "covenant," which is a "conscious act of new beginning" (Sacks 2007: 109). As much as it depicts an open future dependent on choice, the covenant is also a finite act by concrete people. It constitutes a "story" that may ground an "identity," because "Stories create memory, and memory creates identity" (ibid.: 120). The covenant is future and past in one, providing the requisite tension for molding a deficient present in light of unrealized promises. It is a story of old

Identity

to find one's way into the future, an "identity." The problem is that some societies are covenantal, while others aren't. The United States is covenantal, Britain isn't. If America has a national story, retold at each presidential inaugural address, Britain does not have one. If anything, Britain (or rather England) is a "landscape," "the rattle of pin-tables in the Soho pubs, the old maids hiking to Holy Communion through the mists of the autumn morning," in George Orwell's pastel (quoted ibid.: 166). It may be true: "In a multi-ethnic society, you can no longer evoke identity by painting a picture. You have to tell a story" (ibid.). But how do you move from one to the other? Not by means of state policy, Sacks concedes (ibid.: ch. 11), because the "covenant" can be the result only of civic voluntarism, never of coercion (that is the state's currency). It is therefore strangely inconsistent for Sacks to hope that something as paltry as a state-decreed "Britain Day" could push Britain onto the American road (ibid.: 166).

If the covenant has to be discounted for all countries that did not luckily start that way, are there alternatives to ground a collective identity? Two often invoked alternatives are language and religion.[28] Both are easily dismissed, either because of intrinsic weakness as identity marker (language) or because such identity would violate constitutional precepts (religion). However, the fact that both alternatives *are* often raised, even on the part of political elites, merits their closer inspection.

Language is perhaps the strongest particularism that can be found in tightened naturalization rules and in the new civic integration policies for immigrants across Europe. But only in specific contexts, most notably in multinational states such as Canada or Belgium, is language a marker of identity (and in Canada only on the part of the minority nation, Québec). In most other countries, obliging immigrants or citizenship applicants to learn the domestic language is a matter of practical exigency, not of identity. To be German cannot hinge on language if Austria and parts of Switzerland speak German, too. Nevertheless, the German civic integration policy for newcomers, as well as the German naturalization rules, make the relatively demanding, intermediate B1 standard (according to the Common European

Identity

Reference Framework for Languages) a condition for passing the required tests. By contrast, France, which is far more insistent on the domestic purity and international recognition of the French language, is rather lax about its formal integration requirements, asking only for oral competence in the context of naturalization and for the even more elementary A1.1. level within the *Contrats d'acceuil et d'intégration* (CAI) for newcomers (see Michalowski 2007: 124f.). If identity concerns were driving the emphasis on language competence within civic integration, one would expect the opposite outcome, with France setting the hurdle high and Germany putting it low. In reality, the main worry is societal, especially labor market, adjustment. Language thus understood is less of a concern in France, where most immigrants arrive from francophone Africa, and more of a concern in Germany, where most immigrants – even those arriving with ethnic-descent credentials – speak no German at all on arrival. Overall, in the context of civic integration, language is conceived of less in terms of identity than of the functional capacity of the newcomer to adjust and get by without help from the state.

Religion is a more serious candidate for an identity. This is because one cannot adhere to two religions at one time, in contrast to language, the adoption of which is additive and capacity-enhancing, not substitutive (this important observation is made by Zolberg and Litt Woon 1999). However, if language falters for its intrinsic weakness as identity marker, religion falters for constitutional reasons. Making a particular religion obligatory for the acquisition of citizenship, and to propagate religious citizenship identities, would contradict elementary precepts of the constitutional state. Consequently no contemporary Western state would dare advocate such a stance. In fact, liberalism itself was born in early modern Europe in the very differentiation between state and religion, which remains valid today.

But still, there are religious temptations, especially in the confrontation with Muslims and Islam. In Denmark, for instance, the extremist Danish Peoples Party (DPP) insists that Christianity is a defining element of Danish national culture, which newcomers have to adopt or adjust to: "We live in a Christian country, and

Identity

when you come here you must conform to Danish norms, laws and habits" (a DPP member of parliament, quoted in Mouritsen 2006: 76). As Per Mouritsen (ibid.) stresses, this reference to Christianity is sheer particularism, devoid of the missionary zeal of historical Christianity. There is no claim to moral superiority in it; instead it blends with the right of first arrival ("we were here first"), and with a view of "Danish cultural heritage" as "undefinable," "all the 1000 little things," and "the air that we breathe" (DPP leader Kjaersgaards, quoted ibid.: 89, n. 3). To say that such a stance, if turned into a policy, would contradict the precepts of liberal constitutionalism is perhaps not even the relevant objection, because something that is deemed "undefinable" cannot become a matter of policy in the first instance.

A reference to Christianity is also, next to the German language, the one particularism that one can find in the German concept of *Leitkultur*, which was first proposed by circles within the conservative Christian Democratic Union (CDU) in the year 2000, and which was recently revived in the party's 2007 national platform (*Grundsatzprogramm*). That the reference to Christianity was still delicate is indicated by the fact that Christianity did *not* appear in the original formulation of a "liberal German *Leitkultur*" by the CDU leader in parliament, Friedrich Merz. Only the CDU Immigration Commission (CDU 2000) included it. But this was Christianity with a universalistic touch, in terms of the "value system of our Christian-Occidental culture" that had to be "accepted" by immigrants. The duplet "Christian-Occidental" is programmatic, because the values to be inculcated in immigrants were to be not religious but secular – most notably, "freedom, solidarity, and justice," which could be "deduced" from the "Christian understanding of the person" (ibid.).

While the notion of *Leitkultur* disappeared for a while, because it was suspected of being too close to an assimilationist stance, something akin to it has informed the Islamic headscarf laws passed by several German *Land* governments in 2004 and 2005 (see Joppke 2007c; 2009a: ch. 3). As in Baden-Württemberg and Bavaria, these laws prohibit the Islamic headscarf for public school teachers, while explicitly endorsing Catholic wardrobe.

Identity

The crypto-nationalist argument is that the German state is not just any state but a state shaped by the "Christian-Occidental" tradition, which the state had not just the license but the mandate to be partial about and to help reproduce across the generations. The selective exclusion of Islam and endorsement of Christianity rests on a subtle distinction between religion as faith and religion as culture. Of course, the neutral state could not inculcate a faith; anything else would revoke the Westphalian peace formula that had ended the intra-Christian bloodletting in early modern Europe. But the state could see itself as guardian of the secular culture derived from this faith and be partial in the sense that only "this" but not "that" religion has made "us" who we are today.

However secularized, Christian particularism is still problematic. Concretely, it requires the contorted legal construct that veiled Catholic nun teachers in public schools are not expressing a faith but "performing a tradition" (see Joppke 2009a: 75f.). More importantly, the selective exclusion of the Islamic headscarf on the part of public school teachers violates the constitutional equality principle. In its *Ludin* decision of September 2003, which kicked off the flood of *Land* legislations in the following two years,[29] the German Federal Constitutional Court argued that the state was free to exclude religious symbolism from the public space. But if it decided to do so, in deviation from the German tradition of "open" neutrality and factual approximation of the French tradition of "laicist" neutrality, *all* religious symbolisms had to be excluded – the Christian ones as well. Evidently, in the German headscarf conflict, legislatures and courts espoused contradictory self-understandings of the German state: Christian-particularistic versus liberal-universalistic, respectively.

Overall, the grounding of collective identity in religion runs against constitutional obstacles, because the liberal state is obliged to be agnostic or at least impartial about religion.

Instead, the typical solution to the problem of collective identity across Europe today is the one pioneered by republican France, according to which to be national is defined in light of the universalistic precepts of human rights and democracy.

In an interesting discussion of the Danish case, Per Mouritsen

Identity

found that a "Nordic version of the French-Jacobin short circuit" dominated over its main rival, "secularized-Christianity-as-culture" (2006: 84, 77). Accordingly, the program of the Social Democratic Party, traditionally Denmark's strongest political force, defines as "Danish values," which are challenged by globalization, the French republican triptych, "freedom, equality and solidarity" (ibid.: 81). As Prime Minister Rasmussen expressed the Danish particular universalism: "Danish society has been built on some fundamental values, which must be accepted, if you are to live here. In Denmark, politics and religion are separated. In Denmark, there is inviolable respect for human life. In Denmark . . . women are equal to men" (ibid.: 82). Or, as in the so-called Danish cartoon affair, to be Danish is to advocate free speech. Again, this way of being Danish is no different from being French or British or German or Dutch. The national particularisms that immigrants and ethnic minorities are asked to accept across European states are but local versions of the universalistic idiom of liberal democracy.

Liberal Identity and the Exclusion of Muslims

Particular universalism is the main form in which Western states practice exclusion today. Cornered by the dilemma of a particularistic identity that is deemed necessary for integration yet that cannot be supplied by a law or policy that must remain formally non-discriminatory, contemporary states are inclined to call a certain idea of liberalism to the rescue. Liberalism has always had two different sides, one that prescribes autonomy and reason over heteronomy and faith, and thus an ideal way of life; and a second that limits itself to procedural toleration and non-interference in a society marked by an irredeemable multiplicity of ways of life (see Galston 1995; Gray 2000). Of course, both sides of liberalism require one another, as either a single-minded toleration of the intolerant or its ruthless suppression would be destructive of liberalism. But it still makes sense to conceive of both sides of liberalism as variables that may be differently developed in different times and places. In retrospect, the flowering of multiculturalism across Western societies in the past few decades was premised on a prevalence of the toleration over the autonomy mode of liberalism. This does not mean that other core values of liberalism, such as autonomy and reason, were extinct. On the contrary, there was no need to assert them because nobody had questioned them. As Kymlicka (2005) showed in a revealing discussion of "liberal multiculturalism" in Canada, the latter was enabled by the fact that European ethnics had been pushing it, acting and reasoning within a liberal-democratic framework. Conversely, with an eye on Europe, where multiculturalism has been largely discredited by "illiberal" Muslim practices, Kymlicka fathoms that "[t]he debate in Canada might have been very different if, as in Europe, ninety percent of our immigrants were Muslim" (2005: 8).

In fact, in the wake of Islamic terrorism, toleration liberalism has receded behind a less procedural, more substantive variant of liberalism that prescribes a shared way of life, in which, say, men and women are equal and the secular trumps the religious. Such liberalism is potentially an identity, separating liberal from illiberal people. "Identity liberalism" (Tebble 2006) is profoundly paradoxical, because universalism is reduced to the group marker that it notionally cannot be. It made its first appearance in the context of colonialism, where it allowed the hierarchical demarcation between European and non-European ways of life, with the Europeans figuring as "superior people" (Parekh 1994). Though devoid of such hierarchical pretensions, identity liberalism is currently undergoing a revival in the confrontation with politicized Islam. For good or bad, liberalism is the stuff out of which the citizenship identities propagated by contemporary states are made, with exclusionary implications for Muslims. As one author put it appositely, this is a "Schmittian" liberalism that "aims at clarifying the core values of liberal societies and using coercive state power to protect them from illiberal and putatively dangerous groups" (Triadafilopoulos 2008).

A case in point is France, where citizenship universalism has always constituted a distinct national identity, which goes under the name of "republicanism." To see it reinforced by the political

Identity

branches of the state, as in the 2004 anti-headscarf law, may not raise any eyebrows. What does raise eyebrows, however, is its recent reinforcement by France's highest administrative court, the Conseil d'Etat, which so far had been a staunch defender of religious liberties against the political state (see Joppke 2009a: ch. 2). In June 2008 the Conseil d'Etat confirmed the denial of citizenship to a burka-wearing woman on the grounds of her "insufficient assimilation."[30] This is notwithstanding the court-acknowledged fact that she "possessed a good mastery of the French language"[31] and that she was married to a French man (though of Moroccan origins) and was the mother of three French children. In previous rules, the same court had interpreted the "assimilation" required for naturalization in terms of (very basic) French-language competence. In its 2008 turnaround, the court referred to a new clause in the Civil Code that allowed the state to deny citizenship for "insufficient assimilation, other than linguistic."[32] In particular, the court faulted the applicant for "her adoption of a radical practice of her religion, incompatible with the essential values of the French community, especially the principle of the equality of sexes."[33] In fact, the woman had adopted the burka at her husband's request, and she lived "in total submission to the men in her family."[34] Still, this is the first time that the court has refused nationality on the grounds of religious expression. And, paradoxically, this violation of a liberal principle, the freedom of religion, occurred through invocation of another liberal principle, sex equality. This was, indeed, exclusion for the sake of liberal identity.

A second example of liberal exclusion is the invocation of "Dutch norms and values" in the Dutch civic integration policy for immigrants. Many have seen the Netherlands regressing from integration to assimilation, but in the old, transitive way theoretically ruled out by Brubaker (e.g. Entzinger 2006b: 141; Korteweg 2006: 163). Has it? If yes, then only in the sense that liberalism has thickened from a procedural framework for toleration into a substantive way of life, which the majority considers "their" way of life and which is expected to be shared by immigrants and ethnic minorities, too. Duyvendak, Pels, and Rijkschroeff (2009) have interestingly argued that the Netherlands had never been as proverbially multicultural as the stereotype would have it. Instead, not unlike the small Nordic countries, it is marked by a "progressive monoculture," in which, say, men and women are equal, homosexuality is widely accepted, and religion is marginal and strictly private (2009: 138). This impressionistic view is supported by solid empirical evidence. A national survey and ingenious social-psychological experiments by Paul Sniderman and Louk Hagendoorn (2007: 130) found that "[a] large segment of Dutch society takes strong exception to Muslim treatment of women, although not to Muslims themselves" – which qualifies them as "liberal." Accordingly, the "Dutch norms and values" that immigrants are expected to adopt do not consist of a preference for wood clogs, Gouda, and windows without curtains, but the progressive majority outlook. If the Dutch information DVD, disseminated in the context of the new policy of "integration from abroad," contains pictures of nude women on Dutch beaches and of kissing homosexuals, the message is: "This is Holland," a country of progressive people, and who takes issue with this should stay away.

The exclusive and thus identity-forging dimension of particular universalism can be formulated as the notion that the liberal state is only for liberal people. This is, of course, a profoundly illiberal idea, because it casts people into a standard mold and robs them of the possibility to decide for themselves who they want to be. Ever since Kant, it has been a key precept of liberalism that law and public policy can regulate only the external behavior of people, not their inner motivations. Accordingly, the German Constitutional Court established, in its December 2000 decision on Jehova's Witnesses, that citizens are "legally not required to personally share the values of the Constitution."[35] All that can be expected of, say, religious dissenters is that they should respect in their behavior the priority of the secular legal order, and not harm the constitutional rights of third parties. Accordingly, an exacting loyalty requirement, which aims at "an inner disposition, a mindset [*Gesinnung*], not an external behavior," has been deemed contrary to the Basic Law.[36] In fact, as early as 1944 a US appellate court had ruled that "patriotism is not a condition of naturalization; that attachment is not addressed to the heart, demands no affection for or even approval for a democratic system of government, but merely acceptance of the fundamental political habits and attitudes which here prevail, and a willingness to obey the laws" (quoted in Gordon 2007: 371). David Miller articulates the operative principle in these court rulings: "Liberal states do not require their citizens to *believe* liberal principles, since they tolerate communists, anarchists, fascists, and so forth. What they require is that citizens should conform to liberal principles in practice and accept as legitimate policies that are pursued in the name of such principles, while they are left free to advocate alternative arrangements" (Miller 2004: 14).

Citizenship tests that ask for factual knowledge about a country's history, culture, and institutions are unproblematic in this respect, because such matter is merely cognitive: it can be learned and mechanically reproduced. Moving from knowledge to values,[37] even a signed loyalty declaration or an oath to the constitution is unproblematic from a liberal point of view, because it consists of an external behavior that, moreover, only actualizes the contractual underpinnings of liberal citizenship. However, a citizenship test that scrutinizes a candidate's "inner disposition" is problematic, precisely for transgressing the thin line that separates the regulation of behavior from the control of beliefs.

This line has been infamously transgressed in the so-called Interview Guidelines (*Gesprächsleitfaden*), issued by the *Land* government of Baden-Württemberg to aid its naturalization officers in September 2005. The professed purpose was to check whether a citizenship applicant's written "declaration of loyalty" (*Bekenntnis*) to the constitution, which has been a component of the German naturalization procedure since 2000, also corresponded to their actual beliefs or "inner disposition."[38] A legal evaluation of the guidelines found them in violation of national and international law, in two respects (Wolfrum and Röben 2006). Firstly, in being applied only to citizenship applicants from member states of the Islamic League, they "discriminated" against Muslims. In fact, the guidelines, which consisted of thirty questions about applicants' views on parental authority, religion, homosexuality, gender equality, terrorism, and other issues, construed the "liberal democratic order primarily as one that is contrary to the presumed values of a specific group," Muslims (ibid.: 15). Secondly, and more important for our purposes, in touching the intimate sphere of the person, the guidelines violated the liberty rights of the constitution, especially the freedom of negative opinion and conscience. As the two lawyers reiterate the constitutional status quo, "the mere holding of an opinion is no threat to the liberal democratic order, if it is not expressed in concrete actions that are directed against this order" (ibid.: 16). While it was appropriately condemned for its discriminatory, inquisitive morality test, the CDU-ruled *Land* government amazingly refused to backtrack, even after the introduction of a nationwide citizenship test in 2008.[39] Better than any other recent example of "repressive liberalism" (see Joppke 2007a: 14–18), Baden-Württemberg's *Gesprächsleitfaden* epitomizes the illiberal potential of a liberalism that transmutes into an identity, an ethical way of life to which everyone is expected to conform, and which is brought forward with an unabashedly exclusionary intention against liberalism's presumed Other, Islam and Muslims.[40]

Citizenship and Nationhood Revisited

If modern citizenship had always combined "internal inclusion" with "external exclusion" (Brubaker 1992), its externally exclusive dimension has notably weakened in the past half-century. The weakening of the particularistic, identity-lending dimension of citizenship is tantamount to the retreat of nationalism, at least in the West. Habermas's (1987) brief synopsis of nationalism's decline is as good as any. Firstly, especially in Europe, the long peace after 1945, which coincided with the building of a European polity, has blunted the edges between nation-state societies. Secondly, if the "camp," with de-nationalized "inmates" stripped to the condition of bare life, has been the enigmatic experience of the twentieth century, it is one that has pushed for the universalization of rights, beyond the citizenship confine. Thirdly, to the degree that academic history had once provided the cognitive coordinates for nationalist thought, the internationalization and professionalization of academic history has removed this possibility. One sees its imprints in changed history curricula in public schools, which are geared less toward inculcating nationalist loyalty than at disseminating reflexive knowledge.[41] Finally, with the rise of mass communication, mass traveling, and international migration, as a result of which multiple ways of life clamor for coexistence and equal treatment, "all alternatives to a universalistic broadening of moral consciousness are being decimated" (Habermas 1987: 170). To these concrete historical changes Habermas adds the evolutionary advance of "post-conventional" identities, at individual and collective level alike, which are marked by reflexivity and a capacity to step back from one's contingent views and identifications in the light of universal ethical principles. Now any blind identification with a quasi-sacred object, such as the nation, becomes anathema. From this, admittedly Habermasian, angle democratic citizenship does not require a "national identity" but only a "shared political culture" (Habermas 1992: 643), which is more procedural than substantive, captured in his famous notion of "constitutional patriotism."

However one judges the viability of "constitutional patriotism" to forge unity and integration in plural societies, the decoupling of citizenship and nationhood is the incontrovertible exit position for contemporary state campaigns for unity and integration, especially with respect to immigrants. Talcott Parsons (1971), writing decades before globalization would undermine the comprehensively national organization of society, saw modern societies marked by a trend toward increasing "value generalization," which makes for values that are unspecific to any one nation. In fact, what Parsons attributed to the "new lead society," the United States, has come to mark all Western societies: citizenship "dissociated from ethnic membership" and nation-states "emancipated from specific religious and ethnic control" (1971: 114). With Eric Kaufmann (2004), one can depict the underlying process as "decline of dominant ethnicity" – that is, of the notion of the state as property and instrument of self-realization of a particular group.

Arash Abizadeh (2005) persuasively denied that there is "conceptual or metaphysical necessity" for collective identities to be particularistic and thus intrinsically in need of an excluded "Other." Further, he argued that the "particularist thesis" reifies at the theoretical plane the contingent, Westphalian "ideology of indivisible sovereignty" (2005: 46). But this advocate of cosmopolitanism conceded that lesser identities might still be the empirically more potent, especially at the level of the state. A state, to reiterate, is like an individual in that it does not happen twice in the world. This locks both into singularity. Accordingly, when the German interior minister Wolfgang Schäuble called upon "Muslims in Germany" to become "German Muslims," he also found that a generic "constitution" was not sufficient for "successful integration": "Constitutional patriotism, as a matter of reason (and not of emotion), is not sufficient . . . If we want to feel part of a collectivity, then there must be something that connects us at a deeper, human level, at the level of religion and culture, values and identity."[42] The problem is that such an identity would exactly separate "Germans" from "Muslims" and thus forfeit the very attempt at integration. The German state could not impose it except by being openly discriminatory, because a state of "Christian origins and traditions" is one of which Muslims could not be an equal part. Accordingly, when Germany's major Muslim organizations were summoned by the federal government, in the context of the third so-called Islam Conference, to identify with the "German value community" (*deutsche Wertegemeinschaft*), they coolly responded that this was beyond the required liberal minimum. As Schirin Amir-Moazami (2008: 203) expounded the irony, "in this case it is Muslims who remind the state of its own constitutional principles, while the state is trying to impose on Muslims a confession (*Bekenntnis*) that is in violation of the legal status quo."

5

Citizenship Light

In the first part of this concluding chapter, I tackle the question of how the changes of citizenship across its status, rights, and identity dimensions are interrelated. Rather than there being a relationship of strict causality, I argue that there is one of logical complementariness. Secondly, I scrutinize a paradox in the evolution of citizenship, which matters more than ever in the global distribution of wealth, yet strangely not for the people that hold it or have access to it. In a third step, I propose to look at the new European Union citizenship less as a travesty, as which it has appeared in much of the scholarly literature, than as a citizenship of our time.

The Question of Causality

In a state of the art review, Bloemraad, Korteweg, and Yurdakul (2008: 153) noted the "need for a more dynamic and comprehensive understanding of the inter-relationships between the dimensions of citizenship and immigration." To provide such an understanding has been the aim of this book.

Has it lived up to the challenge? Before tackling this question, let me express two caveats, one conceptual, one geographical. On the conceptual side, it must be conceded that the status–rights–identity triptych structuring this book has left out one dimension of citizenship that Bloemraad, Korteweg, and Yurdakul (2008: 156) considered equally important: "political participation." Omitting

Citizenship Light

citizenship's political dimension is no doubt paradoxical, if one considers my starting point of citizenship as membership in a political community. And it is not to deny that political participation matters in the context of citizenship and immigration. In the classic immigration countries, naturalized immigrants have always been a considerable political force, and much of what the few American political scientists with an interest in immigration do is to study exactly their political behavior. Beyond the confines of the domestic, and rather more novel, is a trend toward state-sponsored "transnational political participation" through extending external voting rights to expatriates, which raises significant issues of democratic legitimacy and representation in origin and host societies alike (see Bauböck 2007). In short, whether domestic or transnational, "immigrant political incorporation" matters.[1]

Let me still offer three reasons for excluding it from the heart of my analysis. Firstly, as the iron exclusion of immigrants from the political rights of citizenship testifies, this is the one aspect of citizenship that has changed least and has not opened up in response to immigration. The only exception is a few states' concession of local voting rights to foreigners – the impetus for which slowed down precisely when the acquisition of citizenship came to be considered a more urgent need.[2] And the national vote and right to stand for office has almost everywhere remained a citizenship privilege, with no sign of change around the corner. Secondly, immigrants' general laggardness to naturalize, and their seeming satisfaction with the (non-political) rights of legal permanent residents, which is the gist of the "devaluation of citizenship" diagnosis (see Schuck 1989), suggests that their concerns are more mundane and belly-centered – because they often lead precarious lives, immigrants care more about life's essential functions, above all secure residence and work, than about the loftier goals of political participation.[3]

But, thirdly, giving short shrift to its political dimension is also programmatic and reflective of a real-world change of citizenship, even outside the context of immigration. Because the citizenship that has transpired in these pages, and which has partially gained shape in the very confrontation with immigration, is more the

Roman citizenship of passive rights-holding than the Athenian citizenship of active participation in the political community. What we saw emerging on the status–rights–identity canvas is a citizenship light: easy to access, with rights (and few obligations) that do not sharply distinguish citizens from certain aliens, and capped by thin identities. Citizenship's internally inclusive dynamic has bitten large holes into its externally exclusive crust, which shows in a notorious difficulty for states to legitimize the boundaries that are necessarily set and presupposed by citizenship. It is less and less true that citizenship is "hard on the outside and soft on the inside" (Bosniak 2006: 4). And there is not much difference here between the classic immigrant nations of North America and Australia and the ethnic nation-states of Europe. Accordingly, a recent overview found that "shifts in policy have brought these two categories of societies somewhat closer together," along with the possibility that "common problems, and perhaps even common solutions, might begin to emerge" (Weinstock 2008: 4). Indeed, as Europe has borrowed the *jus soli* provisions of the classic immigrant countries (though in weaker, conditional form) and as the classic immigrant countries have looked to Europe to revamp (as in the United States) or introduce (as in Australia) their citizenship tests, to name just two of the more visible convergent trends, the old distinction between immigrant and non-immigrant societies makes little sense.

Moving to my geographical caveat, I concede that the story of citizenship and immigration unfolded in these pages is a provincial story, limited to the comfort zone of North America, Western Europe, and the British outlets in Oceania. It is a world away from the "differentiated citizenship" that James Holston found in contemporary Brazil – a quasi-feudal citizenship of "legalized privileges and legitimated inequalities" (2007: 4), with limited legal access to landed property or special jail cells for the educated. Even more drastic is the contrast with the "documentary citizenship" that Kamal Sadiq (2005, 2009) observed in India, Malaysia, and Pakistan – that is, a "weakly institutionalized" citizenship that easily enfranchises illegal immigrants on the basis of fraudulent documents and that, in turn, leaves out the mass of the native rural poor, sponsored or tolerated by weak and clannish states in ethnically divided societies.

My story is a provincial story even within Europe, where the twelve Eastern states joining the European Union in 2004 and 2007 sport distinctly less liberal citizenship regimes than their Western neighbors. A comprehensive study on the "new Europe" found that "citizenship in these [new accession] countries is still closely linked to an ethnic interpretation of nationality, transmission to subsequent generations is exclusively based on descent, there is greater hostility towards multiple nationality, and greater emphasis is laid on citizenship links with ethnic kin-minorities in neighbouring countries and expatriates" (Bauböck, Perching, and Sievers 2007: 12). In his review of nationality laws in the EU, Marc Morjé Howard (2006) therefore concludes that there is "no 'common European standard' on citizenship, and none appears to be on the horizon" (Howard 2009: 190).

With these caveats in mind, what has been the story of this book? At one level, one could read it as a story of successive causation, in which changes in one dimension of citizenship helped bring about changes in the other dimensions. This story would go like this:

- Status dimension (1): The liberalization of access to citizenship leads to the ethnic diversification of the citizenry . . .
- Rights dimension (2): . . . which makes social rights, the crown of twentieth-century citizenship, difficult to retain; in turn, other types of right move to the fore: alien rights and minority rights . . .
- Identity dimension (3): . . . and the state responds to this diversification, in which everything and everyone flees the center, with campaigns for unity and integration, which, however, have to be conducted in a liberal-universalistic idiom.

The first problem with this story is that it cannot account for the opening salvo: the liberalization of access to citizenship. There is, in fact, an all-important exogenous variable that has shaped the evolution of citizenship *across* its dimensions: the de-legitimization of racism and extreme nationalism in the West after World War II, and the parallel rise of universal human rights norms. Witness that citizenship's liberalization started with the removal of racial restrictions in early 1950s America, preceding that country's great postwar migrations by almost two decades. While of concrete historical origins, the onslaught on shared humanity that was German Nazism, the rejection of state-level racism and accompanying celebration of human rights has come to constitute the *doxa* or *episteme* of Western societies that no one can sanely put into doubt. Even those who disagree must phrase their claims in the new idiom, which is the idiom of equality and non-discrimination. Short of a collapse of civilization, there is no way back to the world before, the world of blood, hierarchy, and impassable boundaries. This is why the many restrictive trends in citizenship, proliferating post-2001 and traced in the preceding pages across citizenship's status, rights, and identity dimensions, may touch the fringe but never the core of what has evolved in the past half-century.

Secondly, an endogenous story of successive causation obscures the fact that the ethnic diversification of society *preceded* the liberalization of access to citizenship. This is logical, as naturalization presupposes prior residence in the host society. But it reduces the possible impact of changes on citizenship's status on its rights and identity dimensions. Germany, for instance, had become ethnically pluralized, as a result of guest-worker immigration, some four decades before its belated liberalization of citizenship at the turn of the twenty-first century; in Italy, a country of immigration for over two decades now, this liberalization is still waiting to occur. And both countries have moved toward a change in the rights dimension of citizenship, in terms of antidiscrimination laws, not because of a diversified citizenry but on account of the dictate of Brussels. In all cases, the ethnic diversification of society precedes that of the citizenry because of states' (at least temporarily) open immigration policies. From this follows that, in principle, the fact of an ethnically diverse society, and not just of an ethnically diverse citizenry, may create pressure for the establishment of minority rights. Even though, as Jacqueline Gehring (2009) has importantly demonstrated, a sense of solidarity, engendered by shared citizenship, may well be the sociological impetus for agreeing on and instituting minority rights.

A closer look at the origins of ethnic diversification also suggests connecting the evolution of citizenship tightly to that of immigration policy. Because admission into the state is ineluctably dual – firstly into the territory and only secondly into the citizenry – immigration policy is citizenship's perpetual gatekeeper. But then changes in the rights and identity dimension of citizenship may be more the effect of a certain immigration policy than of citizenship's own gatekeeping function on its status dimension. In turn, citizenship's gatekeeping can take on the semblance of liberality, with increasingly blurred lines between citizens and aliens, just because there is an effective immigration policy to ward off the huddled masses.

Thirdly, wherever you situate immigration-based ethnic diversity, at the level of society or citizenry, there is no evidence that it has been causally involved in clipping the social rights crown of citizenship. A compelling analysis of the transformation of the welfare state into "enabling state" (Gilbert 2002), marked by the privatization of services, workfare and return to paid employment, selective targeting of beneficiaries, and a shift in emphasis from rights to responsibilities and duties, makes only spotty reference to the fact of immigration. Instead, among the forces identified as driving the "convergence toward market-oriented social policies" (ibid.: 4–5) across Western societies are the demographic aging and shrinking of the population, the globalization of the economy, and the welfare state's own bad press in the realm of "ideas and normative views" (ibid.: 32–43). The omission of immigration as a causal factor may be the flaw of Gilbert's analysis. But the evidence presented in chapter 3 confirms the bracketing of immigration for understanding current welfare-state retrenchments. At the same time, there is a striking similarity between the post-welfarist enabling state and the civic integration policies for immigrants and citizenship applicants (as discussed in chapter 2). A broader perspective reveals that civic integration is no devious plot against immigrants but embedded within a general restructuring of the welfare state, from public to private responsibility, which is causally disconnected from the fact of immigration.

Next to being too endogenous, the story of successive causation is also captive to a naive functionalism, according to which state policy is rational problem-solving. Organizational sociology has shown that states, like all organizations, do not just look for efficient solutions to objective problems but enact "myth and ceremony" (Meyer and Rowan 1978), screening their environment for legitimate ways of doing things – irrespective of whether there is a need for doing something. In John Meyer et al.'s evocative thought experiment, a recently discovered island society would soon look "something like a modern state with many of the usual ministries and agencies" (1997: 145). From this angle, there are antidiscrimination policies not because the citizenry is ethnically diverse but because other states have such policies, and "this is how one does things." Without suggesting that this *is* the origin of antidiscrimination policy in any one case (in Europe, it certainly is *not*), this gives a hint at what a *really* causal analysis of changing citizenship laws and policies would have to look like.

Finally, the dimensions of citizenship are subject to domain-specific legal regimes and political dynamics. Nationality law is one thing, and even on the rights dimension welfare, alien, multiculturalism, and antidiscrimination laws and policies are all other things. Not to mention that the pronouncements and campaigning on "identity" by state elites is a different matter still, perhaps addressing the majority population more than immigrants. To see all this as "citizenship" is more in the eye of the beholder than in the real world, despite our initial plea for conceptual economy and not to stretch citizenship's meaning beyond that of state membership.

In sum, "to examine more deeply how all dimensions of citizenship interact" (Bloemraad, Korteweg, and Yurdakul 2008: 154) is more easily said than done. At a minimum, such an account must combine and balance the workings of interdimensional influences (as suggested by my story of successive causation) with those of external variables (such as universal human rights norms, welfare restructuring, etc.) and of dimension-specific causalities ("best practice" emulation in differentiated legal and policy fields, etc.). This is no small order, and this book has certainly fallen short of doing this in a rigorous and systematic way.

However, if the status–rights–identity nexus of citizenship suggested in this book is not a straightforwardly causal one, it is still one of logical complementariness. Whatever brought them about, the changes in the three dimensions of citizenship add up to a logically coherent *Gestalt*, in which developments in one dimension logically complement and match, sometimes even lock in and reinforce, developments in the other dimensions. For instance, even if the dethroning of social citizenship is not the result of immigration, immigration will not help to put it back in place. In other words, if not caused by immigration, the dethroning of social citizenship is still commensurate with, even reinforced, by it. Logical complementariness does not prejudge the causes and mechanisms that have brought about developments in each single dimension. Short of espousing single-factor reductionism, causal explanation needs to be local explanation that cannot be decreed from the green table of theory.

The Future of Citizenship: Two Measures of Worth

Having qualified the claim of this book, what future does it project for citizenship? The current evolution of citizenship poses a paradox. On the one hand, in a world of huge and growing disparities of wealth and security, yet one that is more connected than ever by technology and ideas, the objective value of citizenship must further increase. On the other hand, for the lucky ones in possession of it, or for whom its acquisition is within reach, citizenship's value is likely to be low and lower. This paradox is exemplified by two strikingly different recent statements on the "worth" and trends of citizenship in the West, Ayelet Shachar's *The Birthright Lottery* (2009) and Peter Spiro's *Beyond Citizenship* (2008). Shachar points to the startling fact that many of the world's riches and life-chances are divided up by the morally arbitrary fact of birth, considering that 97 percent of the world's population are citizens at birth (only 3 percent are naturalized and thus former immigrants). The near-half of the world's population that is born with the "wrong" citizenship, mostly in the poverty zones of Southeast Asia and sub-Saharan Africa, has to survive on less than $2 a day; children born in the poorest nations are five times more likely to die before the age of five. Is there more need to underline the value of citizenship in the West? At the same time, contrary to the contractual underpinnings of the modern state and the achievement ideology of modern society, citizenship is acquired for most as a "form of inherited property" (Shachar and Hirschl 2007: 254). But whereas the morally corrupting and dysfunctional consequences of inheriting material wealth have been amply debated and curtailed by law for over two centuries now (see most recently Beckert 2007), the transmission of political membership still proceeds much like the "fee tail" or "entail" regime for inheriting landed property in medieval England, in which property transfer is untaxed and infinite in duration, land much like citizenship being passed on "from one generation to another in perpetuity" (Shachar and Hirschl 2007: 270).

While the scholarship on citizenship (including this book) has zeroed in on the "gatekeeping" function of citizenship, bickering about the lot of (always few and privileged) immigrants who are thereby included or excluded, the "wealth-preserving" aspect of hereditary citizenship for the vast rest, our naturalized immigrants included, has faded from view – this is, indeed, the "'black hole' of citizenship theory" (Shachar and Hirschl 2007: 274). Who would disagree that, if inherited citizenship, this "striking exception to the modern trend away from ascribed statuses in all other areas" (Shachar 2009: 13), is to prevail, taxing it or requiring human services in terms of a "birthright privilege levy" may be the minimum that the lucky ones owe those who are born in the wrong places, without any wrongdoing on their part, and without much of a chance of joining the intrinsically small elite of immigrants? Never has the worth of citizenship and its morally uncomfortable consequences for the privileged half of humankind been more effectively expressed.

Contrast this with Peter Spiro's *Beyond Citizenship* (2008), which – he submits – should really have been titled "The End of Citizenship" (2008: 7). As if nothing had happened in the past fifteen years, both in the real world and in the world of scholarship, it reiterates and applies to the case of the United States the "postnational membership" diagnosis that Yasemin Soysal (1994) had met for early 1990s Europe. Yet there is much going for it. With globalization, the "importance of space and territorial boundaries declines" (Spiro 2008: 4), and so does the importance of the one institution defined by space and territory: the state. In a world of multiple citizenships and strengthened alien rights, citizenship in that diminished institution, the state, must mean less than in the past. The "declining legal significance of the status," in turn, reinforces the "waning intensity of bonds among members" (ibid.: 6). The fact that "overinclusive" *jus soli* citizenship has not stirred up much debate in America demonstrates for Spiro the "declining importance of citizenship itself" (ibid.: 30). As he suggests, in a defensible version of our story of successive causation, there is a "feedback loop of diluted ties": "The larger the group of happenstance citizens, the less likely the status will be consequential, which renders existing citizens more accepting of expansive admission criteria and the addition of nominal members, which in turn entrenches the lack of consequence" (ibid.: 31). In the language proposed in our book, the larger the radius of citizenship as status the less it can mean in terms of rights and identity. With respect to rights, citizenship is said to make "very little difference" (ibid.: 81). That is both old, resonating with America's traditionally thin citizenship, and new, as even the mid-1990s onslaught on the welfare rights of immigrants could be redressed so that, again, there is "near equality for the purposes of state assistance" (ibid.). Conversely, except for jury duty, there are no specific obligations of citizenship, because taxes and even military service are imposed or imposable on resident aliens too. With respect to identity, "America's dilemma" is that "inclusion dilutes identity" (ibid.: 157). Predictably, and more questionably, buying into the hyphenated citizenship scenario of contemporary citizenship studies, Spiro sees "the center of community" shifting to "locations other than the state" (ibid.: 137), such as the gated communities and other private bodies that now "regulate our existence" (ibid.: 148). As the state is downgraded to one of many forms of association, "the significance of membership issues outside of the state will grow in proportion to the importance of nonstate communities" (ibid.: 151), and membership in all these groups is conceivable in terms of citizenship, argues Spiro. So, in lieu of one citizenship there are many citizenships for each one of us, without the one that might trump the other memberships.

Juxtaposing these opposite analyses, how can one author see citizenship "back with a vengeance" (Shachar 2009: 2, borrowing from Dauvergne 2007), while the other claims the "irreversibility" of its decline (Spiro 2008: 162)? The answer is: it is all a matter of perspective, and of factoring in or out host states' immigration policies. Shachar's perspective is mainly that of the losers in the "birthright lottery," which condemns the majority of humanity to poverty, starvation, and early death, and it factors out immigration policy so that citizenship law does all the cuts. Spiro's perspective is that of the legal immigrant elite that, having cleared the crucial hurdle of territorial access, may choose between permanent residence and citizenship. The indisputable truth in Spiro's analysis is that the value of an immigrant visa by far surpasses that of formal citizenship. Contrary to the citizenship rhetoric beloved of politicians of all stripes and countries, "the real prize is legal residency, not citizenship. It's all about the green card, not the naturalization certificate" (Spiro 2008: 159). Contemporary campaigning for upgrading citizenship may make cosmetic changes to this reality; it cannot change it at heart. Conversely put, only the immigration policy watchdog has allowed citizenship to take on the lightened contours that it indisputably has throughout the West. Only because the vast majority of humankind is locked out from the purview of Western citizenship by these states' immigration policies (which by definition are vastly more exclusive than inclusive, even in their most generous variants) could citizenship become more porous at the fringes and the distinction between citizen and legal resident alien become blurred.

If Spiro's provocative analysis of a citizenship "almost gone begging for customers" (2008: 91) did not catch an element of truth, contemporary campaigns for upgrading citizenship would be meaningless. These campaigns are desperate, and ultimately futile, rearguard actions against the inevitable lightening of citizenship in the West. The case of Britain, next to the US a prime example of historically thin citizenship, is telling in this respect. The current Labour government's strategy has been to "raise the visibility of national citizenship in response to growing anxieties about identity and migration in our more fluid societies" (Goodhart 2006: 9). Apart from prescribing symbols and ceremony, there is a hard and legal element to this strategy, tying more benefits to formal citizenship than to legal resident status. Concretely, Goodhart advocates a "formal two-tier citizenship," with a "temporary British resident status with fewer rights and duties" and a "more formal, full citizenship" (ibid.: 44). Echoed in the Goldsmith Report (2008), Goodhart's thrust is to draw a thick line between citizenship and all other kinds of status, in lieu of drawing it between citizenship and legal permanent residence *and* all other kinds of status, as is the legal reality in Western countries. The British Labour government under Gordon Brown wisely refused to abolish the permanent residence category, arguing that "it is [not] right to force people to become British citizens should they wish to remain here permanently" (Home Office 2008b: 10). However, it still took significant steps toward redrawing the lines between residence and citizenship, firstly, in excluding temporary residents from all forms of social assistance, and, secondly, in tripling the (relatively) rights-deprived limbo period of "probationary citizenship" for those whose aspiration is merely permanent residence and not the acquisition of citizenship (ibid.: 14).

One wonders: If citizenship in the comfort zone matters more than ever, why this nervous attempt, especially in Europe, to upgrade something the priceless worth of which is beyond doubt? The answer is that the new citizenship talk is to compensate for a significant opening for legal immigration in Europe, highly selective and skill-focused, but deeply unpopular nevertheless. As a result of this opening, the immigration policy watchdog is less available than in the past to permit drift at the citizenship front. Moreover, the function of citizenship talk is to be found less in its illocutionary purpose of integrating newcomers than in its perlocutionary effect of pacifying ill-disposed natives. Witness that the transition to what the current British Labour government dubs "earned citizenship" is nervously in sync with public preferences, distilled as it is from an unprecedented three-month exercise of "consultation" and "listening meetings" with the public (Home Office 2008a, 2008b). The intellectual blacksmith of New Labour's citizenship policy, David Goodhart, does not hide the fact that his proposals are "defensive measures designed to persuade an anxious public that populists do not in fact have the answers and that British citizenship . . . remains valued and protected by mainstream politics" (Goodhart 2006: 55f.).[4] It is no happenstance that the country that prides itself on having become Europe's chief immigration magnet is also the country with the most robust citizenship policy, in its latest projected round even seeking to turn the citizenship tap on or off (dubbed "provid[ing] greater control over the numbers") according to economic or demographic need.[5] Conversely, one might argue that the flower of postnationalism blossomed most strongly in a context of intended zero immigration, when the rhetorical (never factual) denial of territorial access took the drama out of the residence versus citizenship tango.

Almost in passing, David Goodhart concedes a fundamental limit to upgrading or renationalizing citizenship in current times. "The modern nation-state," Goodhart (2006: 17) argues, "is based not on a universal liberalism but on a contractual idea of club membership." If this is the case, citizenship is vitiated by instrumentalism, giving the lie to his principled rhetoric of "progressive nationalism." Along such lines, one economist recently asked whether citizenship was turning into "voluntary club membership," analyzable in terms of the theory of club goods (Straubhaar 2003). Like clubs, states provide goods whose consumption is "non-rivaling" among its members yet from which non-members may still be "excluded." To the degree that, in a world of migration, more and more people choose their state, states become "instrumental associations" (*Zweckgemeinschaften*), like clubs. From this follows, incidentally, a robust admissions policy, according to which the "benefits" for existing members must always exceed the "cost" of accepting new members. Still, extant norms of non-discrimination have to be respected, the two legitimate admissions criteria being a capacity to pay (*Zahlungsfähigkeit*) and a willingness to accept the club rules (*Rechtsbewusstsein*). This mirrors the current emphasis on economic self-sufficiency and civic proceduralism in states' naturalization laws.

However, Thomas Straubhaar (2003: 87) sees one "decisive difference" between states and clubs: "the state can force its citizens to risk their lives for the protection of the community." This echoes Michael Walzer's (1983: 41) observation that states are not like clubs because state membership is involuntary for most, while club membership is always and inherently voluntary. Identity, we suggested earlier, is most strongly invested in the non-chosen aspects of human existence, and states have nonchalantly exploited this fact in the high noon of nationalism.

Only, which state in the West still asks its citizens to "unconditionally subordinate individual interest" to that of the collectivity (Straubhaar 2003: 86)? Even America, where nationalism is stronger than elsewhere in the West, does not ask her native sons to risk their lives on the battlefield – while a good number of poor non-citizen immigrants are doing so every day, in a professional army that provides them with a job and prospects for life. Some thirty years ago, Morris Janowitz noticed a "priority on rights versus obligation in the political process of Western political democracies" (1980: 1), which exposes as empty rhetoric the ritual notion that citizenship rests on a "balance of obligations and rights." As alarmist and fashion-pandering as much of the "decline of citizenship" talk is, an indisputable element of truth is its pointing to a new context of "post-heroic geopolitics," which makes "the role of the patriotic citizen far less crucial to . . . the state" (Falk 2000: 13). Most historical expansions of citizenship rights, especially social rights, such as Britain's Beveridge Plan that promised cradle-to-the-grave welfare benefits for everyone, occurred in the aftermath of war, being compensation for citizens' having put their lives at risk for the collectivity. To the degree that recruitment for battle and participation in war has disappeared as a general citizen obligation in the West, and to the degree that the professional soldier has replaced the citizen soldier, the historical engine of citizenship rights and of strong citizenship identities has irretrievably died – luckily so one should say.[6]

Now that a globalizing economy integrates the West and that the woes of war have become relegated to the Rest, an instrumental attitude to citizenship cannot but grow and grow. If one revisits Rogers Brubaker's classic "ideas and ideals" defining membership in the nation-state (Brubaker 1989a: 3–6), which were "largely vestigial" by the late 1980s, one must conclude that twenty years further on they have become more vestigial still. Of his six "ideas and ideals,"[7] only the norm that membership should be "democratic" still unambiguously holds, as European states in particular have made huge strides toward "providing some means for resident nonmembers to become members" (ibid.: 4). We registered this as the liberalization of the access to citizenship (chapter 2). By contrast, with some exceptions, Western states have largely given up on the idea that state membership should be "unique" (Brubaker 1989a: 4). With the idea of "uniqueness" goes that of the "sacredness" of membership, which had echoed the religious origins of nationalism. It is less citizens than professional soldiers that still "die for [the state] if need be" (ibid.), and this is immediately (and realistically) profaned as "blood for oil." With respect to the idea that membership should be "socially consequential," the post-welfare state has moved toward shifting responsibility from the collectivity to the individual. As this is a trend that has affected citizens and immigrants alike, one can no longer say that the thinning social privileges of membership "define a status clearly and significantly distinguished from that of nonmembers" (ibid.). Finally, the front line of contemporary state campaigns for upgrading citizenship is injecting new life into the notion that state membership should be "based on nation-membership" (ibid.) – that is, a "community of language, mores, or belief" (ibid.). But, as we saw in chapter 4, the collective self that is conveyed in these campaigns has become nationally anonymous, and it is thin and procedural more than thick and cultural.

Instrumentality is even directly inscribed into states' own formal immigration and citizenship rules, which provide access in return for (sizeable amounts of) cash. Widely known are the "investor visas" of Britain, America, and more recently Germany. Much less is known that some countries, including Austria, the latter in curious departure from its usual hard line in this domain, have moved ahead in offering not just immigrant visas but citizenship for cash. For an investment estimated to exceed $2.5 million, one can "buy" Austrian citizenship, without any prior residence, language, or even interview requirement, the paperwork being done by a consultancy that offers to "liaise with the various government agencies and ministries, and then prepare and lodge your application" (in the Austrian case, for the hefty fee of $300,000).[8] An Austrian passport buys its lucky owner visa-free access to 125 countries and territories in the world. Surely, the fact that such schemes usually operate in secret, along with the denial that it is "just a matter of handing money over and getting citizenship,"[9] shows the operation of the norm that citizenship should *not* be instrumental.

However, what goes under the label of "transnational citizenship"[10] is infested to the core by instrumentalism. That is, after all, why states, from Australia to Mexico, have given in to it in terms of accepting dual nationality, which used to be anathema to most of them as recently as ten or fifteen years ago. Rainer Bauböck (2008) wishes to discipline transnational citizenship by means of a "stakeholder" principle. According to this principle, the exercise of full political rights in two or more polities would be limited to those who can prove a "genuine connection" with the respective societies. This would save the essence of citizenship as "equal membership in a self-governing political community" (2008: 7). But politics, while certainly the single most problematic aspect of transnational citizenship, is definitely not the gist of it; economics and personal advancement are. This is why states, on the sending *and* receiving ends, have given in to it. With an eye on East Asia's resourceful diasporas on the North American west coast, Aihwa Ong (1999) has dubbed the new phenomenon "flexible citizenship." It refers "to the strategies and effects of mobile managers, technocrats, and professionals seeking to both circumvent and benefit from different nation-state regimes by selecting different sites for investments, work, and family relocation." It sports such colorful figures as "astronauts," shuttling across borders on business, and "parachute kids," who are "dropped off in another country by parents on the trans-Pacific business commute" (1999: 19). Flexible citizenship is an affront to the classic ideals of nation-state membership, but it is condoned and furthered by these very states as "instrument of flexible accumulation," allowing them "to compete more effectively in the global economy" (ibid.: 130).

European Union Citizenship: A Citizenship of our Time

Instrumental attitudes toward citizenship are indicative of a dissociation of citizenship and nationhood. This key feature of citizenship light is best illustrated by the new European Union citizenship, which is arguably the most innovative and fast-moving citizenship construct in the world today. If one wants to look into the future of citizenship, perhaps it is to be found here. EU citizenship is built entirely around the fact of immigration, or what in Europe is referred to as "free movement." It is Roman to the core, providing rights of free movement within Europe, and giving short shrift to the Greek package of politics, democracy, and duties. It is worth rehashing the Euro-lawyer Joseph Weiler's early diatribe against the "Saatchi and Saatchi European citizenship" (1999: 335): "To conceptualize European citizenship around needs (even needs as important as employment) and rights is an end-of-the-millennium version of bread-and-circus politics." But where in the West (apart from Israel, Weiler's spiritual home) is there more to citizenship than rights and almost no duties, where is it marked by "belongingness and originality," and where does it provide a "shield against existential aloneness" (ibid.: 338)? All these things citizenship may have been when tied up with nationhood. But it is no longer – at the level of European nation-states no less than at European Union level. If the national is "Eros" and the supranational is "civilization" (ibid.: 347), this distinction rests on a romanticized vision of national citizenship, one of "civic responsibility and consequent political attachment" (ibid.: 333), which may exist in the mind of the political theorist but not in the real world.

Certainly, Weiler's (1999) defense of a pluralistic Europe has a long pedigree. From the start, there were two competing visions of Europe, the statist vision of a United States of Europe, analogous to the United States of America, and a supranational vision of an "ever closer union among the peoples of Europe," as expressed in the preamble of the 1957 Treaty of Rome that set up the European Economic Community. Couching the European project in citizenship terms, as happened with the introduction of a EU citizenship in Article 8 of the 1992 Treaty on European Union (Maastricht Treaty), threatened to give victory to the statal unity vision, at the cost of the true supranational potential of a Europe of "multiple demoi," which – as Weiler formulates with an eye on the continent's dark twentieth-century history – "is about affirming the values of the liberal nation-state by policing the boundaries against abuse" (ibid.: 341). However, what Weiler wishes to see at the European level: "citizenship as a hallmark of differentity" (ibid.: 329) and a "decoupling [of] nationality from citizenship" (ibid.: 337), has long been the case at the nation-state level. Establishing such citizenship at the European level can only accelerate a train that has already departed. In sum, there are no statist or nationalist dangers in dubbing Euro-membership "citizenship," because citizenship as "Eros" is chimera at state-level already.

But what *is* European Union citizenship? Originally introduced in 1992, what is now Article 17(1) of the EC Treaty stipulates: "Citizenship of the Union is hereby established. Every person holding the nationality of a Member State shall be a citizen of the Union. Citizenship of the Union shall complement and not replace national citizenship." The last sentence was inserted in the 1997 Amsterdam Treaty, as a defensive measure by member states, when the European Commission had pushed for a residence-based Euro-citizenship that would include third-state nationals (Europe's "immigrants" proper) (Ferrera 2005: 142f.). But this "nay" has no legal meaning, because the peculiarity of EU if compared with state

Citizenship Light

citizenship is set in stone by the preceding sentence: EU citizenship is not grounded in an own EU nationality law but is secondary to holding the citizenship of a member state. This is not unusual in the history of federal citizenships. Before the 1868 Fourteenth Amendment to the US Constitution, and before the 1913 Imperial Citizenship Law, the American and German citizenships, respectively, were derived from subfederal state memberships. By the same token, the derivative quality of EU citizenship is unlikely to be stable, in particular if one considers the "vital connecting function which nationality plays in Community law" (O'Leary 1993: 66) and the notorious tendency of the European Court of Justice to arrogate to itself the definition of such terms.

In this respect mirroring contemporary state citizenships, EU citizenship is essentially about rights – there is a token reference in Article 17(2) of the EC Treaty that EU citizens "shall be subject to the duties imposed [by this Treaty]," only no duties worth the name can be found in the entire text (not even the duty to pay taxes, which anyway could never be an exclusive citizen duty). Instead, suitably figuring ahead of political rights at local and European (notably, not national) levels that in reality no one cares about (in Article 19),[11] the primary Euro-citizen right is the fabled right of free movement, stipulated in Article 18(1): "Every citizen of the Union shall have the right to move and reside freely within the territory of the Member States, subject to the limitations and conditions laid down in this Treaty and by the measures adopted to give it effect."

Because the right of free movement is one of the four classic Euro-freedoms[12] dating back to the EC's first hour as a "common market," Joseph Weiler (1996) had originally dismissed its elevation into *citizen* right as "a cynical exercise in public relations." No new rights were added to already existing rights. There was ground for skepticism, as the "limitations and conditions" proviso in Article 18(1) seemingly folded back "citizens" into "workers" or other economic agents, whose moves (and no one else's!) were regulated and encouraged by the EC Treaty. "Europe," after all, is at heart a functional regime to coordinate the economies of member states, not a territorial state, and as such it is peopled by "factors of production" (Weiler 1996), not citizens. Hence the original polemic against EU citizenship as merely a "market citizenship" (Everson 1995). Even a most recent, last-nail-in-the-coffin attack on the "poverty of postnationalism" reiterates the known line that EU citizen status is a "derivative status that creates no new rights" (Hansen 2009: 6).

This is no longer true. European citizenship is postnational citizenship in its most elaborate form, belatedly vindicating Yasemin Soysal's earlier claim in this respect (1994: 148). What the past critics of an underwhelming EU citizenship could not know, and what current critics overlook, is the activism by the European Court of Justice, which has transformed EU citizenship from derivative status into a free-standing source of rights. Worthy to be labeled "postnational" if there ever was justification of the term, EU citizenship in its presently expansive form is entirely the product of court rules, with only the thinnest relationship to an identity that might warrant the extensive rights that now accrue to Euro-citizens.

In a string of bold and controversial decisions between 1998 and 2004,[13] the European Court of Justice (ECJ) established two fundamental novelties that member states could not have fathomed when launching their window-dressing EU citizenship in 1992: firstly, that there is a right to free movement and residence inherent in EU citizenship, regardless of previous EU law that required a variant of economic activity as a triggering factor; secondly, that there are, next to formal rights of free movement and residence, substantive social rights that accrue to EU citizens qua citizens, outside prior economic status categories.

The battle cry in this stunning rights expansion has been the ECJ diction, given out in its September 2001 landmark judgment on *Grzelczyk*, that "Union citizenship is destined to be the fundamental status of nationals of the Member States."[14] This is either a misnomer or a glimpse into the future, as EU law even in its presently expansive form does not apply to purely internal situations of member states but only to situations where a cross-border component is involved. However, as this limitation entails "reverse discrimination" against domestic citizens, who, for instance, now perversely have lesser family unification rights under national law than border-hopping EU citizens may enjoy in the same country under European law, it is unlikely to be stable. Unless, of course, the ECJ shifts to a lower gear – but this has not been its usual way of operating.

If one reads the ECJ rules on EU citizenship from *Martinez Sala* (1998),[15] which was the first to base equal access to a member-state social benefit on EU citizenship status, to *Trojani* (2004),[16] which effectively allows EU citizens to bootstrap their right of residence by tapping the social-assistance schemes of their host states, one can almost hear the cry of pain of member states, "But we never meant it this way." As one of the few Euro-lawyers sympathizing with the lot of member states points out, the European Court of Justice has raided the worker versus non-worker distinction that secondary Community law, in terms of directives and regulations, continues to uphold (Hailbronner 2005). Indeed, among the "limitations" and "conditions" of longer-term cross-border movement and residence by *non*-economic actors is their possession of "sufficient resources" and of "sickness insurance." This is to avoid benefit tourism and free movers' becoming an "unreasonable burden" on the welfare systems of host states.[17] ECJ case law has blithely ignored, and thereby effectively destroyed, these restrictions. In *Trojani* (2004), the court peculiarly endorsed a bootstrapping strategy on the part of EU citizens that is not unlike the benefit tourism outlawed by secondary Community law. The court argued in this case that, of course, there was no right of residence for non-workers who lack "sufficient resources." However, as long as a person was lawfully present in a host member state on some other basis (in this case, Belgian national law), he or she was still entitled to access non-contributory social assistance on the same conditions as nationals. And recourse to social assistance could "not automatically" lead to the revocation of a residence permit.[18] Held to observe the principle of "proportionality," member states must not equate "recourse to the social assistance system" with the "lack of sufficient resources" that may trigger expulsion. In other words, by having equal access to social assistance, a Euro-citizen can buy him- or herself out of the "lack of sufficient resources" proviso, so that it is effectively void as an obstacle to benefit tourism. "This seems to be logical," finds a Euro-lawyer (Verschueren 2007: 326). The non-initiated is more inclined to call it twisted reasoning, beloved to lawyers, and the stuff out of which European citizenship is made.

The activism by the European Court of Justice has made EU citizenship "socially consequential" of sorts (Brubaker 1989a: 4), but only to the diminishing degree that the national citizenships still exhibit this quality. In fact, such Europeanization must undermine "strong national rights of social and industrial citizenship," without the compensatory rise of strong "supranational rights" in a Europe that remains socially vacuous (Streeck 1997; see also Scharpf 1999). Because, in the absence of strong solidarities at European level, the enthusiasm of nation-states to provide tax-based social benefits from which the rest of Europe cannot be excluded, and that may even be consumable anywhere in Europe, must cool down. Accordingly, when European Union law threatened to make "exportable," and thus usable by return migrants anywhere in Europe, a planned supplementary pension scheme (the so-called *Fink Modell*) that was meant to assist elderly people in coping with the high living costs in Germany, the German government abandoned the idea, which previously had been supported across the political spectrum (see Conant 2004: 306).

The main conflict stake in the social expansion of EU citizenship was a new type of non-contributory "mixed" benefit, which straddles the boundary between social insurance and social assistance, and whose purpose is to "establish a safety net of last resort for the whole citizenry" (Ferrera 2005: 131; see also van der Mei 2002: 552f.). An example is a guaranteed minimum income for the poor elderly, the long-term unemployed, the disabled, and other vulnerable categories. The creation of such schemes, need-based, tax-paid and thus an expression of a "'we-ness' that typically bind[s] the members of a national community – and them only" (Ferrera 2005: 133), was the gist of welfare-state development during its Golden Age in the 1960s and 1970s. No doubt states had intended them for their citizenry only. Article 4 of Regulation 1408 of 1971, which coordinated the social security schemes of

Europe for its "migrant workers," excluded from the ambit of the regulation "social assistance," as which one might think the new welfare policies should be classified.[19] However, the regulation fails to provide a clear definition of either social assistance or social insurance. So it fell to the European Court of Justice to fill the gap, and the court defined the entire mixed benefit schemes emerging since the 1960s, to the consternation of member states, as "social insurance" rather than "social assistance," and thus subject to inclusion in Regulation 1408.

The landmark case is *Frilli* (1972), in which the ECJ defined a supplementary pension benefit, which Belgian law had reserved to Belgian nationals, as "social security," and thus accessible to other Europeans too, on the formal grounds that it "does not prescribe consideration of each individual case, which is a characteristic of assistance, and confers on recipients a legally-defined position giving them the right to a benefit."[20] In sum, to the degree that the new "mixed type" benefits were not charity but right, for which there was no discretion on the part of the granting state, they qualified as "social security" and all Europeans had to be included. In a next step, the ECJ ruled a similar pension supplement in France exportable, with the curious result that "French taxpayers were de facto subsidizing some poor elderly people in Italy's Mezzogiorno" (Ferrera 2005: 134). Making such benefit exportable renders the policy *ad absurdum*, because the purpose of mixed type policies is to guarantee a minimum subsistence level that is determined by the cost of living in *this*, the host state, which is likely to be higher than the living costs in the less developed states or regions into which the benefit is carried.

No wonder that European member states responded to the ECJ's creativity on the social rights front by way of "evasion, overrule, and preemption" (Conant 2004: 317). Interestingly, as nationality-based restrictions of the mixed welfare measures became unsupportable under European law, the only defense left for member states was "control over residence" (Ferrera 2005: 135). This was accomplished in Council Regulation 1247/92 of 30 April 1992, which stipulated that "special non-contributory benefits," as explicitly listed for each country in an annex to the 1971 social-security regulation, had to be granted only in the territory of residence, and only if strict legal residency requirements were fulfilled (on the complexities of establishing residence, see van der Mei 2002: 564–6).

This is precisely where the European Court of Justice's recent inventiveness on European Union citizenship kicked in. As a result, states were no longer protected from an all-European claimants' onslaught on their welfare systems by limiting its possible range to (however expansively defined) "workers." In *Grzelczyk*, the Belgian authority denying a "minimex" minimum subsistence allowance to a French student deemed itself protected by the fact that he was not a "worker," and thus subject to the "sufficient resource" proviso that could impossibly be circumvented by tapping the host state's social coffers.[21] The Belgian and Danish governments submitting opinions in this case reiterated the orthodox line that citizenship of the Union had "no autonomous content," [22] apart from the rights deriving from the EC Treaty and secondary legislation, and the latter clearly upheld the worker versus non-worker distinction. And the French government warned that granting the minimex to a foreign student would "amount to establishing total equality between citizens of the Union established in a Member State and nationals of that State, which would be difficult to reconcile with rights attaching to nationality."[23] This "total equality" is exactly what the ECJ's *Grzelczyk* decision accomplished, in declaring that "Union citizenship is destined to be the fundamental status of nationals of the Member States, enabling those who find themselves in the same situation to enjoy the same treatment in law irrespective of their nationality."[24]

As the ECJ haughtily decreed in *Grzelczyk*, member states had to accept "a certain degree of financial solidarity between nationals of a host Member State and nationals of other Member States," particularly if the difficulties of a Euro-citizen were only, as in this case, "temporary."[25] This astonishing stipulation of a European we-feeling glosses over the fact that there is a fundamental "tension" between freedom of movement and the "principle of solidarity" (Giubboni 2007). In the demonstrable absence of a genuine Euro-solidarity on the part of governments and their citizens, the "financial solidarity" that is exacted on host states and their tax-paying citizens is not freestanding but parasitic upon the national solidarities that it relies upon but does nothing to replenish.

If the logic of Europe is to move from a nationality- to a residence-based sense of community and citizenship, one would think that "immigrants" proper ("third-country nationals" in Euro-jargon) fare well in this. Contrary to the standard pronouncements in the activist world and by most academics, immigrants have indeed done very well in Europe. This is because it is inherently difficult to justify a distinction between two types of internal free movers, one with and another without a European passport (but with legal permanent residence). There is a stinging sense that both types of free mover should be treated equally. As common as this view is, it is a truly radical view, because it erases the citizen–immigrant distinction. While it may be fed by certain "postnational" developments at member state level, above all it shows the power of the de-nationalizing logic of European Union. Equality between both types of mover would be achieved if EU citizenship were redefined "as based on residence and not on nationality" (Besson and Utzinger 2007: 581). While this does correspond to the logic of EU citizenship, it certainly is not at present politically realistic.

Short of this ideal scenario, however, significant progress in binding immigrants into Europe has been made. Those immigrants covered by an association agreement between the EU and their origin country, as a result of European Court of Justice rulings, enjoy "explicit European legal rights" that in many respects approximate, sometimes even perversely exceed, those of member state nationals (Conant 2004: 315). Incidentally, the number of non-EU immigrants protected by an EU association agreement (2.3 million Turks; 1 million Moroccans; 600,000 Algerians; and 250,000 Tunisians) almost matches the number of EU free movers, which stands at 4.9 million.[26] A second immigrant group that has achieved near equality with EU citizens are the family members of EU citizens, who enjoy "quasi-citizenship rights" (Besson and Utzinger 2007: 580). And, considering that the 1971 Council Regulation on social security was extended to third-country nationals in 2003, one must conclude that "[i]n the employment and welfare areas . . . third country nationals now enjoy virtually the same rights and obligations as nationals" (Ferrera 2005: 144).

Of course, the one exception to the near equality of non-EU immigrants with EU citizens is free movement rights, which accrue to EU citizens unconditionally, but to third-country nationals only after five years of legal residence, and then with further strings attached. In this respect, the promise of the 1999 Tampere European Council, which was to grant third-country nationals "rights and obligations comparable to those of EU citizens," has not quite been fulfilled.[27] After the effusive prospect of an EU citizenship based on residence had to be shelved, the emphasis by immigrant advocates indeed shifted toward "approximat[ing]" the legal status of immigrants to that of EU nationals.[28] The démarche of the European Commission and of the advocacy groups aligned with it became the creation of a "civic citizenship" for immigrants, attributed by virtue of residence rather than nationality.

Judged by the major fruit of the "civic citizenship" campaign, which is the 2003 Long-Term Residents Directive,[29] the rights of immigrants trail those of EU citizens in two respects. Firstly, in line with state-level immigrant rights, the EU-level immigrant rights are highly fragmented and stratified, with students, asylum-seekers, refugees, and temporary workers all excluded from the ambit of the directive.[30] Secondly, even the status of the most privileged immigrant group, long-term legal labor migrants, remains subject to the logic of "market citizenship" (Everson 1995). Article 5 of the Long-Term Residents Directive requires "stable and regular resources" and "sickness insurance" as preconditions for long-term resident status. No such conditions are imposed on EU citizens for acquiring permanent resident status. As Mark Bell (2007: 329) astutely observed, "whilst Union citizenship is transiting away from the market citizenship model, this is being reconstructed in respect of third country nationals." A further obstacle not known to EU citizens is making third-country nationals "comply with integration conditions, in accordance with national law,"[31] which enshrines at EU level the civic integration policies toward immigrants now practiced in more and more countries of Europe.

The fact of persistent formal inequality between immigrants and citizens in the European Union is unsurprising – as long as there is an immigration policy at whatever level, national or European, it could not be otherwise. What *is* surprising is the couching of the campaign for immigrant rights in the language of citizenship, and this not by an activist fringe but by the official core of Europe. This shows that European citizenship is "conceptually decoupled from nationality and as a matter of fact from any form of European nationalism" (Besson and Utzinger 2007: 576). Whatever there is in terms of a European identity, it is thin and procedural, epitomized by the so-called Copenhagen Criteria that exclude no state from membership as long as it is a market economy, democratic, and respectful of the rule of law, human rights, and the *acquis communautaire*.[32] As an imaginative lawyer foresees (Davies 2005: 53), in shifting the focus of rights and belonging from nationality to residence, "Europe does not just require the absorption of foreigners, but also the rejection of expatriates." This truly postnational moment, in which citizenship would lapse with one's residence, has not yet been reached, and perhaps it never will arrive. But there *is* the prospect of a "community... defined by its current members more than its history,... constantly reinventing itself and changing, belonging to those who participate, not those selected at birth" (ibid.: 56). This is, indeed, a "model that looks rather American" (ibid.: 55). It is the prospect that European citizenship holds – a blessing for cosmopolitans, but a curse for whom citizenship should not be light but home.

European citizenship used to be ridiculed as a misnomer, but the more interesting way of perceiving it is as the future of the real thing. Constructed at the turn of the new millennium, it is a citizenship of our time, entirely free of the baggage of nationhood and nationalism that, however phantom-like, ensnares the citizenships of old. States deem themselves in control because access to European citizenship is still through holding a national citizenship. But this is deceptive. In reality, the court-driven empowerment of European citizenship casts a long shadow over contemporary state campaigns to upgrade the worth of national citizenship. If the British state seeks to attach more rights to the status of citizenship and in parallel to lessen the attractions of the legal permanent residence alternative, this is entirely futile: European Union law commands the inclusion of all EU foreigners and of long-settled immigrants into any upgraded national citizen privileges. In fact, looking back from the European plane at current attempts to renationalize citizenship, these state campaigns are revealed as just smoke and mirrors – a "symbolic politics" if ever there was one. The future of citizenship is bound to be light, and lighter still with the help of "Europe."[33]

Notes

Chapter 1 The Concept of Citizenship

1. For instance, Dieter Gosewinkel (2001: 1852): "Citizenship means membership in a political community"; or Linda Bosniak (2006: 20): "[T]he domain of citizenship . . . is broadly *political* in nature."
2. Needless to say, there are other possibilities, which cross-cut the normative–factual distinction. See, for instance, Poggi (1978: ch. 1), who distinguishes between politics as internal allocation and politics as external boundary-setting.
3. It would be wrong, though, to characterize Schmitt as a modern-day Hobbes. Schmitt differs from Hobbes in his "virulent anti-individualism" and in his "bellicist" celebration of violence (which Hobbes gives in to as inevitable human vice) (see Holmes 1993: 42).
4. But note that what the "paramount" association is may be historically and biographically variable. From the point of view of Marxist class struggle, the paramount association would be the international working class; from the point of view of contemporary Islamism, it is the global community of believers, the "umma," etc.
5. See Carl Schmitt's famous definition that "sovereign is he who decides on the exception" ([1922] 1985: 5).
6. This is the very un-Schmittian formulation of the same "states-provide-security" nexus by Charles Tilly (1985).
7. Samuel Finer (1997: 367) pointed to the fact that, at the height of its glory, between ca. 480 and 340 BC, ancient Athens was "at war for two years out of every three." Finer also draws a distinctly less comforting picture of classic Greek culture than one can find in Arendt, as "suffused by three very un-civic vices: cupidity, competitiveness, and covetousness" (ibid.: 326).
8. See also Margaret Somers's observation of a "contractualization of citizenship," which she describes as a move "from noncontractual rights and obligations to the principles and practices of quid pro quo market exchange" (Somers 2009: 2).

9 The best contemporary work in this tradition is Koopmans et al. (2005).
10 Especially pertinent in this respect is the distinction by Friedrich Meinecke (a German early twentieth-century historian) between the German *Kulturnation* and the French *Staatsnation*.
11 Further rebuttals of the civic versus ethnic distinction can be found in Joppke (2005: ch. 1) and Shachar (2009: ch. 4).
12 If only until 1997, when a newly elected socialist prime minister reinstituted the status quo ante (with minor modifications).
13 Very similar in this respect is Jacobson (1996).
14 US Supreme Court Justice Blackmun, in his opinion in the famous Bakke case, characterized the logic of affirmative action, the strongest antidiscrimination policy, in these terms: "In order to get beyond racism, we must first take account of race" (438 US 265[*1978*]).
15 For a more detailed critique of "multicultural citizenship," see Joppke (2001a).
16 For instance, Bauböck (2006a) and Shachar (2009). Bloemraad (2000), Bosniak (2006: 20) and Bloemraad, Korteweg and Yurdakul (2008) add a fourth dimension of "political engagement" or "participation," which is otherwise subsumed under "identity." As all these typologies (including the one proposed here) are inductive and ad hoc, their usefulness has to be judged by the result. For a justification of excluding "political participation" as the fourth dimension of citizenship, see the first pages of chapter 5.
17 This is an important qualification. No claim is made, say, that ordinary French do not identify Frenchness with Catholicism. Only the state, constrained by liberal neutrality and non-discrimination norms, must not.

Chapter 2 Status

1 Figures from the late 1990s show that only about 2 percent of the world's population acquires citizenship other than by birthright, through naturalization (Shachar 2003: 359).
2 The apotheosis of voluntarism in marriage is its foundation in romantic love, which is specific to the West (see Luhmann 1982b).
3 This phrase is attributed to the sixteen-year-old Louis XIV, when addressing a recalcitrant Parlement de Paris, not willing to pay for his military campaign against Spain, on 13 April 1655.
4 Since 1790, only "free white persons" had been allowed to naturalize. This racial restriction was lifted for blacks in 1870 and for Asians in 1952.
5 The citizenship clause of the Fourteenth Amendment, which enshrines *jus soli* citizenship, reads: "All persons born or naturalized in the U.S., and subject to the jurisdiction thereof, are citizens of the United States and of the State wherein they reside."
6 In its Dred Scott decision of 1857, the US Supreme Court had ruled that free blacks were not American citizens.

7 In addition, American lawmakers pointed to the negative experience of Europe, where the offspring of "guest workers" were lastingly excluded from receiving states' citizenship by *jus sanguinis*-centered citizenship laws (see Joppke 2000: 150).
8 Alfonso Aguilar, chief of the Office of Citizenship at the US Citizenship and Immigration Service (USCIS), quoted by Lauren Monsen, "Revised US Naturalization Test to Focus on Civic Values, History" (US Department of State), 7 December 2005, at www.america.gov (last accessed 25 July 2008).
9 Note, however, that, starting around 1995, the propensity to naturalize in the United States has notably increased, to 52 percent of all legal foreign-born residents in 2005. During the same period, the number of naturalized citizens from Mexico has risen by 144 percent. Passell (2007: 22) lists several factors likely to be responsible for this: Mexico's recent toleration of dual citizenship; the increase in immigrants from the Middle East, who are the "most likely" to naturalize; the sustained good economy that thwarted the intention to return; and, last but not least, the tying of federal welfare benefits to citizenship (note that in 1996, the year of this welfare reform, new naturalizations reached an all-time peak of 1 million; after several of the welfare restrictions were successively taken back, the number declined to 600,000 to 700,000 annually).
10 The main difference is that naturalization is available in Canada after three years of legal residence, whereas in the US the required minimum period is five years.
11 See Janoski (2006: 2). However, Janoski includes *jus soli* births ("being born of foreign parents on national soil"; ibid.: 15) in his calculation of "naturalization rates," which is rather unconventional. However, for underscoring the greater inclusiveness of North American citizenship regimes, if compared with the European ones, these data are still useful.
12 To quote the key passage from Nottebohm: "[N]ationality is a legal bond having as its basis a social fact of attachment, a genuine connection of existence, interests and sentiments, together with the existence of reciprocal rights and duties" (*Liechtenstein v. Guatemala*, International Court of Justice, 6 April 1955; 1955 ICJ 4).
13 Sweden holds a special status in Brubaker's analysis (1989b: 110), because its approach to naturalization was formally "discretionary" yet substantively, in terms of its low threshold and inclusiveness, "as of right".
14 Note that the 2003 EU Directive on the Status of Third-Country Nationals Who Are Long-Term Residents grants free movement rights in Europe (and thus a de facto European Union citizenship) after five years of legal residence in a member state. While, of course, by far not a reality everywhere, there is an emergent sense in Europe that five years' legal residence time as prerequisite for naturalization is "best practice." This also corresponds

to the recommendation of the Carnegie Comparative Citizenship Project (Aleinikoff and Klusmeyer 2002: 21).

15 In June 2008, the Conseil d'Etat affirmed the refusal to grant citizenship to a Muslim woman who had insisted on wearing a burka during her naturalization interviews. This insistence was deemed "a radical practice of her religion, incompatible with the essential values of the French national community, and notably the principle of the equality of sexes" (Conseil d'Etat, decision no. 286798, 27 June 2008). See my brief discussion of this case in chapter 4 and, for more detail, Orgad (2010).

16 Until 2002, Australia, for instance, allowed its naturalizing immigrants to keep their nationality of origin, but it stripped their emigrants naturalizing abroad of their Australian citizenship.

17 On the distinction between segmentary and functional differentiation, see Luhmann (1982a).

18 Even skeptical minds (most notably Martin 2005; Hansen and Weil 2002) see the benefits of dual citizenship (such as trade, investment, and knowledge transfer) greatly outweighing its costs.

19 In Germany, 44.6 percent of naturalizing immigrants in 2000 kept their citizenship of origin (see Howard 2009: ch. 6). In the Netherlands, which makes even wider exceptions, the de facto acceptance of dual nationality touches 80 percent (see Faist et al. 2007: 927).

20 See especially Hansen and Weil (2001); also, though with an eye on restrictive possibilities, Howard (2006).

21 In 1984, the conservative–liberal (CDU–FDP) coalition government recognized that "no state can lastingly tolerate that a numerically significant part of the population remains outside the political community for generations" (quoted in Hailbronner and Renner 2001: 140). But, while flirting with the idea of a temporary *Kinderstaatszugehörigkeit*, which prefigured the conditional *jus soli* citizenship eventually introduced under an SPD–Green coalition government in 1998, a conservative-led government did not dare to realize it.

22 I discuss this further in chapter 4.

23 There had already been fallout from a tightened immigrant integration policy on citizenship law in the new *Zuwanderungsgesetz* of July 2004, which requires one parent to have a "settlement permit" for *jus soli* citizenship to be granted to his or her child. This settlement permit in turn demands a high level of language proficiency and the taking of civic integration courses (see Hailbronner 2006: 225f.).

24 For Austria and Denmark, see the respective country chapters in Bauböck et al. (2006: vol. 2). See also the brief synopsis in Joppke (2008a: 140–3).

25 The British government announced in 2005 that it would "bring the criteria for settlement nearer to those of citizenship," among other means, by "requiring people *to pass English language/knowledge of the UK tests* before

they are granted permanent settlement rights" (Home Office 2005a: 22, emphasis added). This has been law since April 2007.
26 Edward Rothstein, "Refining the Tests that Confer Citizenship," *New York Times*, 23 January 2006.
27 Lord Filkin, quoted in Crick Commission (2003: 20).
28 At least, in the February 2008 Green Paper, the government was still "consulting on this issue" (Home Office 2008a: 30). To make active citizenship a requirement was eventually rejected (Home Office 2008b: 18). The astonishing matter is not the rejection but the consideration of such an illiberal measure.
29 Such a clause, which is contingent on not making the affected person stateless, was introduced in the Nationality, Immigration and Asylum Act of 2002 (see Dummett 2006: 575). Similar counter-terrorism measures were introduced in many other European states' nationality laws after 11 September 2001.
30 Not incidentally, because the Canadian philosopher Will Kymlicka has advised the British government on the reshaping of its citizenship policy.
31 De Groot (2003: 244) even found it "doubtful" whether the Dutch rule of automatic loss of citizenship after ten years abroad conformed to the 1997 European Convention on Nationality.
32 Mario de Queiroz, "Nationality Extended to Second- and Third-Generation Immigrants," *Inter Press Service News Agency*, 16 February 2006, http://ipsnews.net/news.asp?idnews=32189.
33 Gretchen Lang, "When Roots Translate into a 2d Passport," *International Herald Tribune*, 30 September 2006, p. 19.
34 Article 42 of the Spanish Constitution reads: "[T]he State shall protect the social and economic rights of Spanish workers abroad, and enact a policy to facilitate their return" (quoted in Rubio-Marin 2006: 488).
35 See Sammy Smooha's (2008) comment on the paper (Joppke 2008a) on which I built in this chapter's section on "new restrictions." While disagreeing with many features of my analysis, he concedes that, if compared with Israel, European nationality laws have remained within a "liberal tradition" (Smooha 2008: 11).
36 In early August 2006, the Italian cabinet under Romano Prodi approved a citizenship bill, developed in the interior ministry under Giuliano Amato, which would have reduced the residence time required for naturalization from ten to five years and granted conditional *jus soli* citizenship to the children of immigrants. Like so many things, this noble proposal disappeared in the Byzantine halls of Italian politics.
37 Such pressure, of course, is felt by leftist governments, too, as in the aborted plea for dual citizenship in Germany in 1998 (see above); and the failure of leftist governments in Italy to realize immigrant-friendly citizenship reform proposals in 2000 and in 2006 may be equally attributable to the strong

presence of a right-wing populist party (the Lega Nord) and an accordingly high degree of politicization of immigration-related issues.

38 One year after its introduction in November 2005, one-third of those taking the new citizenship test in Britain had failed it (*Sunday Telegraph*, 15 October 2006, p. 10).

Chapter 3 Rights

1 "Generalized social trust" is defined as "the belief that others will not deliberately or knowingly do us harm, if they can avoid it, and will look after our interests, if this is possible" (Delhey and Newton 2005: 311).
2 Delhey and Newton add that this finding places doubt on the widely used distinction between "generalized" (anonymous) and "particularized" (personal) trust, because the former is "not . . . easily extended to all others in general" but is limited to co-ethnics (2005: 324).
3 Though see Natalia Letki's (2008) important study of Britain, which suggests that poverty is a better predictor than diversity of low levels of trust.
4 A compelling, minimalist case why local diversity may harm economic solidarity, which eschews questionable theorems of nepotistic kin selection, is made by van Parijs (2003). He argues that the skewed communication that results from linguistic, religious, or geographical differences and distances "makes mutual identification, the emergence of a 'we-feeling' less spontaneous, and hence also the trust in reciprocation: the belief that others will not free ride and would do their share too if roles were reversed" (2003: 377).
5 As multiculturalism policies seek to acknowledge and further diversity, they may be looked at as a heightened, reflexive form of diversity. If there is no negative impact of such policies on support for the welfare state, one may conclude that diversity itself also does not have such impact.
6 However, Alesina and Glaeser (2004: 10) immediately distance themselves from any primordial implication of such an argument, maintaining instead that ethnocentric attitudes "are not innate" but are stirred up by right-wing politicians playing the race card. This standard constructivist démarche begs the question why the race card was so easily at hand in the US, but (initially at least) not in Europe. A good critique of Alesina and Glaeser's implicit conspiracy theory is Saunders (2005).
7 About 60 percent of Europeans perceive of the poor as "trapped" in poverty, whereas 60 percent of Americans attribute poverty to "laziness" (Alesina and Glaeser 2004: 184).
8 US Supreme Court, *Graham v. Richardson*, 403 US 365, 14 June 1971; at 371.
9 For an interesting discussion of aliens' stratification by entry category, which he conceives of as part of contemporary "super-diversity," see Vertovec (2007: 1036–40).
10 As reported in Davy (2001), on whose stellar account I mostly rely here and

in the following. The EU Directive on the Status of Long-Term Resident Third-Country Nationals of November 2003 (Council Directive 2003/109/EC) introduced a five-year maximum for proceeding from temporary to permanent resident status. This cut both ways, as Germany had to liberalize its rules, while Britain was free to increase the minimum time from four to five years – which it promptly did.

11 Until the new German immigration law of 2004, which introduced a "one-stop shop procedure" recommended by the European Commission, residence and work permits were issued separately. Work permits were further differentiated between a limited *Arbeitserlaubnis* (tied to a specific employer, region, type of work, or time) and the general *Arbeitsberechtigung* (with no strings attached).

12 This means "primacy of domestic people," which includes national citizens, EU citizens, and permanent legal immigrants.

13 For the tension between the "equal protection" and "preemption" principles as grounds for striking down the state-level welfare restrictions in *Graham*, see Joppke (2001c: 42).

14 See chapter 5.

15 Lord Goldsmith (2008: 12) refers to apparent attempts by the British government to release also permanent residents in Britain from the US detention center at Guantánamo Bay.

16 This notion was codified in the 2006 Military Commissions Act, which subjects aliens suspected as terrorists to special military courts.

17 Julia Eckert draws an interesting parallel between the law for enemies and the "culture of control" that sociologist David Garland (2001) had diagnosed with respect to a criminal law that de-socializes crime and in lieu of rehabilitation and reform opts for "retribution, incapacitation and the management of risk" (quoted in Eckert 2008: 21).

18 Struck down by the Supreme Court in June 2006 also for its capricious limitation to aliens, the Military Order (MA) was resurrected by Congress in terms of the 2006 Military Commissions Act, which upheld MA's citizen–alien distinction (see Katyal 2007: 1366f.).

19 By contrast, President Bush failed in Congress to pass Patriot II, which would have extended the Patriot Act's anti-terrorism provisions from aliens to citizens (see Paye 2005).

20 Lord Hoffmann, in House of Lords, *A and others v. Secretary of State for the Home Department; X and another v. Secretary of State for the Home Department* (2004), UKHL 56, (2005) 2 AC 68, (2005) 3 ALL ER 164, 16 December 2004.

21 Ibid., at par. 33.

22 Ibid., at par. 48.

23 Frances Gibb and Richard Ford, "Terror Laws in Tatters," *The Times*, 17 December 2004, p. 1.

24 It should be mentioned here that the outcome in the United States has been the opposite: in its 12 June 2008 decision *Boumediene v. Bush*, the Supreme Court restored habeas corpus rights for alien terror suspects detained in Guantánamo Bay and declared unconstitutional the 2006 Military Commissions Act on which the stripping of habeas corpus for "alien unlawful enemy combatants" had been based.

25 As does Waters (1990: 157), who refers to them instead as "ethnic groups." Waters's distinction between racial and ethnic groups, the former being positively self-defined and the latter negatively other-defined, echoes Max Weber's famous discussion in *Wirtschaft und Gesellschaft* on "ethnic relations" (*ethnische Gemeinschaftsbeziehungen*) (Weber [1921] 1976: 234–44, especially 234).

26 Article 27 of the 1966 International Covenant on Civil and Political Rights.

27 Article 1 of the 1992 Declaration on the Rights of Persons Belonging to National or Ethnic, Religious and Linguistic Minorities states: "States shall protect the existence and the national or ethnic, cultural, religious and linguistic identity of minorities within their respective territories and shall encourage conditions for the promotion of that identity."

28 For another influential radical variant, which is inspired not by anti-colonialism but by feminism, see Young (1990).

29 One of the few rights with a cultural inflection, which is available to immigrant minorities but not to members of the majority group, is the so-called cultural defense in criminal law, which reduces the culpability of offenders who are deemed conditioned by their origin cultures (see Dundes Renteln 2005).

30 I borrow the useful distinction between "expressive" and "access" racism from Bleich (2003: 9–12).

31 Quoted from Article 1 of Title VII of the 1964 Civil Rights Act, which targets "unlawful employment practices."

32 Still best on the distinction between equality of opportunity and equality of results is Daniel Bell (1973: 408–55).

33 See also John Skrentny (1996: 111–45), who similarly grounded the rise of affirmative action in "administrative pragmatism."

34 US Supreme Court, *Griggs v. Duke Power Co.* (1971), 401 US 424, 91 S.Ct. 849; at 431.

35 Ibid., at 430.

36 The words "indirect discrimination" do not appear in *Griggs*.

37 US Supreme Court, *Regents of the University of California v. Bakke* (1978), 438 US 265, 98 S.Ct 2733.

38 Ibid., at 295.

39 Ibid., at 292.

40 Ibid., at 311 and 313, respectively.

41 Ibid., at 297.

42 See Waters and Vang (2007: 433), who cite evidence that by means of affirmative action minorities have made "remarkable strides in education, particularly post-secondary education."
43 Especially France, which earlier had used penal law to combat "expressive" racism (see Bleich 2003: chs 5 and 6). Why France would strongly support a measure foreign to its legal tradition is persuasively told by Guiraudon (2004).
44 Council Directive 2000/43/EC of 29 June 2000, implementing the principle of equal treatment between persons irrespective of racial or ethnic origin (*Official Journal of the European Communities*, 19 July 2000, pp. 22–6).
45 Ibid., p. 25.
46 Ibid., Article 2.2(b).
47 Ibid., Article 5.
48 Ibid., "whereas" no. 17, p. 23.
49 Cécilia Gabizon, "La France dit non au fichage ethnique," *Le Figaro*, 9 December 2008, p. 2.
50 Sarkozy, quoted ibid.
51 I have discussed these developments in Joppke (2001a, 2004, 2007a, 2007b).

Chapter 4 Identity

1 This chapter profited from a close reading and helpful suggestions by Liav Orgad.
2 In some places, "reasonable" is a qualification of the "doctrines" that people hold, in others a qualification of the people themselves (e.g. Rawls 1997: 805).
3 An excellent account of the evolution of this concept is Müller (2006).
4 Though the price for this, as Abizadeh (2004) showed, is the civic nationalists' lapse into ethnic reasoning, thus blunting the ethnicity versus culture distinction that is dear to them for normative-political reasons.
5 Oral statement by Bernhard Giesen, Holberg Workshop in Honor of Shmuel Eisenstadt, 10–11 June 2007, Hebrew University, Jerusalem.
6 As Akos Kopper (2008) showed in an impressive work, this is not a mere coincidence. The "two sovereignties," that of states and that of autonomous individuals, have always been the dual pillars of modern political life. Both are in tension with each other, states trumping individuals in the age of Westphalia, and – perhaps and somewhat hopefully – the individual trumping the state in a new age of "cosmopolitan sovereignty."
7 This is proved by the negative case of a non-axial country: Japan. Japan's particular aversion to immigration may be explained by its nationalism without universalism, which entails the "impossibility of becoming Japanese by conversion" (Eisenstadt 1999: 157).

8 Simmel (1971) does not use the word "identity"; instead, he speaks of "individuality." In my view both terms can be used interchangeably.
9 See also Charles Taylor (1989: 14), who relates modern identity to autonomy and a positive revaluation of the world of work and everyday life (which is of Christian origins).
10 See only the classic work by George Herbert Mead (1934), which showed that a sense of self requires taking the position of the "generalized other."
11 Following Jon Elster (1983: ch. 2), one could even argue more generally that, like sleep, happiness, or love, identity belongs to a class of "states that are essentially by-products." These are states that cannot be willed. Such a philosophical line cannot be further pursued here.
12 In one of his later works, Rawls (1999: 23) even argues, with J. S. Mill, that "liberal peoples" are united by "shared sympathies," which – among other sources – may derive from "race and descent" (Mill quoted ibid.: n.17).
13 US Citizenship and Immigration Services, *Fact Sheet: USCIS Naturalization Test Design* (22 January 2007), available at www.uscis.gov.
14 "New Citizens Will Need Deeper Knowledge," *New York Times*, 1 December 2006, p. 26.
15 The new master catalogue still contains two flag questions, but toward its very end, under the rubric "symbols," and only asking what the stars and stripes in it represent.
16 Greg Sheridan, "A Test of our Good Faith," *The Australian*, 28 September 2006, p. 12.
17 See also Stone (2006), which is a polemic against Muslims as the "unmentionable problem" of Australian citizenship.
18 Janet Albrechtsen, "Open Market on Democratic Ideals," *The Australian*, 3 May 2006, p. 12.
19 Under German federalism, the regional *Länder* are responsible for naturalization.
20 The only morally inquisitive, Muslim-targeting question in Hesse's proposed citizenship test was: "A woman should not be allowed to move freely in public or travel unless escorted by a close male relative. What is your view on that?" ("Proposed Hesse Citizenship Test," *Spiegel Online*, 9 May 2006).
21 The federal scheme is also cognitively less demanding than the Hesse proposal: the test is passed if the applicant answers seventeen of thirty-three multiple-choice questions correctly (from a list of 300 published questions).
22 *Verordnung zu Einbürgerungstest und Einbürgerungskurs* (5 August 2008, BGBl. 1 S.1649), Anlage 2.
23 Ibid., p. 171.
24 Ibid.
25 "Germany to Introduce Controversial New Citizenship Test," *Spiegel Online*, 11 June 2008.

26 BBC News, "Can You Pass a Citizenship Test?", http://news.bbc.co.uk/1/hi/magazine/4099770.stm (last accessed 12 February 2009).
27 However, this may change should the most recent proposal for a "points test for citizenship" (Home Office 2009), presented in August 2009 for "public consultation," become law. It envisions a two-stage citizenship test, one at the "probationary citizenship" stage that stresses, as previously, the practicalities of everyday life; and a second, more demanding test at the point of requesting citizenship proper, which would include elements of "history" and of the "political and constitutional system of the UK" (ibid.: 22).
28 Of course, one might argue that a "covenantal" identity is a religious identity (in the American case, it certainly is; see Bellah's [1970: ch. 9] notion of civil religion). Accordingly, "religion" cannot possibly be an "alternative" to the covenant. But the different meaning of overtly (as against covertly) religious identities should become clear in the following.
29 For a comprehensive review, see Liedhegener (2008).
30 Conseil d'Etat, 27 June 2008, Mme Faiza M., req. no 286798.
31 Ibid.
32 Loi no. 2003-1119 of 26 November 2003, now Article 21-4 of the Civil Code.
33 Conseil d'Etat, 27 June 2008, Mme Faiza M., req. no 286798.
34 "A Burqa Barrier," *The Economist*, 19 July 2008, p. 51.
35 Decision of the German *Bundesverfassungsgericht* (Federal Constitutional Court) on "Jehova's Witnesses," 19 December 2000 (BVerfGE 102, 370).
36 Ibid.
37 On the distinction between knowledge and values in the context of citizenship tests, see Hampshire (2008b).
38 Interior Ministry of Baden-Württemberg, *Gesprächsleitfaden für die Einbürgerungsbehörden* (Az.: 5-1012.4/12, September 2005; copy on file with author).
39 I thus have to correct my earlier statement that Baden-Württemberg's dubious interview practice "had to be quickly shelved" (Joppke 2008b: 542). Only the questions on homosexuality were apparently dropped. As a spokesperson of the interior ministry declared, the *Land* government remained intent on "clearing any doubt whether the applicants are really conformant with the Basic Law" (Sabine am Orde, "Ein Test für den Pass," *Die Tageszeitung* (TAZ), 11 June 2008, p. 2).
40 One may, of course, question the liberal credentials of a conservative Catholic CDU government in Germany's south. But this cannot be pursued further here.
41 For an informative overview of history textbook battles around the world, see "Where History Isn't Bunk," *The Economist*, 17 March 2007, pp. 65–6.
42 Wolfgang Schäuble, "Muslime in Deutschland," *Frankfurter Allgemeine Zeitung*, 27 September 2006, p. 9.

Chapter 5 Citizenship Light

1 For a comparison of the US and Canada from an "immigrant political incorporation" perspective, see Bloemraad (2006a); for transatlantic comparisons under the same label, see the collection by Hochschild and Mollenkopf (2009).
2 The emblematic case in this respect is Germany. See my discussion in Joppke (1999: ch. 6).
3 This is not to say that exclusion from the political rights of citizenship is not a source of serious vulnerability. An infamous example is the legislative exclusion of legal permanent residents from welfare benefits in mid-1990s America (see Correa 2002). However, this was redressed less by citizen or immigrant political action than by courts and liberal (especially state-level) elites acting on behalf of immigrants.
4 For a critique of Goodhart and New Labour's strategy of "mollifying Middle England," see Pathak (2007: 265).
5 This is the gist of the most recent proposal for a "points test for citizenship," which would apply the logic of the skill-focused points system already in place in immigrant selection to the domain of naturalization (Home Office 2009; the quote in the text is from p. 14). The devious novelty of the proposal is "fundamentally [to break] the automatic link between temporary residence and permanent settlement" (ibid.: 6), so that citizenship acquisition would turn into a citizen selection that is as discretionary and tied up with the "needs of the country" as immigrant selection (ibid.: 4).
6 The relationship between military service and the evolution of citizenship has been at the center of the work by Morris Janowitz, by now largely forgotten (e.g. Janowitz 1978: ch. 6).
7 Brubaker's (1989a: 3) six membership norms are "egalitarian," "sacred," "national," "democratic," "unique," and "socially consequential."
8 "Pledge of Allegiance," *The Economist*, 1 February 2007 (downloaded from www.economist.com).
9 An official at the Austrian Ministry of Economic Affairs, quoted ibid.
10 In Rainer Bauböck's (2007: 2395) definition, transnational citizenship refers to "a triangular relationship between individuals and two or more independent states in which these individuals are simultaneously assigned membership status and membership-based rights or obligations."
11 See Adrian Favell's (2003: 20) observation that "European citizenship [as providing political rights] is not a particularly salient issue to Eurostars" ("Eurostars" being EU member state nationals living and working in another member state).
12 The four Euro freedoms are "free movement of goods, persons, services and capital" (EC Treaty, Article 3c).

13 The best available summary is Craig and de Burca (2008: ch. 23). See also Wind (2009).
14 European Court of Justice, Case C-184/99, *Rudy Grzelczyk v. Centre public d'aide sociale d'Ottignies-Louvain-la-Neuve*, at par. 31.
15 European Court of Justice, Case C-85/96, *Maria Martinez Sala v. Freistaat Bayern*.
16 European Court of Justice, Case C-456/02, *Trojani v. Centre public d'aide sociale de Bruxelles*.
17 Directive 2004/58/EC of 29 April 2004 *on the right of citizens of the Union and their family members to move and reside freely within the territory of the Member States*, preamble at par. 10.
18 ECJ decision on *Trojani*, at par. 45.
19 Council Regulation (EC) no. 1408/71 of 14 June 1971, *on the application of social security schemes to employed persons, to self-employed persons and to members of their families moving within the Community*.
20 Judgment of the European Court of Justice of 22 June 1972, Case 1-72, *Rita Frilli v. Belgian State*, at par. 14.
21 ECJ decision on *Grzelczyk* (op. cit.), at par. 13.
22 Ibid., at par. 21.
23 Ibid., at par. 22.
24 Ibid., at par. 31.
25 Ibid., at par. 44.
26 Combined, Europe's two migrant populations that fall within the ambit of EU law are at circa 9 million, which constitutes slightly under 3 percent of the total EU population (Conant 2004: 314f.).
27 Tampere European Council, 15 and 16 October 1999, *Presidency Conclusions*, at par. 18.
28 Ibid., at par. 21.
29 Council Directive 2003/109/EC of 25 November 2003, *concerning the status of third-country nationals who are long-term residents*.
30 Ibid., Article 3(2).
31 Ibid., Article 5(2).
32 Of course, Article 49 of the Treaty of European Union (Maastricht Treaty) stipulates that any "European state" meeting the listed minimal criteria may file an application to join the EU, and not, say, Japan, so that geography and culture cannot be exorcized from the definition of "Europe."
33 For a gloomier view of the "return of nationalist integration policies across all of Europe," see Favell (2008).

References

Abizadeh, Arash (2004) "Liberal nationalist versus postnational social integration," *Nations and Nationalism*, 10(3), 231–50.
Abizadeh, Arash (2005) "Does collective identity presuppose an other?" *American Political Science Review*, 99(1), 45–60.
Abraham, David (2002) *Citizenship Solidarity and Rights Individualism*. San Diego: Center for Comparative Immigration Studies (Working Paper no. 53).
Aleinikoff, Alexander (2000) "Between principles and politics: U.S. citizenship policy," in Alexander Aleinikoff and Douglas Klusmeyer, eds, *From Migrants to Citizens*. Washington, DC: Carnegie Endowment for International Peace.
Aleinikoff, Alexander, and Douglas Klusmeyer (2002) *Citizenship Policies for an Age of Migration*. Washington, DC: Carnegie Endowment for International Peace.
Alesina, Alberto, and Edward Glaeser (2004) *Fighting Poverty in the US and Europe*. New York: Oxford University Press.
Amir-Moazami, Schirin (2008) "Islam und Geschlecht unter liberal-säkularer Regierungsführung: die Deutsche Islam Konferenz," *Tel Aviver Jahrbuch für deutsche Geschichte* (December).
Appiah, Anthony (2005) *The Ethics of Identity*. Princeton, NJ: Princeton University Press.
Arena, Marta, Bruno Nascimbene, and Giovanna Zincone (2006) "Italy," in Rainer Bauböck et al., eds, *Acquisition and Loss of Nationality*. Amsterdam: Amsterdam University Press, Vol. 2.
Arendt, Hannah ([1958] 1981) *Vita activa oder vom tätigen Leben*. Munich: Piper; Eng. orig. as *The Human Condition*, Chicago: University of Chicago Press.
Arendt, Hannah ([1951] 1979) *The Origins of Totalitarianism*. New York: Harvest.
Aristotle (1981) *The Politics*, trans. T. A. Sinclair. Harmondsworth: Penguin.
Australian Government (2006) *Australian Citizenship: Much More than*

References

a Ceremony (foreword by Andrew Robb). Discussion Paper, Canberra, September.
Australian Government (2007) *Becoming an Australian Citizen*. Canberra.
Baganha, Maria Ioannis, and Constança Urbano de Sousa (2006) "Portugal," in Rainer Bauböck et al., eds, *Acquisition and Loss of Nationality*. Amsterdam: Amsterdam University Press, Vol. 2.
Baldwin, Peter (1997) "State and citizenship in the age of globalization," in Peter Koslowski and Andreas Føllesdal, eds, *Restructuring the Welfare State*. Berlin: Springer.
Banting, Keith, and Will Kymlicka (2006) "Introduction: multiculturalism and the welfare state," in Keith Banting and Will Kymlicka, eds, *Multiculturalism and the Welfare State*. New York: Oxford University Press.
Banting, Keith, Richard Johnston, Will Kymlicka, and Stuart Soroka (2006) "Do multiculturalism policies erode the welfare state? An empirical analysis," in Keith Banting and Will Kymlicka, eds, *Multiculturalism and the Welfare State*. New York: Oxford University Press.
Barth, Fredrik (1969) *Ethnic Groups and Boundaries*. London: Allen & Unwin.
Barry, Kim (2006) "Home and away: the construction of citizenship in an emigration context," *New York University Law Review*, March, 11–59.
Bauböck, Rainer (2006a) "Citizenship and migration – concepts and controversies," in Rainer Bauböck, ed., *Migration and Citizenship: Legal Status, Rights and Political Participation*. Amsterdam: Amsterdam University Press.
Bauböck, Rainer (2006b) "Who are the citizens of Europe?" *Eurozine*, http://www.eurozine.com, 1–7 [last accessed 7 August 2009].
Bauböck, Rainer (2007) "Stakeholder citizenship and transnational political participation: a normative evaluation of external voting," *Fordham Law Review*, 75, 2393–447.
Bauböck, Rainer (2008) "Citizens on the move: democratic standards for migrants' membership," *Canadian Diversity*, 6(4), 7–12.
Bauböck, Rainer, et al. (2006a) "Introduction," in Rainer Bauböck et al., eds, *Acquisition and Loss of Nationality*. Amsterdam: Amsterdam University Press, Vol. 1.
Bauböck, Rainer, Eva Ersbøll, Kees Groenendijk, and Harald Waldrauch, eds (2006b) *Acquisition and Loss of Nationality: Policies and Trends in 15 European States*, 2 vols. Amsterdam: Amsterdam University Press.
Bauböck, Rainer, Bernhard Perching, and Wiebke Sievers, eds (2007) *Citizenship Policies in the New Europe*. Amsterdam: Amsterdam University Press.
Beckert, Jens (2007) "The longue durée of inheritance law," *Archives européennes de sociologie*, 48(1), 79–120.
Bell, Daniel (1973) *The Coming of Post-Industrial Society*. New York: Basic Books.
Bell, Mark (2007) "Civic citizenship and migrant integration," *European Public Law*, 13(2), 311–33.

References

Bellah, Robert N. (1970) *Beyond Belief*. Berkeley: University of California Press.

Bellah, Robert N. (1998) "Is there a common American culture?" *Journal for the American Academy of Religion*, 66(3), 613–25.

Besson, Samantha, and André Utzinger (2007) "Introduction: future challenges of European citizenship – facing a wide-open Pandora's box," *European Law Journal*, 13(5), 573–90.

Betts, Katharine, and Bob Birrell (2007) "Making Australian citizenship mean more," *People and Place*, 15(1), 45–61.

Blair, Tony (2006) *Our Nation's Future: Multiculturalism and Integration*, http://www.number10.gov.uk/ Page11923.

Bleich, Erik (2003) *Race Politics in Britain and France: Ideas and Policymaking since the 1960s*. New York: Cambridge University Press.

Bloemraad, Irene (2000) "Citizenship and immigration: a current review," *Journal of International Migration*, 1(1), 9–37.

Bloemraad, Irene (2002) "The North American naturalization gap: an institutional approach to citizenship acquisition in the United States and Canada," *International Migration Review*, 36(1), 193–228.

Bloemraad, Irene (2006a) *Becoming a Citizen: Incorporating Immigrants and Refugees in the United States and Canada*. Berkeley: University of California Press.

Bloemraad, Irene (2006b) "Becoming a citizen in the United States and Canada: structured mobilization and immigrant political incorporation," *Social Forces*, 85(2), 667–95.

Bloemraad, Irene, Anna Korteweg, and Gökçe Yurdakul (2008) "Citizenship and immigration: multiculturalism, assimilation, and challenges to the nation-state," *Annual Review of Sociology*, 153–79.

Bosniak, Linda (2006) *The Citizen and the Alien*. Princeton, NJ: Princeton University Press.

Bourdieu, Pierre, and Jean-Claude Passeron (1970) *Reproduction in Education, Society and Culture*. London: Sage.

Brubaker, William Rogers (1989a) "Introduction," in R. Brubaker, ed., *Immigration and the Politics of Citizenship in Europe and North America*. Lanham, MD: University Press of America.

Brubaker, William Rogers (1989b) "Citizenship and naturalization: policies and politics," in R. Brubaker, ed., *Immigration and the Politics of Citizenship in Europe and North America*. Lanham, MD: University Press of America.

Brubaker, Rogers (1992) *Citizenship and Nationhood in France and Germany*. Cambridge, MA: Harvard University Press.

Brubaker, Rogers (1999) "The Manichean myth: rethinking the distinction between 'civic' and 'ethnic' nationalism," in Hanspeter Kriesi et al., eds, *Nation and National Identity*. Zurich: Rüegger.

Carens, Joseph (1987) "Aliens and citizens: the case for open borders," *Review of Politics*, 49(2), 251–73.

References

CDU (Christlich-Demokratische Union Deutschlands) (2000) "Arbeitsgrundlage für die Zuwanderungs-Kommission der CDU Deutschlands." Typescript (on file with author).

Cheng, Jennifer (2009) "Promoting 'national values' in citizenship tests in Germany and Australia," in Ricard Zapata-Barrero, ed., *Citizenship Policies in the Age of Diversity*. Barcelona: CIDOB Foundation.

CIC (Commission on Integration and Cohesion) (2007) *Our Shared Future*, http://www.integrationandcohesion.org.uk.

Çinar, Dilek, and Harald Waldrauch (2006) "Austria," in Rainer Bauböck et al., eds, *Acquisition and Loss of Nationality*. Amsterdam: Amsterdam University Press, Vol. 2.

Cole, David (2002) "Enemy aliens," *Stanford Law Review*, 54, 953–1004.

Conant, Lisa (2004) "Contested boundaries: citizens, states, and supranational belonging in the European Union," in Joel Migdal, ed., *Boundaries and Belonging*. New York: Cambridge University Press, 284–317.

Correa, Michael Jones (2002) "Seeking shelter: immigrants and the divergence of social rights and citizenship in the United States," in Randall Hansen and Patrick Weil, eds, *Dual Nationality, Social Rights and Federal Citizenship in the US and Europe*. New York and Oxford: Berghahn Books.

Council of Europe (1997) *European Convention on Nationality*. Strasbourg.

Craig, Paul, and Grainne de Burca (2008) *EC Law*. 4th edn, Oxford: Oxford University Press.

Crepaz, Markus (2006) "'If you are my brother, I may give you a dime!' Public opinion on multiculturalism, trust, and the welfare state," in Keith Banting and Will Kymlicka, eds, *Multiculturalism and the Welfare State*. New York: Oxford University Press.

Crick Commission (2003) *The New and the Old: The Report of the 'Life in the United Kingdom' Advisory Group*. London: HMSO.

Dahl, Robert A. (1989) *Democracy and its Critics*. New Haven, CT: Yale University Press.

Dahrendorf, Ralf (1974) "Citizenship and beyond," *Social Research* (winter), 673–701.

Dauvergne, Catherine (2007) "Citizenship with a vengeance," *Theoretical Inquiries in Law*, 8, 489–507.

Davies, Gareth (2005) "'Any place I hang my hat?' or: Residence is the new nationality," *European Law Journal*, 11(1), 43–56.

Davy, Ulrike (2001) "Integration von Einwanderern: Instrumente-Entwicklungen-Perspektiven," in Ulrike Davy, ed., *Die Integration von Einwanderern*. Frankfurt am Main: Campus.

Davy, Ulrike (2005) "Integration of immigrants in Germany: a slowly evolving concept," *European Journal of Migration and Law*, 7, 123–44.

De Groot, Gerard-René (1989) *Staatsangehörigkeitsrecht im Wandel*. Cologne: Carl Heymanns.

References

De Groot, Gerard-René (2003) "Loss of nationality: a critical inventory," in David A. Martin and Kay Hailbronner, eds, *Rights and Duties of Dual Nationals*. New York: Kluwer Law International.

De Hart, Betty, and Ricky van Oers (2006) "European trends in nationality law," in Rainer Bauböck et al., eds, *Acquisition and Loss of Nationality*. Amsterdam: Amsterdam University Press, Vol. 1.

De Zwart, Frank (2005) "The dilemma of recognition: administrative categories and cultural diversity," *Theory and Society*, 34, 137–69.

Delhey, Jan, and Kenneth Newton (2005) "Predicting cross-national levels of social trust," *European Sociological Review*, 21(4), 311–27.

Dummett, Ann (2006) "United Kingdom," in Rainer Bauböck et al., eds, *Acquisition and Loss of Nationality*. Amsterdam: Amsterdam University Press, Vol. 2.

Dundes Renteln, Alison (2005) *The Cultural Defense*. New York: Oxford University Press.

Duyvendak, Jan Willem, Trees Pels, and Rally Rijkschroeff (2009) "A multicultural paradise? The cultural factor in Dutch integration policy," in Jennifer L. Hochschild and John H. Mollenkopf, eds, *Bringing Outsiders In: Transatlantic Perspectives on Immigrant Political Incorporation*. Ithaca, NY: Cornell University Press.

Dworkin, Ronald (1984) "Rights as trumps," in Jeremy Waldron, ed., *Theories of Rights*. Oxford: Oxford University Press.

Eckert, Julia (2008) "Laws for enemies," in Julia Eckert, ed., "The Social Life of Anti-Terrorism Laws." Bielefeld: transcript Verlag.

Eisenstadt, S. N. (1999) *Fundamentalism, Sectarianism, and Revolution*. Cambridge: Cambridge University Press.

Eisenstadt, S. N., and Bernhard Giesen (1995) "The construction of collective identity," *Archives européennes de sociologie*, 36(1), 72–102.

Elster, Jon (1983) *Sour Grapes*. Cambridge: Cambridge University Press.

Engbersen, Godfried (2003) "The wall around the welfare state in Europe," *Indian Journal of Labour Economics*, 46(3), 479–95.

Ensor, Jonathan, and Amanda Shah (2005) "United Kingdom," in Jan Niessen, Yongmi Schibel, and Cressida Thompson, eds, *Current Immigration Debates in Europe*. Brussels: Migration Policy Group.

Entzinger, Han (2004) "Integration and orientation courses in a European perspective." Expert report written for the Sachverständigenrat für Zuwanderung und Integration. University of Rotterdam (on file with author).

Entzinger, Han (2006a) "The parallel decline of multiculturalism and the welfare state in the Netherlands," in Keith Banting and Will Kymlicka, eds, *Multiculturalism and the Welfare State*. New York: Oxford University Press.

Entzinger, Han (2006b) "Changing the rules while the game is on: from multiculturalism to assimilation in the Netherlands," in Y. Michal Bodemann and

References

Gökçe Yurdakul, eds, *Migration, Citizenship, Ethnos*. New York: Palgrave Macmillan.

Esping-Andersen, Gøsta (1990) *The Three Worlds of Welfare Capitalism*. Princeton, NJ: Princeton University Press.

European Commission (2002) *Promoting Diversity*. Brussels: DG4 Employment and Social Affairs.

Everson, Michelle (1995) "The legacy of the market citizen," in Jo Shaw and Gillian More, eds, *The New Legal Dynamics of European Union*. Oxford: Clarendon Press.

Fagerlund, Jessica (2006) "Finland," in Rainer Bauböck et al., eds, *Acquisition and Loss of Nationality*. Amsterdam: Amsterdam University Press, Vol. 2.

Faist, Thomas, et al. (2007) "Dual citizenship as a path-dependent process," *International Migration Review*, 38(3), 913–44.

Falk, Richard (2000) "The decline of citizenship in an era of globalization," *Citizenship Studies*, 4(1), 5–17.

Favell, Adrian (2003) "Games without frontiers?" *Archives européennes de sociologie*, 44(3), 106–36 [the paginated quotation in the text is from the typescript, available at http://www.sscnet.ucla.edu].

Favell, Adrian (2008) "Immigration, migration and free movement in the making of Europe," in Jeffrey C. Checkel and Peter J. Katzenstein, eds, *European Identity*. New York: Cambridge University Press.

Ferrajoli, Luigi (1994) "Dai diritti del cittadino ai diritti della persona," in Danilo Zolo, ed., *La cittadinanza*. Rome and Bari: Laterza.

Ferrera, Maurizio (2005) *The Boundaries of Welfare: European Integration and the New Spacial Politics of Social Protection*. Oxford: Oxford University Press.

Finer, Samuel (1997) *The History of Government from the Earliest Times*, Vol. 1. Oxford: Oxford University Press.

Fitzgerald, David (2006) "Rethinking emigrant citizenship," *New York University Law Review* (March), 90–116.

Fitzgerald, David (2008) *A Nation of Emigrants: How Mexico Manages its Migration*. Berkeley: University of California Press.

Foblets, Marie-Claire, and Sander Loones (2006) "Belgium," in Rainer Bauböck et al., eds, *Acquisition and Loss of Nationality*. Amsterdam: Amsterdam University Press, Vol. 2.

Freeman, Gary P. (1986) "Migration and the political economy of the welfare state," *Annals of the American Academy of Political and Social Science*, 485, 51–63.

Galeotti, Anna Elisabetta (1993) "Citizenship and equality," *Political Theory*, 21(4), 585–605.

Galston, William (1995) "Two concepts of liberalism," *Ethics*, 105, 516–34.

Garland, David (2001) *The Culture of Control*. Chicago: University of Chicago Press.

References

GCIM (Global Commission on International Migration) (2005) *Migration in an Interconnected World*. New York: GCIM.

Gehring, Jacqueline S. (2009) "Hidden connections: citizenship and anti-discrimination policy in Europe," in Ricard Zapata-Barrero, ed., *Citizenship Policies in the Age of Diversity*. Barcelona: CIDOB Foundation.

Gilbert, Neil (2002) *Transformation of the Welfare State*. New York: Oxford University Press.

Gilens, Martin (1999) *Why Americans Hate Welfare*. Chicago: University of Chicago Press.

Giubboni, Stefano (2007) "Free movement of persons and European solidarity," *European Law Journal*, 13(3), 360–79.

Glick-Schiller, Nancy (1999) "Transmigrants and nation-states," in E. Hirschman, P. Kasinitz, and J. de Wind, eds, *Handbook of International Migration*. New York: Russell Sage Foundation.

Goldsmith, Peter (2008) *Citizenship: Our Common Bond*. London: HMSO.

Goldstone, James A. (2006) "Holes in the rights framework: racial discrimination, citizenship, and the rights of noncitizens," *Ethics and International Affairs*, 20(3), 321–47.

Goodhart, David (2004) "Too diverse?" *Prospect*, 22 January.

Goodhart, David (2006) *Progressive Nationalism: Citizenship and the Left*. London: Demos.

Gordon, Susan M. (2007) "Integrating immigrants: morality and loyalty in US naturalization practice," *Citizenship Studies*, 11(4), 367–82.

Gosewinkel, Dieter (2001) "Citizenship, historical development of," in Neil J. Smelser and Paul Baltes, eds, *International Encyclopedia of the Social & Bahavioral Sciences*. New York: Pergamon, 1852–7.

Graham, Hugh Davis (1990) *The Civil Rights Era*. New York: Oxford University Press.

Graham, Hugh Davis (2002) *Collision Course: The Strange Convergence of Affirmative Action and Immigration Policy in America*. New York: Oxford University Press.

Gray, John (2000) *Two Faces of Liberalism*. Cambridge: Polity.

Groenendijk, Kees, and Paul Minderhoud (2001) "The Netherlands," in Ulrike Davy, ed., *Die Integration von Einwanderern*. Frankfurt am Main: Campus.

Guiraudon, Virginie (2004) "Construire une politique européenne de lutte contre les discriminations," *Sociétés contemporaines*, 53, 11–32.

Gutmann, Amy (2003) *Identity in Democracy*. Princeton, NJ: Princeton University Press.

Habermas, Jürgen (1987) "Geschichtsbewusstsein und posttraditionale Identität," in Jürgen Habermas, *Eine Art Schadensabwicklung*. Frankfurt am Main: Suhrkamp.

Habermas, Jürgen (1992) *Faktizität und Geltung*. Frankfurt am Main: Suhrkamp;

References

Eng. trans. as *Between Facts and Norms*, trans. William Rehg, Cambridge: Polity, 1996.

Hailbronner, Kay (1989) "Citizenship and nationhood in Germany," in Rogers Brubaker, ed., *Immigration and the Politics of Citizenship in Europe and North America*. Lanham, MD: University Press of America.

Hailbronner, Kay (2005) "Union citizenship and access to social benefits," *Common Market Law Review*, 42, 1245–67.

Hailbronner, Kay (2006) "Germany," in Rainer Bauböck et al., eds, *Acquisition and Loss of Nationality*. Amsterdam: Amsterdam University Press, Vol. 2.

Hailbronner, Kay, and Renner, Günter (2001) *Staatsangehörigkeitsrecht*. Munich: C. H. Beck.

Hampshire, James (2008a) "Disembedding liberalism? Immigration politics and security in Britain since 9/11," in Terri E. Givens, Gary P. Freeman, and David L. Leal, eds, *Immigration Policy and Security*. New York: Routledge.

Hampshire, James (2008b) "Liberalism and admission to citizenship." Typescript (on file with author) [to be published by *Journal of Ethnic and Migration Studies*].

Handler, Joel (2004) *Social Citizenship and Workfare in the United States and Western Europe*. New York: Cambridge University Press.

Hansen, Randall (2009) "The poverty of postnationalism: citizenship, immigration, and the new Europe," *Theory and Society*, 38(1), 1–24.

Hansen, Randall, and Patrick Weil, eds (2001) *Towards a European Nationality*. London: Palgrave Macmillan.

Hansen, Randall, and Patrick Weil (2002) "Dual citizenship in a changed world," in Randall Hansen and Patrick Weil, eds, *Dual Nationality, Social Rights and Federal Citizenship in the US and Europe*. Oxford: Berghahn Books.

Hayek, Friedrich (1960) *The Constitution of Liberty*. Chicago: University of Chicago Press.

Hero, Rodney E., and Robert R. Preuhs (2006) "Multiculturalism and welfare policies in the USA: a state-level comparative analysis," in Keith Banting and Will Kymlicka, eds, *Multiculturalism and the Welfare State*. New York: Oxford University Press.

Hobbes, Thomas ([1651] 1998) *Leviathan*, ed. J. C. A. Gaskin. Oxford: Oxford University Press.

Hochschild, Jennifer L., and John H. Mollenkopf, eds (2009) *Bringing Outsiders In: Transatlantic Perspectives on Immigrant Political Incorporation*. Ithaca, NY: Cornell University Press.

Hohfeld, Wesley Newcomb (1919) *Fundamental Legal Conceptions*. Westport, CT: Greenwood Press.

Holmes, Stephen (1993) *The Anatomy of Antiliberalism*. Cambridge, MA: Harvard University Press.

Holston, James (2007) *Insurgent Citizenship: Disjunctions of Democracy and Modernity in Brazil*. Princeton, NJ: Princeton University Press.

References

Home Office (UK) (2002) *Secure Borders, Safe Haven*. London: HMSO.
Home Office (UK) (2004) *Counter-Terrorism Powers*. London: HMSO.
Home Office (UK) (2005a) *Controlling our Borders: Making Migration Work for Britain*. London: HMSO.
Home Office (UK) (2005b) *Improving Opportunity, Strengthening Society: The Government's Strategy to Increase Race Equality and Community Cohesion*. London: HMSO.
Home Office (UK) (2008a) *The Path to Citizenship: Next Steps in Reforming the Immigration System* (February). London: HMSO.
Home Office (UK) (2008b) *The Path to Citizenship: Government Response to Consultation* (July). London: HMSO.
Home Office (UK) (2009) *Earning the Right to Stay: A New Points Test for Citizenship* (July). London: HMSO.
Howard, Marc Morjé (2005) "Variation in dual citizenship policies in the countries of the EU," *International Migration Review*, 39(3), 697–720.
Howard, Marc Morjé (2006) "Comparative citizenship: an agenda for cross-national research," *Perspectives on Politics*, 4(3), 443–55.
Howard, Marc Morjé (2009) *The Politics of Citizenship in Europe*. New York: Cambridge University Press.
ILA (International Law Association) (2000) *Final Report on Women's Equality and Nationality in International Law*. London: ILA.
Isin, Engin F., and Bryan S. Turner, eds (2002) *Handbook of Citizenship Studies*. London: Sage.
Jacobson, David (1996) *Rights across Borders*. Baltimore: Johns Hopkins University Press.
Janoski, Thomas (2006) "Making strangers into citizens: regimes, barriers and the politics of naturalization." Typescript (on file with author).
Janowitz, Morris (1978) *The Last Half-Century: Societal Change and Politics in America*. Chicago: University of Chicago Press.
Janowitz, Morris (1980) "Observations on the sociology of citizenship: obligations and rights," *Social Forces*, 59(1), 1–24.
Joppke, Christian (1995a) *East German Dissidents and the Revolution of 1989: Social Movement in a Leninist Regime*. New York: New York University Press.
Joppke, Christian (1995b) "Toward a new sociology of the state: on Rogers Brubaker's *Citizenship and Nationhood in France and Germany*," *Archives européennes de sociologie*, 36(1), 168–78.
Joppke, Christian (1998) "Immigration challenges the nation-state," in Christian Joppke, ed., *Challenge to the Nation-State: Immigration in Western Europe and the United States*. Oxford: Oxford University Press.
Joppke, Christian (1999) *Immigration and the Nation-State: the United States, Germany, and Great Britain*. Oxford: Oxford University Press.
Joppke, Christian (2000) "Mobilization of culture and the reform of citizenship law: Germany and the United States," in Ruud Koopmans and Paul Statham,

References

eds, *Challenging the Politics of Ethnic Relations in Europe*. Oxford: Oxford University Press.

Joppke, Christian (2001a) "Multicultural citizenship: a critique," *Archives européennes de sociologie*, 42(2), 431–47.

Joppke, Christian (2001b) "The legal-domestic sources of immigrant rights," *Comparative Political Studies*, 34(4), 339–66.

Joppke, Christian (2001c) "The evolution of alien rights in the United States, Germany, and the European Union," in Alexander Aleinikoff and Douglas Klusmeyer, eds, *Citizenship Today*. Washington, DC: Carnegie Endowment for International Peace.

Joppke, Christian (2003) "Citizenship between de- and re-ethnicization," *Archives européennes de sociologie*, 44(3), 429–58.

Joppke, Christian (2004) "The retreat of multiculturalism in the liberal state: theory and policy," *British Journal of Sociology*, 55(2), 237–57.

Joppke, Christian (2005) *Selecting by Origin: Ethnic Migration in the Liberal State*. Cambridge, MA: Harvard University Press.

Joppke, Christian (2007a) "Beyond national models: civic integration policies for immigrants in Western Europe," *West European Politics*, 30(1), 1–22.

Joppke, Christian (2007b) "Transformation of immigrant integration: civic integration and antidiscrimination in the Netherlands, France, and Germany," *World Politics*, 59(2), 243–73.

Joppke, Christian (2007c) "State neutrality and Islamic headscarf laws in France and Germany," *Theory and Society*, 36(4), 313–42.

Joppke, Christian (2008a) "Comparative citizenship: a restrictive turn in Europe?" *Journal of Law and Ethics of Human Rights*, 2, 128–68.

Joppke, Christian (2008b) "Immigration and the identity of Citizenship," *Citizenship Studies*, 12(6), 533–46.

Joppke, Christian (2009a) *Veil: Mirror of Identity*. Cambridge: Polity.

Joppke, Christian (2009b) "Successes and failures of Muslim integration in France and Germany," in Jennifer L. Hochschild and John H. Mollenkopf, eds, *Bringing Outsiders In*. Ithaca, NY: Cornell University Press.

Katyal, Neal (2007) "Equality in the war on terror," *Stanford Law Review*, 59(5), 1365–94.

Kaufmann, Eric (2004) *The Rise and Fall of Anglo-America*. Cambridge, MA: Harvard University Press.

King, Desmond (1999) *In the Name of Liberalism*. Oxford: Oxford University Press.

Kiwan, Dina (2008) "A journey to citizenship in the United Kingdom," *International Journal of Multicultural Societies*, 10(1), 60–75.

Koopmans, Ruud, Paul Statham, Marco Giugni, and Florence Passy (2005) *Contested Citizenship*. Minneapolis: University of Minnesota Press.

Kopper, Akos (2008) "Cosmopolitan sovereignty and the proliferation and stratification of citizenship." Doctoral dissertation, Jacobs University, Bremen.

References

Korteweg, Anna C. (2006) "The murder of Theo van Gogh," in Y. Michal Bodemann and Gökçe Yurdakul, eds, *Migration, Citizenship, Ethnos*. New York: Palgrave Macmillan.

Koslowski, Rey (2000) *Migrants and Citizens*. Ithaca, NY: Cornell University Press.

Kukathas, Chandran (2003) *The Liberal Archipelago*. Oxford: Oxford University Press.

Kymlicka, Will (1995) *Multicultural Citizenship*. Oxford: Clarendon Press.

Kymlicka, Will (2005) "Testing the bounds of liberal multiculturalism?" Typescript (on file with author).

Kymlicka, Will (2007) *Multicultural Odysseys*. New York: Oxford University Press.

Kymlicka, Will, and Keith Banting (2006) "Immigration, multiculturalism, and the welfare state," *Ethics and International Affairs*, 20(3), 281–304.

Laborde, Cécile (2002) "From constitutional to civic patriotism," *British Journal of Political Science*, 32, 591–612.

Lacroix, J. (2002) "For a European constitutional patriotism," *Political Studies*, 50(5), 944–58.

Ladeur, Karl-Heinz (2002) "The German proposal of an 'anti-discrimination' law: anticonstitutional and anti-common sense," *German Law Journal*, 3(5), 1–3.

Letki, Natalia (2008) "Does diversity erode social cohesion?" *Political Studies*, 36, 99–126.

Levitas, Ruth (2005) *The Inclusive Society? Social Exclusion and New Labour*. 2nd edn, London: Palgrave Macmillan.

Liedhegener, Antonius (2008) "Religionsfreiheit und die neue Religionspolitik," *Zeitschrift für Politik*, 55(1), 84–107.

Luhmann, Niklas (1982a) *The Differentiation of Society*. New York: Columbia University Press.

Luhmann, Niklas (1982b) *Liebe als Passion*. Frankfurt am Main: Suhrkamp; Eng. trans. as *Love as Passion*, trans. Jeremy Gaines and Doris L. Jones, Cambridge: Polity, 1986.

Luhmann, Niklas (1986) *Ökologische Kommunikation*. Opladen: Westdeutscher Verlag; Eng. trans. as *Ecological Communication*, trans. John Bednarz, Jr., Cambridge: Polity, 1989.

Lukes, Steven (1973) *Individualism*. Oxford: Blackwell.

MacIntyre, Alasdair (1995) "Is patriotism a virtue?" in Ronald Beiner, ed., *Theorizing Citizenship*. Albany: State University of New York Press, 209–28.

Mann, Michael (1970) "The social cohesion of liberal democracy," *American Sociological Review*, 35(3), 423–39.

Marshall, T. H. ([1950] 1992) *Citizenship and Social Class*. Concord, MA: Pluto Press.

Martin, David (2005) "Dual nationality," in Matthew J. Gibney and Randall

References

Hansen, eds, *Immigration and Asylum: From 1900 to the Present*, Vol. 1. Santa Barbara: ABC CLIO.

Martin, Susan (2002) "The attack on social rights: US citizenship devalued," in Randall Hansen and Patrick Weil, eds, *Dual Nationality, Social Rights and Federal Citizenship in the US and Europe*. Oxford: Berghahn Books.

Marx, Karl ([1843] 1978) "On the Jewish question," in Robert C. Tucker, ed., *The Marx–Engels Reader*. New York: Norton.

Mead, George Herbert (1934) *Mind, Self, and Society*. Chicago: University of Chicago Press.

Meyer, John, and Brian Rowan (1978) "Institutionalized organizations: formal structures as myth and ceremony," *American Journal of Sociology*, 83(2), 340–63.

Meyer, John, John Boli, George M. Thomas, and Francisco O. Ramirez (1997) "World society and the nation-state," *American Journal of Sociology*, 103(1), 144–81.

Michalowski, Ines (2007) "Bringschuld des Zuwanderers oder Staatsaufgabe? Integrationspolitik in Frankreich, Deutschland und den Niederlanden." Doctoral dissertation, University of Münster and Institut d'etudes politiques, Paris.

Miller, David (2003) "Social justice in multicultural societies," in Philippe van Parijs, ed., *Cultural Diversity vs Economic Solidarity*. Brussels: de Broek.

Miller, David (2004) "Immigrants, nations, and citizenship." Paper presented at the conference on Migrants, Nations, and Citizenship, New Hall, Cambridge, 5–6 July.

Miller-Idriss, Cynthia (2006) "Everyday understandings of citizenship in Germany," *Citizenship Studies*, 10(5), 541–70.

Miller-Idriss, Cynthia (2009) *Blood and Culture*. Durham, NC: Duke University Press.

Morris, Lydia (2002) *Managing Migration: Civic Stratification and Migrants' Rights*. London: Routledge.

Mouritsen, Per (2006) "The particular universalism of a Nordic civic nation," in T. Modood, A. Triandafyllidou, and R. Zapata-Barrero, eds, *Multiculturalism, Muslims and Citizenship*. London: Routledge.

Moyse, Françoise, and Pierre Brasseur (2006) "Luxembourg," in Rainer Bauböck et al., eds, *Acquisition and Loss of Nationality*. Amsterdam: Amsterdam University Press, Vol. 2.

Müller, Jan-Werner (2006) "On the origins of constitutional patriotism," *Contemporary Political Theory*, 5, 278–96.

Murguia, Janet, and Cecilia Muños (2005) "From immigrant to citizen," *American Prospect Online*, 11 October, http://www.prospect.org.

Myles, John, and Sébastian St-Arnaud (2006) "Population diversity, multiculturalism, and the welfare state: should welfare state theory be revised?" in Keith Banting and Will Kymlicka, eds, *Multiculturalism and the Welfare State*. New York: Oxford University Press.

References

Neuman, Gerald L. (1998) "The effects of immigration on US nationality law." Typescript (on file with author).

Noiriel, Gérard (1996) *The French Melting Pot*. Minneapolis: University of Minnesota Press.

Norman, Wayne (1995) "The ideology of shared values," in Joseph Carens, ed., *Is Quebec Nationalism Just?* Montreal: McGill–Queen's University Press.

OECD (2007) *International Migration Outlook: Annual Report*. Paris: OECD.

O'Leary, Siofra (1993) "The evolving concept of community citizenship." Doctoral dissertation, Department of Law, European University Institute, Florence.

Ong, Aihwa (1999) *Flexible Citizenship: The Cultural Logics of Transnationality*. Durham, NC: Duke University Press.

Orentlicher, Diane (1998) "Citizenship and national identity," in David Wippmann, ed., *International Law and Ethnic Conflict*. Ithaca, NY: Cornell University Press.

Orgad, Liav (2010) "Illiberal liberalism: cultural restrictions on migration and access to citizenship in Europe," *American Journal of Comparative Law* (forthcoming; all citations are from the typescript, in author's possession).

Parekh, B. (1994) "Superior people," *Times Literary Supplement*, 25 February, 11–13.

Parsons, Talcott (1971) *The System of Modern Societies*. Englewood Cliffs, NJ: Prentice Hall.

Passell, Jeffrey S. (2007) *Growing Share of Immigrants Choosing Naturalization*. Washington, DC: Pew Hispanic Center, 28 March; http://pewhispanic.org/reports/report.php?ReportID=74.

Pathak, Pathik (2007) "The trouble with David Goodhart's Britain," *Political Quarterly*, 78(2), 261–71.

Paye, Jean-Claude (2005) "The end of habeas corpus in Great Britain," *Monthly Review*, 57(6), 34ff.

Pocock, J. G. A. (1995) "The idea of citizenship since classical times," in Ronald S. Beiner, ed., *Theorizing Citizenship*. Albany: State University of New York Press, 29–52.

Poggi, Gianfranco (1978) *The Origins of the Modern State*. Stanford, CA: Stanford University Press.

Popitz, Heinrich (1992) *Phänomene der Macht*. 2nd edn, Mohr: Tübingen.

Preuss, Ulrich K. (1995) "Problems of a concept of European citizenship," *European Law Journal*, 1(3), 267–81.

Putnam, Robert D. (2007) "E pluribus unum: diversity and community in the twenty-first century," *Scandinavian Political Studies*, 30(2), 137–74.

Rawls, John (1971) *A Theory of Justice*. Cambridge, MA: Harvard University Press.

Rawls, John (1985) "Justice as fairness: political not metaphysical," *Philosophy and Public Affairs*, 14(3), 223–51.

References

Rawls, John (1987) "The idea of an overlapping consensus," *Oxford Journal of Legal Studies*, 7(1), 1–23.
Rawls, John (1993) *Political Liberalism*. New York: Columbia University Press.
Rawls, John (1997) "The idea of public reason revisited," *University of Chicago Law Review*, 64(3), 765–807.
Rawls, John (1999) *The Law of Peoples*. Cambridge, MA: Harvard University Press.
Rosanvallon, Pierre (2000) *The New Social Question*. Princeton, NJ: Princeton University Press.
Rubio-Marin, Ruth (2000) *Immigration as a Democratic Challenge*. Cambridge: Cambridge University Press.
Rubio-Marin, Ruth (2006) "Spain," in Rainer Bauböck et al., eds, *Acquisition and Loss of Nationality*. Amsterdam: Amsterdam University Press, Vol. 2.
Sabbagh, Daniel (2007) *Equality and Transparency: A Strategic Perspective on Affirmative Action in American Law*. London: Palgrave Macmillan.
Sacks, Jonathan (2007) *The Home We Build Together*. London: Continuum.
Sadiq, Kamal (2005) "When states prefer non-citizens over citizens," *International Studies Quarterly*, 49, 101–22.
Sadiq, Kamal (2009) *Paper Citizens*. New York: Oxford University Press.
Sandel, Michael (1994) "Review of political liberalism," *Harvard Law Review*, 107, 1765–94.
Sapiro, Virginia (1984) "Women, citizenship, and nationality: immigration and naturalization policies in the United States," *Politics and Society*, 13(1), 1–26.
Saunders, Peter (2005) "Review of *Fighting Poverty in the US and Europe* by A. Alesina and E. Glaeser," *Policy*, 21(3), 60–2.
Scharpf, Fritz (1999) *Governing in Europe*. Oxford: Oxford University Press.
Scheffler, Samuel (2007) "Immigration and the significance of culture," *Philosophy and Public Affairs*, 35(2), 93–125.
Schmitt, Carl ([1932] 1963) *Der Begriff des Politischen*. Berlin: Dunker & Humblot; Eng. trans. as *The Concept of the Political*, trans. George Schwab, Chicago: University of Chicago Press, 1996.
Schmitt, Carl ([1922] 1985) *Political Theology*. Chicago: University of Chicago Press.
Schnapper, Dominique (2006) *Providential Democracy*. New Brunswick, NJ: Transaction Books.
Schuck, Peter H. (1989) "Membership in the liberal polity: the devaluation of American citizenship," in Rogers Brubaker, ed., *Immigration and the Politics of Citizenship in Europe and North America*. Lanham, MD: University Press of America.
Schuck, Peter H., and Rogers M. Smith (1985) *Citizenship without Consent*. New Haven, CT: Yale University Press.
Scott, James C. (1998) *Seeing Like a State*. New Haven, CT: Yale University Press.

References

Shachar, Ayelet (2003) "Children of a lesser state," in Stephen Macedo and Iris Marion Young, eds, *Child, Family, and State*. New York: New York University Press, 345–97.

Shachar, Ayelet (2006) "The race for talent," *New York University Law Review*, 81, 148–206.

Shachar, Ayelet (2009) *The Birthright Lottery: Citizenship and Global Inequality*. Cambridge, MA: Harvard University Press.

Shachar, Ayelet, and Ran Hirschl (2007) "Citizenship as inherited property," *Political Theory*, 35(3), 253–87.

Simmel, Georg ([1908] 1971) "Group expansion and the development of individuality," in Donald Levine, ed., *Georg Simmel: On Individuality and Social Forms*. Chicago: University of Chicago Press.

Skrentny, John (1996) *The Ironies of Affirmative Action*. Chicago: University of Chicago Press.

Skrentny, John (2002) *The Minority Rights Revolution*. Cambridge, MA: Harvard University Press.

Smith, Rogers (2001) "Citizenship: political," in Neil J. Smelser and Paul Baltes, eds, *International Encyclopedia of the Social & Behavioral Sciences*. New York: Pergamon, 1857–60.

Smith, Rogers (2003) *Stories of Peoplehood*. New York: Cambridge University Press.

Smooha, Sammy (2008) "Response to Joppke," *Journal of Law and Ethics of Human Rights*, 2(1), article 7; http://www.bepress.com/lehr/.

Sniderman, Paul, and Louk Hagendoorn (2007) *When Ways of Life Collide*. Princeton, NJ: Princeton University Press.

Somers, Margaret (2009) *Genealogies of Citizenship*. New York: Cambridge University Press.

Soysal, Yasemin (1994) *Limits of Citizenship: Migrants and Postnational Membership in Europe*. Chicago: University of Chicago Press.

Soysal, Yasemin (1996) "Changing parameters of citizenship and claims-making: organized Islam in European public spheres," *Theory and Society*, 26(4), 509–27.

Spiro, Peter J. (2008) *Beyond Citizenship: American Identity after Globalization*. Princeton, NJ: Princeton University Press.

Starr, Paul (1992) "Social categories and claims in the liberal state," in Mary Douglas and David Hull, eds, *How Classification Works*. Edinburgh: Edinburgh University Press.

Stone, John (2006) "The unmentionable problem of Australian citizenship," *National Observer* [Melbourne], 70, 12–24.

Straubhaar, Thomas (2003) "Wird die Staatsangehörigkeit zu einer Klubmitgliedschaft?" in Dietrich Thränhardt and Uwe Hunger, eds, "Migration im Spannungsfeld von Globalisierung und National-Staat," *Leviathan* [special edn] 22, 76–89.

References

Straw, Jack (2007) "The way we are," *World Today* [Chatham House], May, 14–16.
Streeck, Wolfgang (1997) *Citizenship under Regime Competition*. Oslo: ARENA working papers, no. 6.
Sunstein, Cass R. (1995) "Rights and their critics," *Notre Dame Law Review*, 70, 727–68.
Tajfel, Henry (1970) "Experiments in intergroup discrimination," *Scientific American*, 223(5), 96–102.
Taylor, Charles (1989) *Sources of the Self: The Making of Modern Identity*. Cambridge, MA: Harvard University Press.
Taylor, Charles (1992) *Multiculturalism and "The Politics of Recognition"*. Princeton, NJ: Princeton University Press.
Taylor-Gooby, Peter (2005) "Is the future American?" *Journal of Social Policy*, 34(4), 661–72.
Tebble, Adam J. (2006) "Exclusion for democracy," *Political Theory*, 34(4), 463–87.
Teles, Steven M. (1998) "Why is there no affirmative action in Britain?" *American Behavioral Scientist*, 41(7), 1004–26.
Tilly, Charles (1985) "War making and state making as organized crime," in Peter Evans, Dietrich Rueschemeyer, and Theda Skocpol, eds, *Bringing the State Back In*. New York: Cambridge University Press.
Torpey, John (2005) *Making Whole What Has Been Smashed: On Reparations Politics*. Cambridge, MA: Harvard University Press.
Triadafilopoulos, Phil (2008) "Illiberal means to liberal ends? Immigrant integration policies in Europe." Typescript (on file with author) [to be published by *Journal of Ethnic and Migration Studies*].
Van der Mei, Anne Pieter (2002) "Regulation 1408/71 and co-ordination of special non-contributory benefit schemes," *European Law Review*, 27 (October), 551–66.
Van Oers, Ricky, Betty de Hart, and Kees Groenendijk (2006) "Netherlands," in Rainer Bauböck et al., eds, *Acquisition and Loss of Nationality*. Amsterdam: Amsterdam University Press, Vol. 2.
Van Parijs, Philippe (2003) "Cultural diversity against economic solidarity," in P. van Parijs, ed., *Cultural Diversity versus Economic Solidarity*. Brussels: de Boeck.
Veil, Simone (2008) *Comité de réflexion sur le preambule de la constitution: rapport au président de la république*. Paris.
Verschueren, Herwig (2007) "European (internal) migration law as an instrument for defining the boundaries of national solidarity systems," *European Journal of Migration and Law*, 9, 307–46.
Vertovec, Steven (2007) "Super-diversity and its implications," *Ethnic and Racial Studies*, 30(6), 1024–54.
Vink, Maarten P., and Gerard-René de Groot (2008) "Citizenship attribution in

References

Western Europe: international framework and domestic trends." Typescript (on file with author) [to be published by *Journal of Ethnic and Migration Studies*].

Waldron, Jeremy (1992) "Minority cultures and the cosmopolitan alternative," *University of Michigan Journal of Law Reform*, 25(3–4), 751–92.

Walzer, Michael (1970) "The problem of citizenship," in Michael Walzer, *Obligations: Essays on Disobedience, War, and Citizenship*. New York: Simon & Schuster.

Walzer, Michael (1983) *Spheres of Justice*. New York: Basic Books.

Walzer, Michael (1997) *On Toleration*. New Haven, CT: Yale University Press.

Waters, Mary (1990) *Ethnic Options*. Berkeley: University of California Press.

Waters, Mary, and Zoua M. Vang (2007) "The challenges of immigration to race-based diversity policies in the United States," in Keith Banting, Thomas J. Courchene, and F. Leslie Seidle, eds, *Belonging? Diversity, Recognition and Shared Citizenship in Canada*, Vol. 3. Montreal: Institute for Research on Public Policy.

Weber, Eugene (1977) *Peasants into Frenchmen*. Palo Alto, CA: Stanford University Press.

Weber, Max ([1919] 1965) *Politik als Beruf*. Tübingen: Mohr; Eng. trans. as *Politics as a Vocation*, trans. H. H. Gerth and C. Wright Mills, Philadelphia: Fortress Press, 1965.

Weber, Max ([1921] 1976) *Wirtschaft und Gesellschaft*. Tübingen: Mohr; Eng. trans. as *Economy and Society*, trans. Keith Tribe, London: Routledge, 2008.

Weil, Patrick (2001) "Access to citizenship," in Alex Aleinikoff and Douglas Klusmeyer, eds, *Citizenship Today*. Washington, DC: Carnegie Endowment for International Peace.

Weil, Patrick (2002) *Qu'est-ce qu'un Français?* Paris: Grasset.

Weiler, Joseph (1996) *The Selling of Europe*. New York University School of Law, Jean Monnet Center, Working Paper no. 96 [non-paginated]; http://www.jeanmonnetprogram.org/papers/96/9603.

Weiler, Joseph (1999) *The Constitution of Europe*. Cambridge: Cambridge University Press.

Weinstock, Daniel M. (2008) "The theory and practice of citizenship in the 21st century: a few international trends," *Canadian Diversity*, 6(4), 3–6.

Wind, Marlene (2009) "Post-national citizenship in Europe: the EU as a 'welfare rights generator'?" *Columbia Journal of European Law*, 15(2).

Wirth, Louis (1945) "The problem of minority groups," in Ralph Linton, ed., *The Science of Man in the World Crisis*. New York: Columbia University Press.

Wolfrum, Rüdiger, and Volker Röben (2006) "Gutachten zur Vereinbarkeit des Gesprächsleitfaden für die Einbürgerungsbehörden des Landes Baden-Württemberg mit Völkerrecht." Typescript (on file with author).

Wonjung Park, Julian (2008) "A more meaningful citizenship test? Unmasking

References

the construction of a universalist, principle-based citizenship ideology," *California Law Review*, 96, 999–1047.

Young, Iris Marion (1990) *Justice and the Politics of Difference*. Princeton, NJ: Princeton University Press.

Zolberg, Ari, and Long Litt Woon (1999) "Why Islam is like Spanish," *Politics and Society*, 27(1), 5–38.

Index

Abizadeh, Arash 144
affirmative action (US) 103–5, 109
  Bakke decision (US Supreme Court) 104–6
Aleinikoff, Alexander A. 44–5, 48
Alesina, Alberto 76–9
Algeria 169
alien rights 32, 82–96
  compared with rights of citizens 73–4
  entrusted to judiciary (Ely) 96
  "hybrid legal status" (Bosniak) 88
  reversible 91–6
  stratified 84–91
  see also postnational membership; rights
Amir-Moazami, Schirin 144
antidiscrimination 101–10
  accommodation strategies (De Zwart) 109
  affirmative action (US) 103–5, 109
  denial strategies (De Zwart) 109
  diversity as link between multiculturalism and 105–6
  EU policies 106–8
  replacement strategies (De Zwart) 109–10
  see also discrimination; ethnicity; gender; multiculturalism; race; religion
Appiah, Anthony 122–3
Arendt, Hannah
  on aliens as "rightless" 96

citizenship as "right to have rights" 27, 82
  on the *polis* 7, 82
  "rights of man" and stateless people 82
  on state sovereignty 46
Aristotle 6–7
  citizenship as virtue 30
assimilation
  integration vs. 46–7, 97–8, 112–13
Augustine of Hippo 8
Australia vii, 35, 44
  Australian Citizenship Act (2007) 67
  citizenship test 67, 123, 126–7
  dual citizenship 67, 160
  global economy and 72
  naturalization process 67, 126–7
  re-ethnicizing citizenship 63
Austria
  citizenship for sale 160
  on "citizenship policy index" (Howard) 42
  employment permits (*Befreiungsschein*) 87
  immigration statistics 35–6
  long-term residence status 86
  naturalization as of right 69
  naturalization rates 41
  new restrictions in naturalization 53, 55, 61
  populist politics 71
  re-ethnicizing citizenship 64

Index

Axial Age (Eisenstadt) 118–19
Aznar, José 64

Baganha, Maria Ioannis 65
Bakke decision (US Supreme Court) 104–6
Baldwin, Peter 89, 90
Bancroft, George 47
Banting, Keith 76, 78
Bauböck, Rainer 70, 148, 160
Belgium
   access to labor market for immigrants 87
   on "citizenship policy index" (Howard) 42
   citizenship reform (2000) 50, 61
   ECJ decisions 165, 167, 168
   immigration statistics 35–6
   integration requirements 46–7
   long-term residence status 86
   mixing *jus sanguinis* and *jus soli* citizenship principles 45
   naturalization rates 41
   return to *jus domicilii* 61
Bell, Mark 170
Bellah, Robert 121–2
Besson, Samantha 171
Betts, Katharine 71–2, 126
Bingham, Lord Chief Justice 95
Birrell, Bob 72, 126
Blackmun, Justice Harry 83–4
Blair, Tony 131–2
Bloemraad, Irene 39–40, 145, 151
Blunkett, David 58
Bosniak, Linda 6, 83, 87–8, 147
Bourdieu, Pierre 12–13
Brandt, Willy 128–9
Brazil 147
Brown, Gordon 156
Brubaker, Rogers vi
   Citizenship and Nationhood in France and Germany 14–20
   citizenship as identity 30
   citizenship as "nation membership" 111
   compared to Soysal 22
   cultural idiom approach 50
   exclusive/inclusive citizenship 6
   "ideas and ideals" of citizenship 159
   national citizenship 14–20, 28
   on naturalization 45–6
Burke, Edmund 82
Bush, George W. 92–3

Canada
   as-of-right naturalization 45–6
   compared to US (Bloemraad) 39–40
   "ideology of shared values" (Norman) 117
   immigration statistics 35–6
   multiculturalism of 40, 61, 138
Cantle Commission (UK) 57
capitalism
   Disraeli's "two nations" 11
   growth of citizenship 11–14
   inequalities of 9, 11
   presupposes civil rights 11
   social class 11, 12
   victory over socialism 13
Carens, Joseph 29
Carnegie Endowment for International Peace 48
Cheney, Richard 92–3
Chirac, Jacques 19
Christian Democratic Union (CDU) (Germany) 135
Christianity 134–6
citizenship
   alien (Bosniak) 6, 83
   aspects/dimensions of 28–30, 148–52
   as birthright 34, 44, 54, 152–3
   causes of change 148–52
   changing concepts of vi–viii
   in classic social theory 9
   as club membership 157–8
   competition with legal permanent residency 91–2, 155–6
   contemporary study of viii, 1, 31
   as contract 60, 62–3, 79
   convergence across Western states vii, 31, 147, 152–61
   de-ethnicization 43–53, 70
   deprivation of 61, 62, 71
   devaluation of 63, 146
   differentiated (Holston) 147
   documentary (Sadiq) 147–8
   dual 31, 47–50, 52, 63–7, 91, 124, 160–1
   earned (UK) 58–60, 157

Index

citizenship (*cont.*)
  emigration and 63–7
  in Europe (East vs. West) 148
  European Union 161–72
  flexible (Ong) 160–1
  future of 152–61
  "genuine connection" 45, 66
  global viii
  Greek vs. Roman 6–8, 67, 147, 161
  as identity vii, 30, 32–3, 111–44, 148, 151–2
  inclusive/exclusive vi, 6, 14–20, 142–4
  instrumentalism and 159–61
  involuntary nature of 16, 36–7
  jus domicilii 45, 61
  jus sanguinis 19–20, 34, 40–3, 43, 53
  jus soli 19–20, 34, 37, 53, 63, 147
  liberalizing trends 41–53
  light 33, 145–72
  multicultural (Kymlicka) 23–6
  national (Brubaker) 14–20
  and nationhood 14–20, 142–4
  naturalization 32, 38–43, 45–7, 53–63
  as political membership and participation 1–7, 145–7
  postnational (Soysal) 20–2, 23, 28, 32, 154
  probationary (UK) 60–2
  re-ethnicization 63–7, 70
  as "right to have rights" (Arendt) 27, 82
  as rights vi–viii, 7, 9–14, 20–1, 27, 29, 32–3, 73–110, 148, 150, 156, 161
  for sale 160
  sectoral (Dahrendorf) 5
  social (Marshall) 9–14, 27–8
  as status vii–viii, 12, 28–9, 31–2, 34–72, 79, 148–9
  tests 54–61, 123–30, 140
  transnational 61, 160–1
city-states 7, 8
Clarke, Charles 96
Clinton, Bill 39
Cole, David 93
Cole, G. D. H. 4
colonialism
  European 106–7
  multiculturalism and 99

Commission on Integration and Cohesion (CIC) (UK) 132
communitarianism 116–17
community *see* political community
Conant, Lisa 167
Conseil représentative des associations noires (CRAN) (France) 108
Convention on the Reduction of Cases of Multiple Nationality (1963) 48
Council of Europe Nationality Convention (1997) 48, 50, 64–5
Crepaz, Markus 76
Crick (Sir Bernard) Commission (UK) 56, 58–9, 129, 130
Croatia 70
culture
  assimilation 46, 68–9
  and citizenship light 33
  compared to identity 121–2
  ethnic vs. civic 17–20
  "new institutionalism" (Meyer) 20–1, 151
  "societal" (Kymlicka) 23–4
  "survivance" (Taylor) 24
  see also diversity; multiculturalism

Dahrendorf, Ralf 5
Davy, Ulrike 86, 89, 90–1
De Hart, Betty 64
De Zwart, Frank 109
Declaration of the Rights of Man and Citizen (1798) 82
Declaration on the Rights of Persons Belonging to National or Ethnic or Linguistic Minorities (1992) 98
democracy
  congruence between rulers and ruled 31–2
Denmark
  Christian identity 134–5, 136–7
  on "citizenship policy index" (Howard) 42
  Danish Peoples Party (DPP) 134–5
  EU citizenship and 168
  new restrictions in naturalization 53, 61
  populist politics 71
  rejects dual nationality 50
Devlin, Lord 112

Index

discrimination
  direct 102
  indirect 102–3, 107
  racial vii, 26–8, 43, 102–3, 106
  reverse 103
  sexual 28, 37, 43, 102
  see also antidiscrimination; ethnicity; gender; multiculturalism; race; religion
Disraeli, Benjamin 11
diversity
  as fact and multicultural citizenship 23
  as fact and social citizenship 74–82
  link between antidiscrimination and multiculturalism 105–6
  as policy norm 105–8
  see also antidiscrimination; multiculturalism
Dominican Republic 66
Dred Scott decision (US Supreme Court) 38
Durkheim, Emile 9, 113
Duyvendak, Jan Willem 139–40

economy *see* capitalism; feudalism; labor and employment; socialism; welfare state
Eisenstadt, S. N. 117, 118–19
Ely, John Hart 96
emigration and emigrants
  dual citizenship 49
  EU 171
  "re-ethnicizing" citizenship 63–7, 70
  voting rights 66, 146
  see also immigration and immigrants
employment *see* labor and employment
Entzinger, Han 79–80
equality
  antidiscrimination and 102–5
  and citizenship 5–6, 10
  vs. feudalism 8
  vs. inclusion 13
  isonomy 5
  and multicultural citizenship (Kymlicka) 24–5
  of opportunity vs. results 102
Esping-Andersen, Gøsta 13, 79
ethnicity
  definition of minority groups 96–7
  re-ethnicizing citizenship 32, 52, 63–7
  and the state 24–5, 31
  see also race; religion
Europe
  antidiscrimination policies 106–10
  both restrictive and liberalizing nationality laws 67–72
  colonialism 138
  compared to North America 31
  consolidation of residence status 85–6
  decline of nationalism 142–3
  East vs. West 148
  liberalizing nationality laws 43–50
  naturalization rates 41
  rise of restrictions in nationality laws 53–63
  tolerating dual nationality 49–50
  trend toward territorial citizenship 44–5
  welfare spending 76–80
European Convention for the Protection of Human Rights (ECPHR) (1950)
  and UK anti-terror laws 94–5
European Court of Justice (ECJ) 89, 163–9, 171
  Frilli decision 167
  Grzelczyk decision 164–5, 168
  Martinez Sala decision 165
  Trojani decision 165
European Union (EU)
  Amsterdam Treaty 162–3
  citizenship 161–72
  Long-Term Residents Directive 170
  Maastricht Treaty 162
  new states in EU 148
  non-EU immigrants 169–71
  Race Directive 106–7
  welfare rights 165–70
European Year of Intercultural Dialogue (2008) 132
expatriates *see* emigration and emigrants

Fanon, Frantz
  The Wretched of the Earth 99
Ferrajoli, Luigi 29
Ferrera, Maurizio 166, 167, 170

Index

feudalism
  "city of man" (Augustine) 8
  inequality under 11
Finland 42, 50, 64, 69
Fischer, Joschka 52
Fitzgerald, David 67
France
  antidiscrimination policies 107
  assimilation requirement in naturalization 47
  on "citizenship policy index" (Howard) 42
  civic nationhood 17–20
  Conseil répresentative des associations noires (CRAN) 108
  consolidation of residence status 85
  discretionary approach in naturalization 45
  dual citizenship 47
  and *Grzelczyk* decision (ECJ) 168
  headscarf controversy 47
  immigration statistics 35–6
  labor market access for immigrants 87
  language requirement in integration policy 134
  Napoleonic *Code civil* 19
  National Front 19
  naturalization rates 41
  new restrictions in naturalization 53
  Republican identity 138–9
  Veil Committee (2008) 107–8
  see also French Revolution
Freeman, Gary 74
French Revolution
  and creation of modern citizenship 8–9
  democratic revolution 11–12
  invention of national citizen 15
  Rights of Man and Citizen 27, 29, 82
Friedrich, Caspar David 128
Frilli decision (ECJ) 167

Galeotti, Anna Elisabetta 25
Gehring, Jacqueline 149
gender
  body politic and 114
  Cable Act (US) 37
  discrimination in nationality laws 28, 37, 43, 48–9

multiculturalism and 24–5
Muslim treatment of women 140
see also antidiscrimination; discrimination; multiculturalism
German Federal Constitutional Court (*Bundesverfassungsgericht*)
  Jehova's Witnesses decision 140
Germany
  access to labor market for immigrants 87
  Aliens Act (1990) 86
  antidiscrimination policies 106
  anti-veiling laws 101
  on "citizenship policy index" (Howard) 42
  citizenship reforms 50–3
  consolidation of residence status 86
  discretionary approach in naturalization 45
  dual citizenship 49–50, 52
  ethnic nationhood 17–18
  Fink pension model 166
  Framework Curriculum for the Citizenship Test (2008) 128
  guest workers 149
  Immigration Act (*Zuwanderungsgesetz*) (2004) 86–7
  immigration statistics 35–6
  introducing *jus soli* and *jus domicilii* 45
  Jehova's Witnesses decision (German Federal Constitutional Court) 140
  jus sanguinis tradtion 40–1
  language and citizenship 17, 54, 133
  large immigrant intake 51
  Leitkultur and Christianity 135–6
  naturalization process 41–2, 127–9, 141–2
  Nazi racism 26–7, 116, 128–9, 149
  new restrictions in naturalization 53–6
  postwar identity 116
  reunification 51
Giesen, Bernhard 117
Gilbert, Neil 150
Glaeser, Edward 76–9
global citizenship *see under* citizenship
globalization
  "demise" of nation-state 5

208

Index

tightening access to citizenship and 71–2
transnationalization of migration 67
Goethe, Johann Wolfgang von 128
Goldsmith, Peter 90, 91–2, 156
Gonzales, Emilio 124–5
Goodhart, David 74–6, 156, 157
Graham, Hugh Davis 102
Graham v. Richardson decision (US Supreme Court) 83, 87–8
Greece (ancient)
  active political participation 67
  citizenship in 6–7
  metics 36
  polis 1
  virtuous citizenship 30, 121
Greece (modern) 42
Griggs v. Duke Power Company (US Supreme Court) 102–3
Grzelczyk decision (ECJ) 164–5, 168

Habermas, Jürgen
  constitutional patriotism 115–16
  decline of nationalism 142–3
Hagendoorn, Louk 140
Hague Convention on Nationality (1930) 47
Hailbronner, Kay 165
Hansen, Randall 84
Hart, H. L. A. 112
Hegel, Georg F. W. 21
Hirschl, Ran 153
Hobbes, Thomas 2–3, 113, 114
Hohfeld, Wesley Newcomb 82
Holston, James 147
Howard, John 126
Howard, Marc Morjé 52
  "citizenship policy index" 41–3, 69
  explaining new restrictions 70
  no common European standards on citizenship 148
human rights vii–viii, 21, 26–7, 29, 82–4, 94–6, 149
  see also liberalism; rights; universalism

identity
  citizenship as vii, 18, 30, 32–3, 111–44, 148

compared to culture 121–2
EU and Copenhagen criteria 171
individual- and group-level (Simmel) 119–20
liberalism as 138–42
modern (Taylor) 98
vs. political values 120–1
"post-conventional" 143
recognition 99–100
religious 134–6
universalism paradox 33, 111–13, 123–37
see also citizenship; culture; values
immigration and immigrants
  alien rights 82–96
  asylum-seekers 170
  in EU 169–70
  exclusion from welfare (US) 22
  illegal viii, 85, 90
  inventing the foreigner 15
  linkage of immigration with citizenship policy 150
  as political issue 70–1
  polyethnic rights (Kymlicka) 26
  postcolonial 28
  postwar vi, 26–8, 74
  potential enemies (à la Schmitt) 92
  poverty and 15
  refugees and stateless people 27, 60
  skills and 60, 85
  statistics of 35–6
  unpopularity of 156–7
  see also alien rights; emigration and emigrants
inclusion
  discourse of (vs. equality) 13
  as obligation 79
  see also integration
India 147–8
individualism
  liberalism and 4
  Simmel on 119–20
  see also liberalism
integration
  vs. assimilation 46–7, 97–8, 112–13
  civic 53–63, 123–42
  unity in liberal states 113–23
  see also inclusion
International Court of Justice (ICJ)
  Nottebohm decision 45

209

Index

International Covenant on Civil and Political Rights (1966) 98
Ireland 35–6, 41–2
Isin, Engin F.
  Handbook of Citizenship Studies (with Turner) 1
Islamic League 141
Israel 51, 82
Italy 42, 51, 66, 70

Jackson, Justice Robert H. 93, 95
Janowitz, Morris 158
Jehova's Witnesses decision (German Federal Constitutional Court) 140
Jews 27, 116, 128–9
Juncker, Jean-Claude 69

Katyal, Neal 93
Kaufmann, Eric 143
Klusmeyer, Douglas 44–5, 48
Kopper, Akos 116
Korteweg, Anna 145, 151
Kukathas, Chandran 114
  critique of recognition 99–100
Kymlicka, Will
  critique of "benign neglect" 99
  on liberal multiculturalism in Canada 138
  Multicultural Citizenship 23–6
  multiculturalism and welfare state 76, 78
  polyethnic rights 100
  social unity 117, 120

labor and employment
  access to for immigrants 85–8
  flexible citizenship (Ong) 160–1
  guest workers 20
  skills of immigrants 57, 60, 85, 156–7
  welfare to workfare 79–80, 150–1
  see also alien rights; inclusion; integration; welfare state
language
  Common European Reference Framework for Languages 133–4
  identity marker vs. practical exigency in integration and citizenship policy 133–4
  naturalization process and 53–4, 59, 69, 124

Laski, Harold 4
Le Pen, Jean-Marie 19
legal permanent residency
  competition with citizenship 91–2, 155–6
  in Europe (and compared with US) 85–6
  trumping citizenship ties in the EU 171
  see also alien rights
Leitkultur (Germany) 135–6
liberalism
  and changing citizenship vii, 148–52
  exclusion of Muslims 137–42
  as identity 137–42
  identity and unity in the liberal state 113–23
  justification of multiculturalism (Kymlicka) 24–5
  liberalization of access to citizenship 31, 42–4, 50–3, 67–72
    Europe 50–3
  paradox of universalism 123–37
  as "politics of indifference" (Kukathas) 99–100
  requires inclusive citizenship (Walzer) 36
  Schmitt's view of 4
  state neutrality 31, 111–12, 114–15, 117
  US citizenship and the 14th Amendment (US) 38
  virtuous citizenship and 30
  see also individualism
Litt Woon, Long 134
Luhmann, Niklas 14
Luxembourg 35–6, 41–2, 50, 68–9, 71

MacIntyre, Alasdair 118–19
Makarov, A. 27
Malaysia 147–8
Mann, Michael 113, 114
Marshall, T. H. vi, 17, 90
  Citizenship and Social Class 9–14
  citizenship as claims-making 14
  "ideal" of citizenship 25
Marx and 11–12
rights and 29

Index

sets tone for liberal postwar sociology 27–8
social citizenship 9–14
"unified civilization" through citizenship 33
Martinez Sala decision (ECJ) 165
Marx, Karl
   Marshall and 11–12
   view of citizenship 9
Mathews v. *Diaz* (US Supreme Court) 88
meritocracy 12
Merz, Friedrich 135
Mexico 38–9, 66
Meyer, John 20–1, 151
military service
   and the evolution of citizenship 158–9
Mill, John Stuart 112
Miller, David 141
Miller-Idriss, Cynthia 30
minority groups
   antidiscrimination 101–8
   defining 96–7
   multiculturalism 97–101
   rights of 74, 96–110, 149–50
   social spending and 76–8, 79–80
   see also antidiscrimination; discrimination; ethnicity; multiculturalism; race
Mitterrand, François 86
Morocco 169
Morris, Lydia 84–5
Mouritsen, Per 135, 136–7
multicultural citizenship 23–6
   see also citizenship; Kymlicka; multiculturalism
multiculturalism
   vs. antidiscrimination 74, 108–10
   Britain 131–3
   Canada 40, 61, 138
   decline of 108–10
   defining 97–9
   diversity link 105–6
   European 22
   Kymlicka's approach 23–6
   as result of citizenship evolution 14
   rights and 32, 97–101
   turn away from in Dutch politics 55–6

United States 105–6
   see also ethnicity; Kukathas; Kymlicka; minority groups; race; religion; rights; Taylor
Muslims
   Britishness and 131–2
   Dutch values and 140
   exclusion of 137–42
   identity and 33, 134–6
   imposing liberal values on 141–2
   individual vs. polyethnic rights 100–1
   new restrictions in naturalization 32, 53, 55
   veiling 101, 135–6, 139
   see also minority groups; multiculturalism; religion
Myles, John 78

nation-states
   closure through citizenship (Brubaker) 16
   as clubs 157–8
   "demise" of 5
   encode rights (Arendt) 82
   ethnic vs. civic 17–20
   and free movement within EU 161–4
   identity and viii, 111–44
   immigration policy as prior to citizenship policy 150
   instrumental attitudes toward 159–61
   nation-building preventing liberal citizenship (Germany, Israel) 51
   national citizenship 14–20
   obligations of citizens 158–9
   postnational membership (Soysal) 20–2, 72, 73, 154
   as protection (Hobbes to Schmitt) 2–3
   reject dual citizenship 48
   sovereignty 46
   state-level racism 26–7
   territorial 8
   "total state" (Schmitt) 4
   uniqueness 117–18
   see also citizenship; nationalism; naturalization; politics
national citizenship 14–20
   see also Brubaker; citizenship; nation-states

Index

National Front (France) 19
nationalism viii
  decline of 142–3
  patriotism 118–19
Nationality Convention of the Council of Europe (1997) 48, 50, 64–5
naturalization
  civic integration 46, 53–63, 123–30
  discretion to as-of-right 45–6
  and liberalism as identity 140–2
  low Mexican ratio in US 38–9
  new restrictions 32, 53–63
  probationary citizenship (UK) 60, 62
  public ceremonies 58
  statistics of 41
  see also citizenship
Netherlands
  access to labor market for immigrants 87
  antidiscrimination (replacement strategies) 109–10
  on "citizenship policy index" (Howard) 42
  civic integration policy 55–6, 58, 139–40
  consolidation of residence status 86
  immigration statistics 35–6
  Linking Act (1998) 90
  multiculturalism and welfare 79–80
  nationalism in integration policy 58
  Nationality Act (1984) 55
  naturalization rates 41
  new restrictions in nationality law 53–6, 61
  populist politics 71
  re-ethnicization of citizenship 63–4
  rejects dual nationality 50
  welfare benefits for immigrants 89–90
Neuman, Gerald 37
New Zealand 35–6
Norman, Wayne 117
North America
  citizenship evolution compared to Europe 31
  turn to non-discriminatory citizenship 43
  see also Canada; United States
Norway 35–6

Nottebohm decision (International Court of Justice) 45

Oers, Ricky van 64
Ong, Aihwa 160–1
Orgad, Liav 128, 129
Organization for Economic Cooperation and Development (OECD)
  immigration statistics 35–6
  unemployment 79
Orwell, George 133

Pakistan 147–8
Parekh, B. 138
Parijs, Philippe van 80
Parsons, Talcott 113, 114, 143
Pels, Trees 139–40
Perching, Bernhard 148
Pocock, J. G. A. 7, 8
Poland 40
political community
  ancient world 6–8
  citizenship as membership in 1–5
  also a cultural community 111
  incompatible with political liberalism (Rawls) 115
  participation in 145–7
  participation in other spheres 5, 154–5
  R. Smith on 3
  see also citizenship; liberalism; nation-states; politics
politics
  of citizenship 51–3, 70–2
  of difference vs. politics of universalism (Taylor) 98–9
  external voting rights 66
  of identity (Brubaker) 18
  and liberalism 4–5
  vs. morality (Schmitt) 2
  normative vs. factual 1–2
  relationship to other spheres (Schmitt) 2–3
  terrorism and aliens 92–6
  tied up with violence (Weber) 3
  see also nation-states; violence
Popitz, Heinrich 2–3, 5
Portugal
  on "citizenship policy index" (Howard) 42

Index

emigrants and re-ethnicization of citizenship 65
liberalization of citizenship 50, 65
mixing *jus soli* and *jus sanguinis* citizenship principles 44, 45
postnational membership (Soysal) 20–3, 28, 32, 154
EU and 164–72
vs. reality of alien rights 82–4, 85
social rights as crown of 88
see also citizenship; globalization; liberalism; universalism
Powell, Justice Lewis F. 104
Preuss, Ulrich 7
Prussia 16
public opinion
hostile to immigrants 52, 156–7
mobilized on citizenship and immigration (Howard) 52–3, 70–1
support for the welfare state 76
welfare and multiculturalism 74–80
Putnam, Robert 75

Quakers 119–20

race vii, 26–8, 43, 102–3, 106
access racism (Bleich) 102
expressive racism (Bleich) 102
state-level racism 26–7, 149
see also antidiscrimination; discrimination; ethnicity; minority groups
Rasmussen, Anders Fogh 137
Rawls, John
political liberalism 114–17
public political culture 121
Regents of the University of California v. Bakke see Bakke decision (US Supreme Court)
religion 134–6
see also ethnicity; race; Muslims
rights, alien *see* alien rights
rights, antidiscrimination *see* antidiscrimination
rights, civil
decoupled from citizenship 29
impaired for aliens after 2001 84, 92–6
and Marshall vi, 10–11
property 4

Roman tradition 7–8
US civil rights laws 101–6
rights, defined 83
rights, human *see* human rights
rights, minority 74, 96–110, 149–50
see also minority groups
rights, multicultural *see* multiculturalism
rights, political
external voting 66, 146
Greek tradition 6–7
less important for immigrants 146
local voting rights for immigrants 146
and Marshall 10, 12
tied to citizenship status 29, 96, 146
rights, social
in the EU 164–71
immigrants' exclusion from in the US 22, 88–9, 91
for immigrants in Europe 88–91
for immigrants in the US 88–9
and Marshall 9–14
from redistributive to procedural rights 81
restricting immigrants' access to benefits in the UK 90
Rijkschroeff, Rally 139–40
Robb, Andrew 126
Röben, Volker 141–2
Rome (ancient)
citizenship as legal status 7–8
citizenship as passive rights-holding 67, 147
European Union citizenship as Roman 161
Rosanvallon, Pierre 80–2
Rosberg, G. 88
Runnymede Trust 131

Sabbagh, Daniel 105
Sacks, Jonathan
social covenant 124, 132–3
on values and identity 120–1
Sadiq, Kamal viii, 147
St-Arnaud, Sébastian 78
Sarkozy, Nicolas 107–8
Schäuble, Wolfgang 144
Scheffler, Samuel 122
Schiller, Friedrich von 128

213

Index

Schmitt, Carl 138
Der Begriff des Politischen 2–5
Schröder, Gerhard 52
Schuck, Peter H.
  consent and citizenship 38, 62
  devaluation of citizenship 63, 146
security
  post-2001 obsession 92–6
  see also terrorism
Shachar, Ayelet
  birthright citizenship 34
  The Birthright Lottery 152–3, 155
Sievers, Wiebke 148
Simmel, Georg 119–20
Skrentny, John 103–4
Slovenia 70
Smith, Jacqui 60
Smith, Rogers M.
  citizenship as membership in political community 1, 3
  consent and citizenship 38, 62
  people-making identity 122
Sniderman, Paul 140
social citizenship 9–14
  see also citizenship; Marshall; social rights; welfare state
social classes
  Disraeli's "two nations" 11
  informal inequality 12
  see also capitalism
social closure
  citizenship as (Brubaker) 15–17
  Weber's concept of 15
socialism 13
solidarity
  as condition of minority rights 106, 149–50
  vs. diversity 74–6, 80–2
  EU and 168–9
  see also trust; welfare state
Somers, Margaret 60
Soysal, Yasemin
  civil/social vs. political rights 29
  Limits of Citizenship 20–2
  postnational membership 23, 28, 32, 72–3, 82–3, 88, 154
Spain 42, 64
Spiro, Peter
  Beyond Citizenship 152, 153–5
Starr, Paul 108

status vii–viii, 28–9, 34–72
  access to 31–2, 34–72
  basic aspect of citizenship 28–9
  causes of change 148–52
  concept of citizenship (Marshall) 12
  to contract (Handler) 13, 79
  see also citizenship
Straubhaar, Thomas 158
Straw, Jack 129–30
Sunstein, Cass 83
Supreme Court (US)
  Bakke decision 104–6
  Dred Scott decision 38
  Graham v. *Richardson* decision 83, 87–8
  Griggs v. *Duke Power Company* decision 102–3
  Mathews v. *Diaz* decision 88
Sweden
  on "citizenship policy index" (Howard) 42
  discretionary approach to naturalization 45
  dual nationality 49–50
  immigration statistics 35–6
  liberalization of citizenship 50
  naturalization rates 41
Switzerland
  immigration statistics 35–6
  long-term residence status 86

Taylor, Charles
  multiculturalism 98–9
  politics of recognition 110
  "survivance" of cultures 24
Taylor-Gooby, Peter 78
Tebble, Adam J. 138
terrorism
  alien rights and politics 92–6
  civic integration and 53, 55, 61
  effects of 53, 71, 73–4, 126
  security concerns 32, 92–6
  see also security
Torpey, John 110
Triadafilopoulos, Phil 138
Trojani decision (ECJ) 165
trust
  diversity and 75–6
  see also diversity; solidarity; welfare state

Index

Tunisia 169
Turkey 66, 169
Turner, Bryan S.
  Handbook of Citizenship Studies
    (with Isin) 1

United Kingdom
  access to labor markets for
    immigrants 87
  antidiscrimination policies 106–8
  anti-terrorism laws and policies 94–6
  Anti-terrorism, Crime and Security
    Act (2001) 94–5
  Borders, Citizenship and Immigration
    Act (2009) 59–60
  Citizenship Day 131
  on "citizenship policy index"
    (Howard) 42
  civic integration 58–60, 71, 129–31,
    156–7
  Crick Commission 56, 58–9, 129,
    130
  decriminalizing homosexuality 112
  discretionary approach to
    naturalization 45
  dual citizenship 47
  ethnic social unrest of 2001 57
  Immigration and Asylum Act (1999)
    90
  immigration statistics 35–6
  Immigration, Asylum and Nationality
    Act (2006) 71
    mixing *jus soli* with *jus sanguinis*
      citizenship principles 44, 45
  Nationality, Immigration and Asylum
    Act (2002) 57–8
  naturalization process 41–2, 53–4,
    56–61, 124, 129–32
  Our Shared Future (CIC) 132
  permanent residency 91–2
  postwar social theory 10
  Prevention of Terrorism Act (2005)
    96
  probationary citizenship 60–1, 62
  race and Britishness 131–2
  restricting temporary immigrants'
    access to benefits 90
  restrictive *cum* liberal citizenship
    71
  skilled immigrants 157–8
  *Strategy to Increase Race Equality
    and Community Cohesion* (Home
    Office) 130
  two-tier citizenship (Goodhart) 156
  welfare state 158
United Nations Universal Declaration of
    Human Rights (1948) 27
United States
  alien rights 83–4, 87–9
  antidiscrimination 101–6
  anti-terrorism 92–4
  as-of-right naturalization 45–6
  Cable Act (1922) 37
  and Canada compared on
    naturalization 39–40
  citizenship test 124–5
  Civil Rights Act (1964) 104
  civil rights laws and policies 101–2
  covenantal nation (Sacks) 133
  decline of citizenship 153–5, 158–9
  democratic revolution and citizenship
    11–12
  Dred Scott decision (Supreme Court)
    38
  dual citizenship 47
  ethnicity vs. race 97
  and Europe compared on welfare-
    spending 76–8
  evolution of nationality law 37–8
  immigration law (de-racialized) 104
  immigration statistics 35–6
  Mexican immigrants and
    naturalization 38–9
  naturalization process 16, 37, 45–6,
    58, 124–5
  Patriot Act (2002) 93
  relabeling blacks as African-
    Americans 97
  welfare state compared to Europe
    76–8
universalism
  and alien rights 84
  exclusion of Muslims and 137–42
  feudalism as opposed to 8
  French republicanism 138–9

  identity paradox of 33, 111–13,
    123–37
  inherent in citizenship 6, 23, 31, 83,
    147

Index

universalism (*cont.*)
  liberalism and 23, 116
  multiculturalism as opposite of 23, 74
  patriotism as opposite of 118
  personhood and postnational membership (Soysal) 20–2
  trend toward universalistic citizenship 31
  see also citizenship; liberalism; rights
Urbano de Sousa, Constança 65
Utzinger, André 171

values
  civic 11, 17–18
  generalization of (Parsons) 143
  identity vs. political 120–1
  political 120–1
  see also identity; Kymlicka; liberalism; Rawls; Sacks
Veil (Simone) Committee (France) 107–8
Verdonk, Rita 56
violence
  legitimate use of (defining the state) 3
  state as protection from 2–3
  see also Hobbes; politics; Schmitt; Weber

Waldron, Jeremy 23–4
Walzer, Michael 31, 158
Waters, Mary 97
Weber, Max
  ignoring citizenship 9
  legitimate use of violence (defining the state) 3
  occidental city 8

Politics as a Vocation 3
  social closure 15
Weil, Patrick 18–19, 50–1
Weiler, Joseph 161, 162, 163–4
welfare state
  aliens' access to (US and Europe) 88–91
  as based on "insurance society" (Rosanvallon) 80–1
  benefit tourism (EU) 165
  as closed system (Freeman) 74
  current retrenchments 13–14, 73, 74–82, 150–1
  and diversity 74–82
  EU social rights 165–70
  Europe and America compared 76–8
  exclusion of immigrants (US) 22, 88–9, 91
  social citizenship 9–14
  social trust 75–6
  spending patterns in Europe and the US 76–7
  tying welfare benefits to legal permanent residence (UK) 90, 156
  to workfare state 13, 78–9, 150–1
  see also capitalism; rights; social citizenship
Wilde, Oscar 30, 112
Wirth, Louis 96–7
Wojung Park, Julian 125
Wolfenden Committee Report (UK) 112
Wolfrum, Rüdiger 141–2

Yurdakul, Gölçe 145, 151

Zolberg, Ari 134

Made in the USA
Middletown, DE
18 January 2021